Op Amp Handbook

Third Edition

Op Amp Handbook

Fredrick W. Hughes
Electronics Training Consultant

PTR Prentice Hall, *Englewood Cliffs, New Jersey 07632*

Library of Congress Cataloging-in-Publication Data
Hughes, Fredrick W.
    Op-amp handbook.

    Includes index.
    1. Operational amplifiers.   2. Integrated circuits.   I. Title.
TK7871,58.06H83 1993   621.39'5--dc20   92-40507
ISBN 0-13-030792-0

Editorial/production supervision and
    interior design: *Ray Pajek*
Buyer: *Mary Elizabeth McCartney*

Copyright © 1993 by PTR Prentice Hall, Inc.
A Simon & Schuster Company
Englewood Cliffs, NJ 07632

The publisher offers discounts on this book when
ordered in bulk quantities. For more information, contact:

    Corporate Sales Department
    PTR Prentice Hall
    113 Sylvan Avenue
    Englewood Cliffs, NJ 07632

    Phone: 201-592-2863
    Fax: 201-592-2249

Printed in the United States of America
10 9 8 7 6 5 4 3 2 1

ISBN 0-13-030792-0

Prentice-Hall International (UK) Limited, *London*
Prentice-Hall of Australia Pty. Limited, *Sydney*
Prentice-Hall Canada Inc., *Toronto*
Prentice-Hall Hispanoamericana, S.A., *Mexico*
Prentice-Hall of India Private Limited, *New Delhi*
Prentice-Hall of Japan, Inc. *Tokyo*
Simon & Schuster Asia Pte. Ltd., *Singapore*
Editora Prentice-Hall do Brasil, Ltda., *Rio de Janeiro*

Contents

Preface

The third edition of this book continues with a straightforward, practical approach that enables students to grasp the concepts necessary to understand and use the operational amplifier (op amp). This edition is greatly enhanced by the addition of 17 new practical experiments; a description of discrete-component differential amplifiers in the first chapter; the addition of the operational transconductance amplifier (OTA) and the current-differencing amplifier (CDA); or Norton op amp, in chapter 7; actual voltage waveform photographs of selected experimental circuits in Appendix A; a review of basic test equipment and circuit-testing procedures in Appendix B; and a 50-question Op Amp Final Examination at the end of the book.

The book has been popular among schools because of its easy-to-learn approach. The first and second editions had a separate chapter for experiments, but this edition uses existing and newer experiments keyed to their specific units. Chapters 1 through 7 follow a new format, which consists of the following:

Section 1 - Text Material
Section 2 - Terminology Exercise
Section 3 - Problems and Exercises
Section 4 - Experiments
Section 5 - Summary Points
Section 6 - Self-Checking Quiz (with answers at the back of the book)

In each chapter, the text material includes theory, functional diagrams, nomenclature, and basic practical circuits. Many of the circuit drawings have component values given, and the circuits can be constructed directly from the book. The text is followed by a terminology exercise that enables the reader to recognize and use new terms. Third, problems and exercises are given to reinforce the theory and help the reader gain a working knowledge of the subjects. Fourth, comprehensive experiments are provided to give the reader the manipulative skills needed to work with op amp circuits. Fifth, summary points serve as a review for the main topics in the chapter. Sixth, a self-checking quiz gives the reader immediate follow-up to determine his or her mastery of the theory and circuit operations previously studied. This type of chapter format provides instructors with student-centered instructional material that does not require lesson plan preparation, and it allows students to progress forward at the class pace or by themselves.

The prerequisites for successfully using this book go little beyond knowledge of fundamental algebra and basic dc/ac circuit theory. However, bipolar transistor theory is helpful, and it is recommended that this book be used in post-solid-state device courses as a bridge between a study of discrete devices and integrated circuits.

There are many fine books and manuals concerning op amps on the market. However, this book takes a direct, easy-to-read approach that develops the basic understanding and practical skills essential to working with op amps for readers at various levels: the electronics student, the technician, the engineer, and the instructor.

CHAPTER CONTENTS

Chapter 1 begins with a description of the discrete differential amplifier, in order to form a basis for understanding the inner workings of the op amp. The chapter goes on to explain the function of an op amp, its nomenclature, IC-package pin identification, and important characteristics and parameters. Basic dual-voltage power supplies needed to operate op amps are also discussed.

Chapter 2 describes the operation of basic op amp circuits: voltage comparators, the inverting amplifier, the noninverting amplifier, voltage followers, summing amplifiers, and the difference amplifier.

Chapter 3 presents basic signal-processing circuits, such as the integrator, the differentiator, the low-pass filter, the high-pass filter, the bandpass filter, and the notch filter. This chapter provides the necessary formulas for determining output voltages, cut-off frequencies, and bandwidth capabilities.

Chapter 4 deals with oscillators. It describes the square-wave generator, the sawtooth-wave generator, the triangle-wave generator, the sine-wave oscillator, the quadrature oscillator, and a basic function generator.

Chapter 5 discusses the application of op amps to audio circuits in the forms of voltage amplifiers, equalization preamps, active tone control circuits, basic audio mixers, and miscellaneous other audio circuits.

Chapter 6 describes associated circuits found with op amps that provide protection and stability. This chapter also presents basic op amp testing and troubleshooting techniques. Four op amp tester circuits with construction hints are given to aid the reader with building projects.

Chapter 7 describes other specialized op amps and their uses, such as JFET-input amplifiers, operational transconductance amplifiers, and current-differencing amplifiers.

Chapter 8 presents practical step-by-step design procedures for twenty basic op amp circuits. These circuits, while easy enough to give the beginner a straightforward approach to designing, provide the experienced designer with instant, time-saving applications.

Chapter 9 is a collection of sixty-two practical op amp circuits with a brief description of each. This furnishes a reference for readers interested in constructing circuits or creating electronic systems.

Appendix A presents voltage waveform photographs of selected experiments. In Appendix B, a brief review of basic test equipment and their operation is given, which will facilitate the reader's performance of the op amp experiments. Appendix C lists ten op amp manufacturers' specification sheets, which contain information for further study or circuit construction of op amp circuits presented in the text.

Although there are countless integrated-circuit (IC) op amps available, the 741 op amp is used throughout this book because it is inexpensive and reliable, does not burn out easily, and can readily be found in most electronics supply houses.

This book will help the beginner with its easy-to-understand approach to learning about op amp circuits; it will make the instructor's job less difficult with its individualized-instruction format; and it will present different ideas and approaches to the experienced person.

SPECIAL NOTE FOR INSTRUCTORS

There is a 50-question multiple-choice final examination at the end of this book. The answers to the questions are given in the instructor's guidebook.

SPECIAL NOTE TO STUDENTS

You have chosen an exciting and fast-moving career in electronics. It is hoped that this book will make it easier for you to learn the skills required to design, test and/or service op amp circuits and related equipment. Good luck to you.

Fredrick W. Hughes

Op Amp Handbook

CHAPTER **1**

OPERATIONAL AMPLIFIER FUNCTIONS AND CHARACTERISTICS

Operational amplifiers (op amps) are specially designed and packaged electronic circuits that can be used for various purposes with only a few external components. Until recently, op amps were constructed of discrete components within a sealed package and were so costly that few engineers and technicians ever became involved with them. Today however, with improved integrated-circuit (IC) technology, these inexpensive IC packages are found in nearly every aspect of electronics.

Originally, op amps were used for analog computing circuits, control circuits, and instrumentation. Their main function was to provide linear (voltage and current) mathematical operations, such as comparison, addition, subtraction, differentiation, integration, and amplification. Now they are found virtually everywhere—in audio reproduction, communication systems, digital processing systems, consumer electronics, and many unique hobbyist's devices.

Op-amp configurations may have a single input and single output, differential input and differential output, or differential input and single output. The latter configuration is the most widespread in the electronics industry and will be used as the basis of this book. Anyone involved in electronics should know how the op amp functions and what its characteristics are, and should be able to recognize and work with basic circuit configurations.

1-1-1 THE DISCRETE DIFFERENTIAL AMPLIFIER

The heart of an operational amplifier is the *differential amplifier*, which is defined as a circuit having two inputs with an output voltage equal to the difference between the input voltages. A basic differential amplifier is shown in Figure 1-1. Notice that it has two similar transistors; in this case both are NPN types. Both transistor circuits have common emitter configurations with a common emitter resistor (R_E). The difference between the two input voltages V_1 and V_2 is called the voltage input differential (V_{id}). This difference voltage is what determines the value of the voltage at the output of the circuit. The difference between the two output voltages at the collectors of Q_1 and Q_2 (V_{C1}-V_{C2} or vice versa) is referred to as the voltage output differential (V_{od}).

The function of the circuit components: Resistors R_{B1} and R_{B2} develop the signal at the inputs of Q_1 and Q_2, respectively. Transistors Q_1 and Q_2 are linear amplifying devices which can also be used as switches by driving Q_1 and Q_2 into saturation or outoff. Resistor R_E is the common emitter resistor for Q_1 and Q_2. Notice that R_E is not bypassed with a capacitor. This means that an input signal at Q_1 affects the current through Q_1, which in turn causes the voltage across R_E to change. This change in voltage is applied to the emitter of Q_2, which causes a change in current flow through this transistor. Likewise, an input signal to Q_2 will cause a change in the current flow through Q_1. Resistors R_{C1} and R_{C2} develop the output signal for transistors Q_1 and Q_2, respectively.

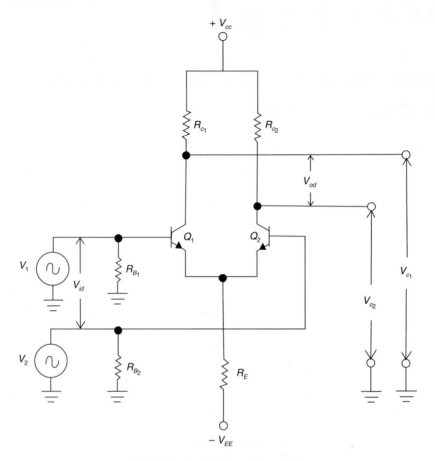

FIGURE 1-1 Basic differential amplifier

Even though the differential amplifier has two inputs and two outputs, it is not necessary to use both inputs and both outputs at the same time. A differential amplifier can be connected as a single-input, single-output device; a single-input, differential-output device; or a differential-input, differential-output device. The following descriptions will show how the circuit responds with different input conditions.

1-1-1-1 Input Voltages In Phase

The circuit shown in Figure 1-2a is redrawn to facilitate understanding. In an ideal situation, all of the components in the circuit are perfectly matched, meaning: $R_{C1} = R_{C2}$, $Q_1 = Q_2$ and $R_{B1} = R_{B2}$. If the input voltages are in phase and the same amplitude, then each side of the circuit should amplify the same way, and the signals should be identical at the outputs. The graph in Figure 1-2b shows the output voltages. When the input signal increases at each input, the output signal decreases at each output. When the input signals decrease at the inputs, the output signals increase at the outputs. The negative feedback caused by R_E will be ̣ same for each transistor. Since both outputs increase and decrease simultaneously, the dif- ̣ce voltage, V_{od}, between the two outputs should be zero. However, in reality the circuit

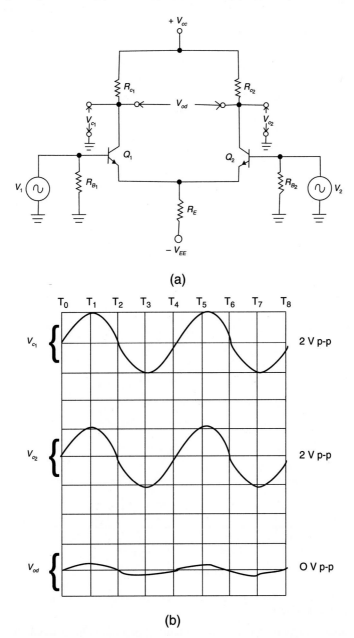

FIGURE 1-2 Input voltage in phase (a) schematic diagram (b) output voltage waveforms

components are never perfectly matched, so one input signal will be amplified more than the other, resulting in a slight difference at the outputs. The ability of a difference amplifier to have zero volts between the two outputs under these input conditions is called *common mode rejection*. With 100 percent rejection, V_{od} would equal zero. Notice that if V_1 and V_2 are the same amplitude, the differential voltage V_{id} (V_1-V_2), is equal to zero. In other words, if the

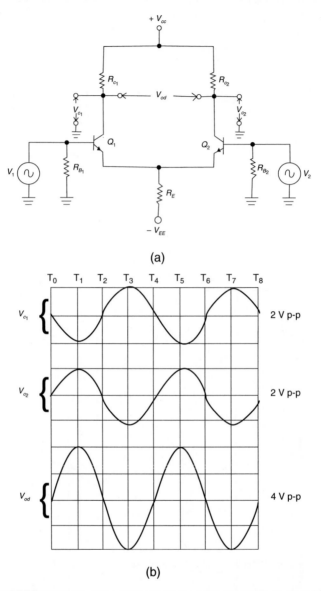

FIGURE 1-3 Input voltage 180° out of phase (a) schematic diagram (b) output voltage waveforms

input differential voltage is zero, then the output differential voltage should be zero.

1-1-1-2 Input Voltages 180° Out of Phase

When the input signals to the differential amplifier are 180° out of phase as shown in Figure 1-3a, one transistor will conduct more than the other, depending on the polarity of the input signal. When the input signal to Q_1 decreases, the output voltage, V_{C1}, increases. At the same time, the input signal to Q_2 increases and the output voltage, V_{C2}, decreases. Likewise, the output voltages go in opposite directions when the input signals reverse themselves.

The amplitude of each output signal is equal to the input signal multiplied by the gain of the amplifier. The graph shown in Figure 1-3b indicates the output voltage of each transistor to be 2 Vp-p each. Since the two output voltages are 180° out of phase, the differential output voltage, V_{od}, is equal to 4 Vp-p. When the input signals are 180° out of phase, the amplitude of V_{od} is equal to the amplitude of one input signal multiplied by two times the gain of the amplifier. Also, the input differential voltage will be twice as large in amplitude as a single input signal, hence the differential output signal will be larger than a single output voltage . Notice that output voltage V_{C1} is in phase with input voltage V_2, and that output voltage V_{C2} is in-phase with input voltage V_1.

1-1-1-3 One Input Grounded

A differential amplifier can be connected with a single input and a differential output as shown in Figure 1-4a. The Q_1 side of the circuit acts like an emitter-follower amplifier. The voltage drop across R_E, as a result of the input signal at Q_1, is applied to the emitter of Q_2 which acts as a common base amplifier. The voltage across R_E is in phase with the input signal. As a result, the output voltage of Q_2, or V_{C2}, is in phase with the input signal (remember there is no phase reversal with a common base amplifier). The output voltage of Q_1, or V_{C1}, is out of phase with the input signal. Therefore, the output voltages of V_{C1} and V_{C2} are out of phase with each other.

The voltage across R_E will always be less than the input signal voltage V_1, since this part of the circuit acts like a voltage follower. Therefore, the output voltage of Q_2, or V_{C2}, will always be less than the output voltage of Q_1, or V_{C1}. The graph shown in Figure 1-4b indicates the amplitudes of both output voltages. The differential output voltage, V_{od}, is the difference between V_{C1} and V_{C2}. Since these voltages are out of phase, the differential output voltage will be greater in amplitude than either single output voltage.

1-1-2 WHAT IS AN OP AMP?

The IC op amp is a solid-state device capable of sensing and amplifying DC and AC input signals.

A typical IC op amp consists of three basic circuits, a high-input impedance differential amplifier, a high-gain voltage amplifier, and a low-impedance output amplifier (usually a push-pull emitter follower). Figure 1-5 shows a block diagram of an op amp. Notice that it usually requires a positive and a negative power supply. This allows the output voltage to swing positive and negative with respect to ground.

The most important characteristics of an op amp are:
1. *Very high input impedance,* which produces negligible currents at the inputs.
2. *Very high open-loop gain.*
3. *Very low output impedance,* so as not to affect the output of the amplifier by loading.

The standard op amp schematic symbol is represented by a triangle, as illustrated in Figure 1-6. The input terminals are at the base of the triangle. The inverting input is represented by the minus sign. A DC voltage or AC signal placed on this input will be 180° out of phase at the output. The noninverting input is represented by the plus sign. A DC voltage or AC signal placed on this input will be in phase at the output. The output terminal is shown at the apex of the triangle.

Power-supply terminals and other leads for frequency-compensation or null-adjusting

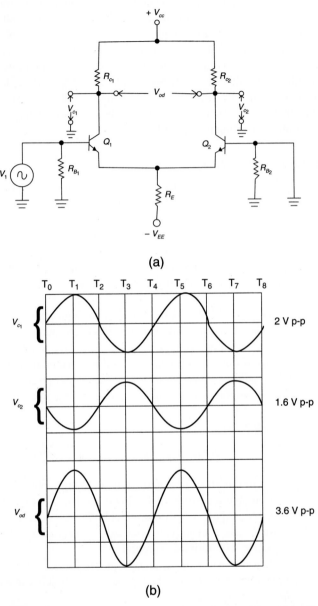

(a)

(b)

FIGURE 1-4 One input grounded (a) schematic diagram (b) output voltage
waveforms

are shown extending above and below the triangle. These leads are not always shown in schematic diagrams, but they are implied. Power connections are understood, whereas the other
leads may not be used at all.

The type of op amp or the manufacturer's part number is centered within the body of
the triangle. A general circuit not indicating a specific op amp might use the symbols A_1, A_2,
., or OP-1, OP-2, etc.

Although we can use the op amp without knowing exactly what goes on inside it, we

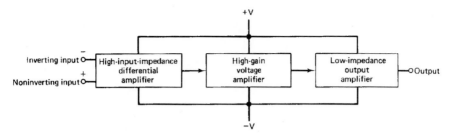

FIGURE 1-5 Block diagram of op amp

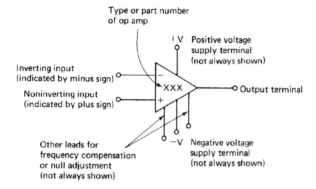

FIGURE 1-6 Standard op-amp schematic symbol

can better understand its operating characteristics by having some idea of its internal circuitry. Figure 1-7 shows the schematic diagram of the popular 741 op-amp IC. Other op amps are similar. Resistors and capacitors are held to an absolute minimum in IC design, using transistors wherever possible. No coupling capacitors are used, allowing the circuit to amplify DC as well as AC signals. The 30-pF capacitor shown provides internal frequency compensation, which will be discussed later in this chapter.

The op amp consists basically of three stages: a high-input-impedance differential amplifier, a high-gain voltage amplifier with a level shifter (permitting the output to swing positive and negative), and a low-impedance output amplifier.

There are many circuit variations in the production of ICs. Each manufacturer will design their own circuit version of an industry standard, including more or fewer components, depending on the special features they want to incorporate into the circuit. The circuit shown in Figure 1-7 is one version of the standard 741 op amp IC. The basic function of the various components are as follows:

Q_1 **and** Q_2 are the differential amplifier inputs. A differential input signal is placed between the bases of these transistors (pins 2 and 3).

Q_3 **and** Q_4 are in series with Q_1 and Q_2, respectively, which increases the maximum input signal capacity of the input differential amplifier.

Q_5 **and** Q_6 form a controlled current source for the differential amplifier. If R_E in the basic differential amplifier is replaced with a transistor, the current through the circuit will be constant, which provides more stability and improves the amplifying characteristics of the circuit. Two transistors are used here so the current through the differential amplifier can be

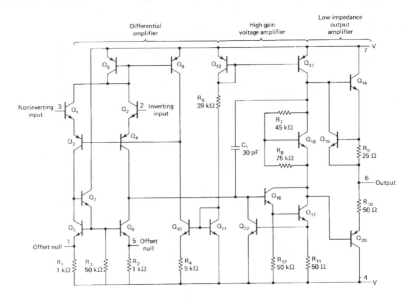

FIGURE 1-7 Typical op-amp schematic diagram

adjusted. The emitters Of Q_5 and Q_6 have external pins (1 and 5), which can be used with a potentiometer to balance the current through the differential amplifier. This technique is referred to as input-current-offset nulling and will be explained more fully later on.

Q_7 provides a constant current source to the base of Q_5 and Q_6.

Q_8 has its base and collector shorted, which in effect produces a diode used for temperature compensation to improve the stability of Q_9 and R_{10}. Notice that Q_{11} and Q_{12} also act as temperature-compensating diodes.

Q_9 **and** Q_{10} provide a constant current source to the base of Q_3 and Q_4.

Q_{11}, Q_{12} **and** Q_{13} establish the current requirements and stability for Q_{16}, Q_{17}, and Q_{18}.

The output of the differential stage is taken at the junction Of Q_4 and Q_6 and is applied to the emitter-follower circuit formed by Q_{16} and R_{12}.

Q_{16} is the emitter follower circuit which acts as a *voltage level shifter*. Because of the direct coupling, the DC level at the emitters rises from stage to stage toward the positive voltage. With this increase in DC level, the output voltage swing is limited and may even distort the output signal. The shifter circuit moves the overall circuit operating point (or reference point) back toward the negative voltage. It is ideal if the quiescent output operating point (pin 6) is at zero volts. This means that the output signal can swing nearly to the maximum of the positive and negative supply voltages.

The signal is taken from the cathode resistor of Q_{16} and applied to the base of Q_{17}.

Q_{17} is a common emitter amplifier that drives Q_{14} and Q_{20}, the output transistors.

Q_{18}, R_7 **and** R_8 are components designed to bias the output transistors in the linear region. The signal at the collector of Q_{18} is fed to the base of Q_{14}, while the signal at the emitter of Q_{18} is fed to the base of Q_{20}. In effect, Q_{18} acts as a phase-splitter. The two signals fed to the output stage are 180° out of phase.

Q_{14} **and** Q_{20} form the output complementary symmetry stage. These two transistors operate where one is conducting more than the other during an input signal. The output (pin 6) is at the junction of R_9 and R_{10}, which are the emitter circuits of Q_{14} and Q_{20}. When the output signal goes positive, Q_{14} is conducting more and, in effect, is pulling the output up toward the positive voltage supply. Similarly, when the output signal goes negative, Q_{20} is conducting more and pulling the output down toward the negative voltage supply. Considering conventional current flow, where the current flows from positive to negative, Q_{14} would be called a *source transistor* since it connects the output to the positive voltage supply. Transistor Q_{20} connects the output to the negative voltage supply and is referred to as the *sink transistor.* This type of circuit, where the components in the output stage are stacked one on top of the other, is referred to as a *totem-pole output.*

Q_{15}, is a current-limiting protection circuit for Q_{14}. If Q_{14} conducts too much current, the increased voltage drop across R_9 causes Q_{15} to conduct more, which in turn tends to cut off Q_{14}.

Q_{22}, forms a feedback circuit from the driver, Q_{17}, to the emitter-follower circuit, Q_{16}, and protects output transistor Q_{20}. If the signal being fed through the amplifier is so large that it may overdrive output transistor Q_{20}, the increased voltage drop across R_{11} causes Q_{22} to conduct more, which in turn decreases the gain of Q_{16} and Q_{17}. All of these individual stages tend to affect each other and control the current through the overall circuit to a safe limit.

1-1-3 HOW AN OP AMP FUNCTIONS

Ideally, the gain of an op amp would be infinite; however, practically, the gain may exceed 200,000 in the open-loop mode. In the open-loop mode there is no feedback from the output to the inputs, and the voltage gain (A_v) is maximum, as shown in Figure 1-8a. In a practical circuit, the slightest voltage difference at the inputs will cause the output voltage to attempt to swing to the maximum power-supply level. The maximum voltage at the output will be about 90 percent of the supply voltages because of the internal voltage drops of the op amp. (Refer to Figure 1-7 and note components Q_{14}, R_9, R_{10}, and Q_{20}.) The output is said to be at saturation and can be represented (for either polarity) by $+V_{sat}$ and $-V_{sat}$. As an example, an op-amp circuit in the open-loop mode using a ±15-V supply would have its output swing from +13.5 V to –13.5 V. With this type of circuit the op amp is very unstable and the output will be 0 V for a 0-V difference between the inputs, or the output voltage will be at either extreme, with a slight voltage difference at the inputs. The open-loop mode is found primarily in voltage comparators and level-detector circuits.

The versatility of the op amp is demonstrated by the fact that it can be used in so many types of circuits in the closed-loop mode, as shown in Figure 1-8 b. External components are used to feed back a portion of the output voltage to the inverting input. This feedback stabilizes most circuits and can reduce the noise level. The voltage gain (A_v) will be less than (<) maximum gain in the open-loop mode.

Closed-loop gain must be controlled to be of any value in a practical circuit. By adding a resistor R_{in} to the inverting input, as shown in Figure 1-8c, the gain of the op amp can be controlled. The resistance ratio of R_F to R_{in} determines the voltage gain of the circuit and can be found by the formula

$$A_v = \frac{R_F}{R_{in}}$$

The minus sign indicates that the op-amp circuit is in the inverting configuration and is disregarded for calculations. For example, if R_{in} = 10 kΩ and R_F = 100 kΩ, then A_v would equal 10. An input voltage of 0.01 V would yield an output voltage of 0.1 V. If R_{in} were changed to 1 kΩ , the A_v would increase to 100. Now, an input voltage of 0.01 V would yield

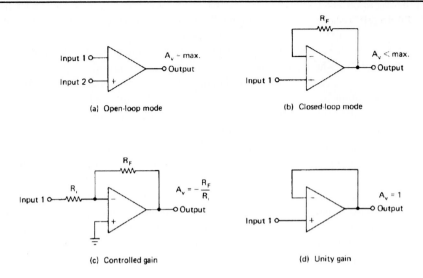

FIGURE 1-8 Op-amp gain.

an output voltage of 1 V.

If both R_{in}, and R_F are the same value, the A_v equals 1, or unity gain. A direct connection from output to input also results in unity gain, as shown in Figure 1-8d. In this noninverting configuration, the voltage out equals the voltage in, and A_v equals +1.

These various types of gain will be used in basic circuits later in this book to better acquaint you with the functions of op amps. One important function to remember is the relationship of input polarity to output polarity. Simply stated, if the inverting input is more positive than the noninverting input, the output will be negative. Similarly, if the inverting input is more negative than the noninverting input, the output will be positive. Figure 1-9 shows this important function, where the noninverting input is at ground or zero volts.

1-1-4 OP AMP CHARACTERISTICS AND PARAMETERS

Understanding the characteristics and parameters of an electronic device will enable you to better understand the circuit in which it is used. Knowing what to expect from op amps will aid you in servicing or designing circuits in which they are used. This section lists the pertinent information on the characteristics and parameters of op amps used in most circuits.

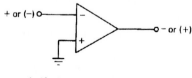

1. If input is more positive than + input, output will be negative.

2. If − input is more negative than + input, output will be positive.

FIGURE 1-9 Input/output polarity relationship.

1-1-4-1 Input Impedance

Ideally, the input impedance of an op amp should be infinite, but in practice is about 1 MΩ or more. Some special op amps may have an input impedance of as much as 100 MΩ. The higher the input impedance, the better the op amp will perform. The input capacitance of an op amp may become important at high frequencies. Typically, this capacitance is less than 2 pF, when one input terminal is grounded.

1-1-4-2 Output Impedance

Ideally, the output impedance of an op amp should be zero. In actuality, each op amp is different and its output impedance may range from 25 to several thousand ohms. For most applications, the output is assumed to be zero and will function as a voltage source capable of providing current for a wide range of loads. With high input impedance and low output impedance, the op amp becomes an impedance-matching device.

1-1-4-3 Input Bias Current

Theoretically, the input impedance is infinite; therefore, there should not be any input current. However, there do exist small input currents, on the order of microamperes down to picoamperes. The average of these two currents is termed the input bias current. This current can cause an unbalance in the op amp, which can affect the output. Generally, the lower the input bias current, the smaller the imbalance will be. Op amps using field-effect transistors (FETs) at the inputs have the least amount of input bias current.

1-1-4-4 Output-Offset Voltage

Output-offset voltage (error voltage) is caused by the input bias current. When both inputs are the same voltage, the output of an op amp should be zero volts. Since this is seldom the case, a small voltage will usually appear at the output. This situation can be minimized or corrected somewhat by offset nulling, which is applying an input-offset voltage or current.

1-1-4-5 Input-Offset Current

Both input currents should be equal to obtain zero output voltage. However, this is impossible and there will be an input offset current to maintain the output at zero volts. In other words, to set the output to zero volts, one input may require more current than the other. This offset current may range up to 20 mA.

1-1-4-6 Input-Offset Voltage

Ideally, the output voltage of an op amp should be zero when the voltage at both inputs is zero. However, owing to the high gain of an op amp, a slight circuit imbalance can cause an output voltage. By applying a small offset voltage at one of the inputs, the output voltage can be brought back to zero.

1-1-4-7 Offset Nulling

There are different methods to introduce an input-offset voltage to zero or null the output voltage. Op-amp manufacturers have taken this into account and their data sheets usually give the best recommendations for a particular op amp. Figure 1-10 if shows how to null a typical op amp. Offset null terminals have been shown in Figures 1-6 and 1-7. The following procedure describes the steps for nulling the output voltage.

1. Make sure that the circuit has all the correct components, including the null circuit. (Null circuits are usually not shown on normal schematic diagrams.)
2. Reduce input signals to zero. If any series input resistor is about 1 percent larger than the signal source impedance, nothing else need be done at this point. If the series resistor is equal to or less than the source impedance, replace each source with a resistor equivalent to its impedance.
3. Connect the load to the output terminal.
4. Apply DC power and wait a few minutes for the circuit to settle down.
5. Connect a sensitive voltmeter (capable of reading a few millivolts) or a DC-coupled oscilloscope across the load to read the output voltage (V_{out}).
6. Adjust the variable resistor until V_{out} reads zero.
7. Remove any added components to the input and reconnect the source inputs, making sure not to touch the offset-voltage adjusting resistor.

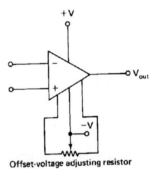

Offset-voltage adjusting resistor

FIGURE 1-10 Offset nulling.

1-1-4-8 Effects of Temperature

Changes in temperature affect all solid-state devices, and op amps are not immune to this problem. DC circuits using op amps tend to be more susceptible than do AC circuits. A change in temperature can cause a change in offset current and offset voltage and is termed drift. A drift caused by temperature will upset any adjusted op-amp imbalance and produce errors in the output voltage.

1-1-4-9 Frequency Compensation

Because of the op amps high gain and the phase shift from one internal circuit to another, a point is reached at some high frequency where enough output signal could be fed back to the input and cause oscillations. Frequently, compensation capacitors are added to the op amp, either internally or externally, to prevent these oscillations by decreasing the op amp's gain as frequency increases.

1-1-4-10 Slew Rate

Slew rate is the maximum rate of change of the op amp output voltage and can be stated thus:

$$\text{slew rate} = \frac{\text{maximum change in output voltage}}{\text{change in time}} = \frac{\Delta V_{out(max)}}{\Delta t}$$

The 741 general-purpose op amp has a slew rate of 0.5 V/μs, which means that the output voltage can change a maximum of 0.5 V in 1 μs. Capacitance limits this slewing ability, and the output voltage will be delayed from the input voltage, as shown in Figure 1-11. Most often, the frequency-compensation capacitor, either internal or external, causes slew-rate limiting in an op amp. At high frequencies or high rates of signal change, slew-rate limiting becomes more pronounced. Slew rate is a large-signal-performance parameter. Slew rate is usually specified at unity gain. Op amps with higher slew rates have wider bandwidths.

1-1-4-11 Frequency Response

The gain of an op amp decreases with an increase in frequency. The gain given by manufacturers is generally at zero hertz or DC. Figure 1-12 shows a voltage-gain versus frequency-response curve. In the open-loop mode, the gain falls off very rapidly as frequency increases. When the frequency increases tenfold, a tenfold decrease in gain results. The breakover point occurs at 70.7 percent of the maximum gain. The frequency bandwidth is normally considered at the point where the gain falls to 70.7 percent of maximum.

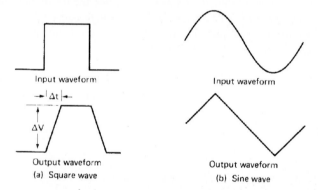

FIGURE 1-11 Example of slew-rate limiting on waveforms.

Therefore, the open-loop bandwidth is about 10 Hz, for this example. Fortunately, op amps usually require degenerative feedback in amplifier circuits, and this feedback increases the bandwidth of the circuit. For a closed-loop gain of 100, the bandwidth has increased to about 10 kHz. Lowering the gain to 10 increases the bandwidth to about 100 kHz. The unity-gain point occurs at 1 MHz and is called the unity-gain frequency. The unity-gain frequency establishes the reference point at which many op amps are specified by manufacturers.

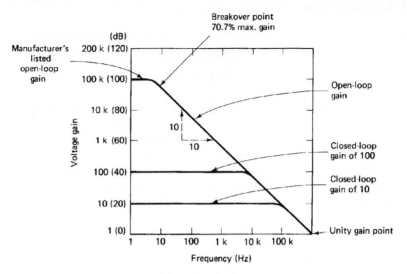

FIGURE 1-12 Voltage gain versus frequency.

1-1-4-12 Gain-Bandwidth Product

The gain-bandwidth product is equal to the unity-gain frequency. It not only tells us the upper useful frequency of a circuit, but allows us to determine the bandwidth for a given gain. For example (referring to Figure 1-12, which shows a frequency-response curve for a frequency-compensated op amp, such as the 741), if you multiply the gain and bandwidth of a specific circuit, the product will equal the unity-gain frequency:

gain-bandwidth product   = gain X bandwidth = unity-gain frequency
(GBP)   = 100 X 10 kHz = 1,000,000 Hz (1 MHz)
or
GBP   = 10 X 100 kHz = 1,000,000 Hz (1 MHz)

Therefore, if we wanted to know the upper frequency limit or bandwidth of a circuit with a gain of 100, we would divide the unity-gain frequency by gain:

$$\text{bandwidth} = \frac{\text{unity-gain frequency}}{\text{gain}}$$

$$(BW) = \frac{1,000,000}{100} = 10 kHz$$

1-1-4-13 Noise

Op amps are as susceptible to noise as any other electronic circuit. External noise is generated by electrical devices and the inherent noise of electronic components (resistors, capacitors, etc.), ranging in frequency from 0.01 Hz to the megahertz range. Proper circuit construction techniques can minimize external noise. Internal noise of an op amp results from the internal components, bias current, and drift. Noise is also amplified by the op amp, just as offset voltage and signal voltage are. The noise gain is expressed

$$\text{noise gain} = 1 + \frac{R_F}{R_{\text{in}}}$$

Internal noise can be minimized by keeping series input resistors and the feedback resistor as low in value as practically possible to satisfy circuit requirements. Also, bypassing the feedback resistor with a small capacitor ($\approx$3 pF) reduces the noise gain at high frequencies.

1-1-4-14 Common-Mode Rejection Ratio (CMRR)

Common-mode rejection is a feature associated with differential amplifiers. If the same in-phase voltage is applied to the inputs of the amplifier, the output will be zero. Only a difference of potential at the inputs will produce a voltage at the output. For instance, a 1020-Hz signal is applied to the inverting input of the op amp shown in Figure 1-13. The same frequency is applied to the noninverting input but is 180° out of phase. This is the differential signal. However, the 1020-Hz signal has picked up a 60-Hz hum. The 60 Hz is in phase at the two inputs and represents the common-mode signal. The differential amplifier will tend to reject the 60-Hz common-mode signal while amplifying the differential 1020-Hz signal. The ability of an op amp to amplify the differential signal while rejecting the common-mode signal is called the common-mode rejection ratio (CMRR). This ratio can be expressed as

$$\text{CMRR} = \frac{A_D}{A_{\text{cm}}}$$

where A_D is the differential gain and A_{cm} the common-mode gain. The CMRR is usually expressed in decibels, where the higher the rating, the better the rejection.

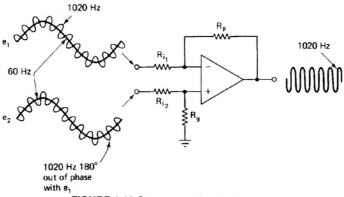

FIGURE 1-13 Common mode rejection.

1-1-4-15 Short-Circuit Protection

An op amp can produce damaging current if its output is shorted to ground, $+V_C$ supply, or $-V_C$ supply, unless it is provided with short-circuit protection. Transistor Q_{15} shown in Figure 1-7 is a current-limiting device that provides this protection. Most newer-type op amps have this short-circuit protection built in, while some older types do not.

1-1-4-16 Electrical Limitations

Like all solid-state devices, op amps have electrical limitations that must not be exceeded, to ensure proper operation and to prevent possible destruction. These limitations are referred to as absolute maximum ratings.

Supply voltage ±V. The safe maximum allowable voltage that can be applied to the device, including both positive and negative supplies.

Power dissipation. The safe amount of power the device is capable of dissipating on a continuous basis while operating within a specified temperature range.

Differential-input voltage. The safe maximum voltage that can be applied between the two inputs without excessive current flow.

Input voltage. The maximum voltage that can safely be applied between either input terminal and ground (circuit common). The magnitude of this input voltage should never exceed the magnitude of the supply voltage (typically 15 V).

Output short-circuit duration. The length of time that the op amp can withstand a direct short circuit from the output terminal to ground or either voltage supply terminal.

Operating-temperature range. The range of temperature over which the op amp will perform within the rated specifications. Commercial-grade devices operate from 0 to +70°C, industrial-grade devices operate from –25 to +85°C, and military-grade devices operate from –55 to +125°C.

Storage-temperature range. The safe range of temperature over which the device can be stored, typically –65 to +150°C.

Lead temperature. The temperature that the device will withstand for a specific period of time during the lead soldering process. This rating is typically 300°C for a period of 10 to 60 s.

1-1-4-17 Understanding Specification Sheets

In designing or constructing op amp circuits it is important to know the parameters and electrical limitations of a particular device to be able to predict performance and protect the circuit from over-voltage conditions. Figure 1-14 shows a typical manufacturer's specification or data sheet.

The data sheet will usually give a brief description of the device, list its salient features, indicate its absolute maximum ratings, and show pin-out diagrams. Electrical characteristics and parameters are usually shown with ranges indicated by minimum (MIN), typical (TYP), and maximum (MAX). Very often other information and circuits are given showing special testing conditions and applications.

Special attention should be paid to the maximum operating supply voltage of a device and its maximum power dissipation.

μA741
FREQUENCY-COMPENSATED OPERATIONAL AMPLIFIER
FAIRCHILD LINEAR INTEGRATED CIRCUIT

GENERAL DESCRIPTION — The μA741 is a high performance monolithic Operational Amplifier constructed using the Fairchild Planar* epitaxial process. It is intended for a wide range of analog applications. High common mode voltage range and absence of latch-up tendencies make the μA741 ideal for use as a voltage follower. The high gain and wide range of operating voltage provides superior performance in integrator, summing amplifier, and general feedback applications. Electrical characteristics of the μA741A and E are identical to MIL-M-38510/10101.

- NO FREQUENCY COMPENSATION REQUIRED
- SHORT CIRCUIT PROTECTION
- OFFSET VOLTAGE NULL CAPABILITY
- LARGE COMMON MODE AND DIFFERENTIAL VOLTAGE RANGES
- LOW POWER CONSUMPTION
- NO LATCH-UP

ABSOLUTE MAXIMUM RATINGS

Supply Voltage	
μA741A, μA741, μA741E	±22 V
μA741C	±18 V
Internal Power Dissipation (Note 1)	
Metal Can	500 mW
Molded and Hermetic DIP	670 mW
Mini DIP	310 mW
Flatpak	570 mW
Differential Input Voltage	±30 V
Input Voltage (Note 2)	±15 V
Storage Temperature Range	
Metal Can, Hermetic DIP, and Flatpak	−65°C to +150°C
Mini DIP, Molded DIP	−55°C to +125°C
Operating Temperature Range	
Military (μA741A, μA741)	−55°C to +125°C
Commercial (μA741E, μA741C)	0°C to +70°C
Lead Temperature (Soldering)	
Metal Can, Hermetic DIPs, and Flatpak (60 s)	300°C
Molded DIPs (10 s)	260°C
Output Short Circuit Duration (Note 3)	Indefinite

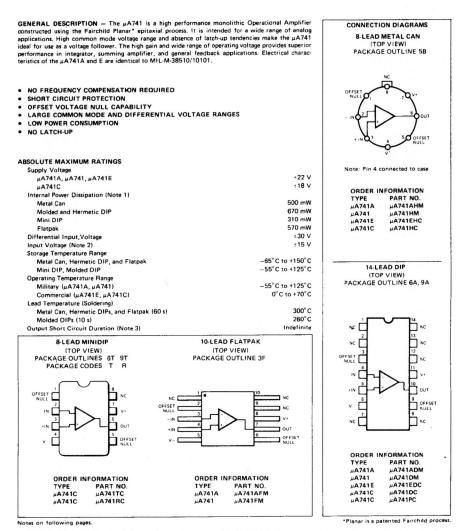

CONNECTION DIAGRAMS

8-LEAD METAL CAN
(TOP VIEW)
PACKAGE OUTLINE 5B

Note: Pin 4 connected to case

ORDER INFORMATION

TYPE	PART NO.
μA741A	μA741AHM
μA741	μA741HM
μA741E	μA741EHC
μA741C	μA741HC

14-LEAD DIP
(TOP VIEW)
PACKAGE OUTLINE 6A, 9A

ORDER INFORMATION

TYPE	PART NO.
μA741A	μA741ADM
μA741	μA741DM
μA741E	μA741EDC
μA741C	μA741DC
μA741C	μA741PC

8-LEAD MINIDIP
(TOP VIEW)
PACKAGE OUTLINES 6T 9T
PACKAGE CODES T R

ORDER INFORMATION

TYPE	PART NO.
μA741C	μA741TC
μA741C	μA741RC

10-LEAD FLATPAK
(TOP VIEW)
PACKAGE OUTLINE 3F

ORDER INFORMATION

TYPE	PART NO.
μA741A	μA741AFM
μA741	μA741FM

Notes on following pages.

*Planar is a patented Fairchild process.

FIGURE 1-14 Typical data sheet (courtesy Fairchild Camera and Instruments Corporation)

1-1-5 POWER-SUPPLY REQUIREMENTS FOR OP AMPS

Most op amps require a dual ± power supply for proper operation. Using this type of power source allows the output of the op amp to swing positive and negative with reference to ground. This feature is particularly useful in DC circuits and special audio applications.

The simplest power source is batteries, as shown in Figure 1-15a. Two 9-V dry-cell batteries can be connected in series, with the common connection being reference ground. The

FAIRCHILD LINEAR INTEGRATED CIRCUITS • μA741

μA741A

ELECTRICAL CHARACTERISTICS ($V_S = \pm15V$, $T_A = 25°C$ unless otherwise specified)

PARAMETERS (see definitions)	CONDITIONS		MIN	TYP	MAX	UNITS
Input Offset Voltage	$R_S \leqslant 50\Omega$			0.8	3.0	mV
Average Input Offset Voltage Drift					15	μV/°C
Input Offset Current				3.0	30	nA
Average Input Offset Current Drift					0.5	nA/°C
Input Bias Current				30	80	nA
Power Supply Rejection Ratio	$V_S = +10, -20; V_S = +20, -10V, R_S = 50\Omega$			15	50	μV/V
Output Short Circuit Current			10	25	35	mA
Power Dissipation	$V_S = \pm20V$			80	150	mW
Input Impedance	$V_S = \pm20V$		1.0	6.0		MΩ
Large Signal Voltage Gain	$V_S = \pm20V, R_L = 2k\Omega, V_{OUT} = \pm15V$		50			V/mV
Transient Response	Rise Time			0.25	0.8	μs
(Unity Gain)	Overshoot			6.0	20	%
Bandwidth (Note 4)			.437	1.5		MHz
Slew Rate (Unity Gain)	$V_{IN} = \pm10V$		0.3	0.7		V/μs
The following specifications apply for $-55°C \leqslant T_A \leqslant +125°C$						
Input Offset Voltage					4.0	mV
Input Offset Current					70	nA
Input Bias Current					210	nA
Common Mode Rejection Ratio	$V_S = \pm20V, V_{IN} = \pm15V, R_S = 50\Omega$		80	95		dB
Adjustment For Input Offset Voltage	$V_S = \pm20V$		10			mV
Output Short Circuit Current			10		40	mA
Power Dissipation	$V_S = \pm20V$	$-55°C$			165	mW
		$+125°C$			135	mW
Input Impedance	$V_S = \pm20V$		0.5			MΩ
Output Voltage Swing	$V_S = \pm20V$,	$R_L = 10k\Omega$	±16			V
		$R_L = 2k\Omega$	±15			V
Large Signal Voltage Gain	$V_S = \pm20V, R_L = 2k\Omega, V_{OUT} = \pm15V$		32			V/mV
	$V_S = \pm5V, R_L = 2k\Omega, V_{OUT} = \pm2V$		10			V/mV

NOTES
1. Rating applies to ambient temperatures up to 70°C. Above 70°C ambient derate linearly at 6.3mW/°C for the metal can, 8.3mW/°C for the DIP and 7.1mW/°C for the Flatpak.
2. For supply voltages less than ±15V, the absolute maximum input voltage is equal to the supply voltage.
3. Short circuit may be to ground or either supply. Rating applies to +125°C case temperature or 75°C ambient temperature.
4. Calculated value from: $BW(MHz) = \dfrac{0.35}{Rise\ Time\ (\mu s)}$

FIGURE 1-14 *continued*

output will be a ±9-V power supply. Adding two more 9-V batteries in series will produce a ±18-V power supply, if needed or desired. Although this battery supply has portability, each battery must be fresh for proper circuit operation.

A single battery, such as an automobile 12-V rechargeable battery, can utilize a resistive voltage divider network to produce a ±6-V power supply, as shown in Figure 1-15b. If this circuit is used in an automotive application, remember that the ground reference for the op-amp circuitry is not the same as the battery ground for the vehicle.

Battery-operated power supplies have the disadvantage of maintaining the rated voltage up to maximum, through either recharging or replacement. Electronic dual power supplies operating from commercial electric service are shown in Figure 1-16. Two step-down 12-V transformers can be used to construct a ±15-V dual power supply with the ground reference connecting the two supplies together (Figure 1-16a).

The same dual power supply can be constructed more easily and is less bulky and less costly by using a 24-V center-tapped transformer, as shown in Figure 1-16b.

The power supplies discussed provide the basic voltages for op-amp operation. Many op-amp applications require these voltages to be regulated and as free as possible from noise. Basic zener-diode voltage regulation is shown in Figure 1-17a, it is good practice to have V_{in}, from the rectifier about 2 V greater than the total regulated voltage. For example, a ±15-V supply would be 30 V from $-V$ to $+V$; therefore, V_{in} should be about 32 V.

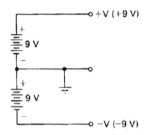

(a) ±9-volt battery power supply

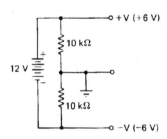

(b) ±6-volt battery power supply

FIGURE 1-15 Battery dual power supplies.

The value of the limiting resistor R_s (the resistor of the pi-type filter in Figure 1-17a) can be found by the formula

$$R_s = \frac{V_{in} - 2V_z}{I_z}$$

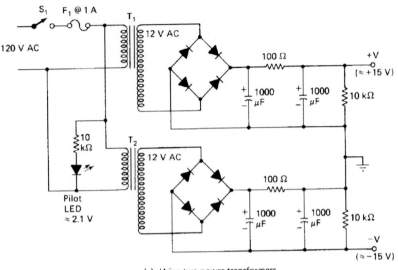

(a) Using two power transformers

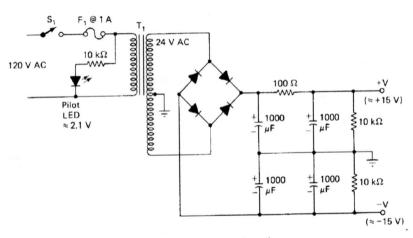

(b) Using a center-tapped transformer

FIGURE 1-16 Dual polarity power supplies.

where V_z is the zener-regulated voltage of each diode and I_z the current through the diodes without a load on the power supply. Generally, I_z can be set for half of the maximum allowable current. For example, $I_{z_{max}}$ for a 1-W 15-V zener diode can be found by the formula

$$I_{z_{max}} = \frac{P_{max}}{V_z} = \frac{1\text{W}}{15\text{V}} = 66.6\text{mA}$$

Then

$$I_z = \frac{I_{z_{max}}}{2} = 33.3\text{mA}$$

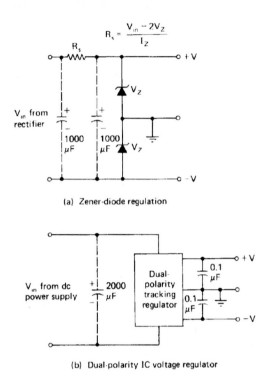

(a) Zener-diode regulation

(b) Dual-polarity IC voltage regulator

FIGURE 1-17 Dual polarity voltage regulation.

Of course, I_z can be set higher, depending on the load placed on the power supply, but it should never exceed $I_{z_{max}}$ or there is a definite possibility of destroying the zener diodes when there is no load current present.

For precision op-amp applications requiring very stable power supplies, an IC dual-polarity-tracking voltage regulator may be used, as shown in Figure 1-17b. These types of voltage regulators provide different voltages (LM325 = ±15 V, LM326 = ±12 V) and should be connected to the power supply according to the manufacturer's specification sheet.

In critical applications of low-level inputs and high gain, the power-supply requirements are extremely stringent. Voltage changes or noise on the power-supply lines can be coupled into an op amp and appear as equivalent input signals. Manufacturers take this into account in the design of op amps by minimizing these effects. The ability of an op amp to reject power-supply-induced noise and drift is called the power-supply rejection ratio (PSRR). Stated another way, the PSRR is the ratio of the change in input offset voltage to the change in power-supply voltage producing it. Ratings may be given for each power supply separately or together, giving a typical value and a maximum limit. The unit of measure may be μV/V or dB.

Some special op amps are designed to operate from single-voltage (usually positive) power supplies. Standard op amps may in some limited applications use a single power supply. In the quiescent state (no input signals present) the output should measure about halfway between ground and the maximum voltage supply.

1-1-6 TYPES OF OP AMPS AND PACKAGE CONFIGURATIONS

Op amps have been around for quite a number of years. But it was not until 1963, when Fairchild Semiconductor introduced the first usable IC op amp, the µA702, that the present trend in op amp usage was set. Since that time, solid-state manufacturers have improved and developed a vast amount of diversified types of op amps into the broad spectrum of devices available today. Some op amps have become so specialized that they are fabricated into specific circuit configurations, such as voltage comparators and voltage followers. The characteristics of op amps are constantly being improved, but regardless of the various manufacturers, op amps having similar characteristics are placed into group and/or family types.

General-purpose op amps (group 1). General-purpose op amps have a gain-bandwidth product of approximately 1 MHz, a fairly high gain, and input impedance of several mega-ohms, and they operate from power supplies of approximately ±5 to ±22 V.

The 709 family. The Fairchild µA709 IC op amp had significant improvements over the µA702, so that it became the first recognized industry standard and is still in use today. The µ702 had very limited common-mode input range, relatively low voltage gain, and used odd supply voltages, such as +12 V and -6 V. The uA709 overcame many of these problems and operates from a ±15-V supply. It has an input resistance of about 250 kΩ , an output resistance of about 150 Ω , a voltage gain of about 45,000, but no output short-circuit protection. It also has the problem of latch-up, where certain values of common-mode input signals would drive the output voltage to some level where it would remain. Some members of the 709 family are the Fairchild µ709, Motorola MC 1709, National Semiconductor LM709, and Texas Instruments SN72709.

The 101 family. The next evolutionary step came in 1967, when National Semiconductor Corporation introduced the LM 101. The 101 design solved many of the 709 problems, and in addition has an increased gain to 160,000 and a useful power-supply range from ±5 V to ±20 V. Op amps 101A, 107, and 301A belong to the 101 family.

The 741 family. In 1968, Fairchild Semiconductor introduced the µA741, the first internally compensated IC op amp. This op amp offers many features, that make their application nearly foolproof: overload protection on the input and output, no latch-up when the common-mode range is exceeded, and freedom from oscillations in most standard circuit configurations. The 741 is probably the most widely used industry standard today. It is readily available at most electronics component stores. This family includes the 741A, the 747 dual op amp, the 748, the LM 148 (quad-741 op amp), and the 1558 dual op amp.

The other numerous general-purpose op amps available have improved characteristics or are specialized versions of the basic families mentioned. Other groups and families emphasize extremely high input impedances. Some offer very wide bandwidth with high slew rates, while others are designed to operate at high voltages and currents. A general outline of the various groups is given in Table 1-1.

IC op amp package configurations. Integrated-circuit op amps are available in four commonly used packages, as shown in Figure 1-18a. The metal TO-type package is approximately 0.300 to 0.450 in. in diameter and 0.130 to 0.185 in. high, with 8 to 10 leads coming out of the bottom. The flat package has a body about 0.250 to 0.270 in. square and 0.050 to 0.070 in. thick, usually with five leads coming out each side. This package may be of metal, glass, or plastic. The dual-in-line package (DIP) can be made of metal, glass, ceramic, or plastic. It measures about 0.750 in. long, 0.270 in. wide, and 0.190 in. thick, with seven leads protruding downward from each side. The mini-DIP is about half the size of a standard 14-pin DIP and has four leads protruding downward from each side.

Table 1-1: Uses and features of op-amp groups.

Group	Use	Salient Features
I	General purpose	DC up to 1-MHz bandwidth
II	DC and low-level performance	Extremely high input impedance, low bias current, etc.
III	AC and high-level performance	Wide bandwidth and high slewing rates
IV	High voltage and power	Capable of driving loads directly
V	Unique devices	Special op amps, such as programmable, digitally addressable, etc., types

The lead identification shown in Figure 1-18b is usually self-explanatory. The positive supply voltage is connected to the $+V$ terminal, and the negative supply voltage is connected to the $-V$ terminal. Input and output terminals are clearly indicated. The balance terminals (sometimes designated Offset Null) are connected to a potentiometer for null adjusting. Terminals marked NC means no connection and are included for physical ruggedness of the package.

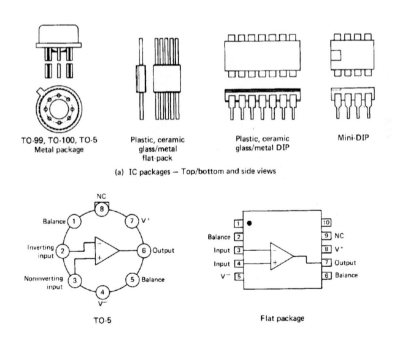

FIGURE 1-18 IC op-amp packages.

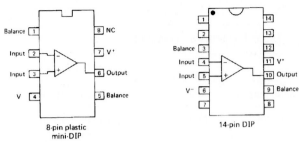

(b) Single op-amp IC packages

FIGURE 1-18 *continued.*

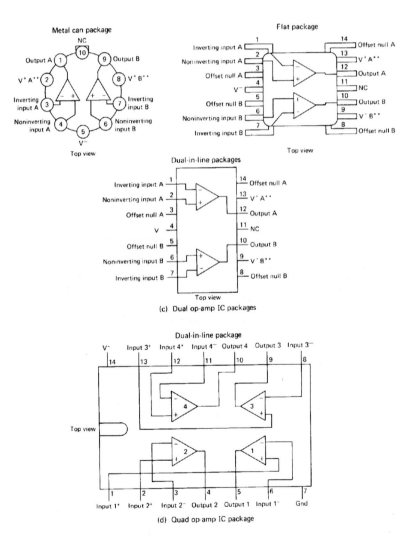

(c) Dual op-amp IC packages

(d) Quad op-amp IC package

FIGURE 1-18 continued

SECTION 1-2 TERMINOLOGY EXERCISE

Write a brief definition for each of the following terms:
1. Differential amplifier
2. V_{id}
3. V_{od}
4. Voltage level shifter
5. Source transistor
6. Sink transistor
7. Totem-pole output
8. Common mode rejection
9. Open-loop gain
10. Closed-loop gain
11. $A_v = -R_F/R_{in}$
12. $A_v = R_F/R_{in} + 1$
13. Output-offset voltage
14. Input-offset voltage
15. Input-offset current
16. Offset nulling
17. Op amp frequency compensation
18. Slew rate
19. Frequency response
20. Unity gain
21. GBP
22. CMRR
23. Noise gain (Show formula)
24. Data sheet

SECTION 1-3 PROBLEMS AND EXERCISES

1. Draw a block diagram of an op amp.
2. Draw the schematic symbol of an op amp and identify all parts.
3. What is the controlled gain of an op amp when $R_{in} = 2.2$ kΩ and $R_F = 68$ kΩ?
4. What is the controlled gain of an op amp when R_{in} 4.7 kΩ and $R_F = 4.7$ kΩ?
5. Draw a schematic symbol of an op amp, indicating offset nulling.
6. Draw two examples of slew-rate limiting on voltage waveforms.
7. What is the gain-bandwidth product of an op-amp circuit with a gain of 45 and a bandwidth of 50 kHz?
8. What is the upper frequency limit of an op-amp circuit with a gain of 25 and a unity-gain frequency of 1 MHz?
9. Draw a voltage gain versus frequency graph for an op amp with a unity-gain frequency of 1 MHz and an open-loop gain of 200,000. Indicate a closed-loop gain of 10,000 and 100.
10. Find the value of R_s for a zener diode regulator for a $\pm$ 12-V supply where $I_z = 80$ mA

and $V_{in} = 30$ V.

11. Referring to Figure 1-14 list the maximum rating for the following terms:

    a.   Power supply voltage   _____

    b.   Power dissipation   _____

    c.   Lead temperature for soldering   _____

    d.   Output short circuit duration   _____

    e.   Input offset voltage   _____

    f.   Input offset current   _____

    g.   Input bias current   _____

    h.   Output short-circuit current   _____

12. Referring to Figure 1-14, identify the pins for an 8-lead mini-DIP op amp IC:

Pin number   *Description*

    1

    2

    3

    4

    5

    7

    8

SECTION 1-4 EXPERIMENTS

This chapter presents some basic experiments to familiarize you with op-amp characteristics and provide working skills in their use. Some of the experiments show how to determine specific op-amp parameters. The experiments are arranged in order from basic operation to more complex procedures. You are not compelled to follow this sequence, but a newcomer to op amps may find it very helpful to do so.

Step-by-step procedures and directions are used to ensure success of the experiments and minimize the chances of damaging the ICs and equipment. There are a few questions at the end of each experiment to aid you in proving that you understand the specific characteristic or parameter.

The popular 741 op-amp IC is used in all the experiments. Be sure you use one of high quality (no surplus rejects) to ensure accurate results in the experiments. No pin identification is shown on the schematic diagrams, but you can refer to Figure 1-18 for proper numbering, depending on the style of package you use. Other types of op amps may be used, provided that you have a "spec" sheet and pin identification guide for the one you select.

Circuit connections can be temporarily "tack"-soldered, perhaps on a perforated board, or better yet, some sort of breadboard can be used. Regardless of the method you use, be sure to keep the leads as short as possible to reduce stray pickup and provide good results.

1-4-1 *Safety Precautions*

The experiments in this manual do not use a voltage greater than 30 V ($\pm$ 15 V); therefore, the chance of getting an electrical shock is greatly reduced. However, all voltages do have the potential to burn materials and start fires, destroy electronic components, and present hazards to the person performing the operations. Common sense and an awareness of electrical circuits is important whenever you are working on these experiments. An electronic technician or student may have to work with high voltages, power tools, and machinery. Before actual work is performed, sufficient instruction should be acquired in the proper use and safety requirements of all electronic devices.

It takes a very small amount of current to pass through the human body from an electrical shock to injure a person severely or fatally. The 60-Hz current values affecting the human body are as follows:

Current Value	Effects
1 mA (0.001 A)	Tingling or mild sensation.
10 mA (0.01 A)	A shock of sufficient intensity to cause involuntary control of muscles, so that a person cannot let go of an electrical conductor.
100 mA (0. 1 A)	A shock of this type lasting for 1 second is sufficient to cause a crippling effect or even death.
Over 100 mA	An extremely severe shock that may cause ventricular fibrillation, where a change in the rhythm of the heartbeat causes death almost instantaneously.

The resistance of the human body varies from about 500,000 Ω when dry to about 300 Ω when wet (including the effects of perspiration). In this case, voltages as low as 30 V can cause sufficient current to be fatal (I = voltage/wet resistance = 30 V/300 Ω = 100 mA).

Even though the actual voltage of a circuit being worked on is low enough not to present a very hazardous situation, the equipment being used to power and test the circuit (that is, power supply, signal generator, meters, oscilloscopes) is usually operated on 120 V AC. This equipment should have (three-wire) polarized line cords that are not cracked or brittle. An even better safety precaution is to have the equipment operate from an isolation transformer, which is usually connected to a workbench. To minimize the chance of getting shocked, a person should use only one hand while making voltage measurements, keeping the other hand at the side of the body, in the lap, or behind the body. Do not defeat the safety feature (fuse, circuit breaker, interlock switch) of any electrical device by shorting across it or by using a higher amperage rating than that specified by the manufacturer. These safety devices are intended to protect both the user and the equipment.

Hand tools can be dangerous and cause severe injuries. Diagonal cutters, wire. strippers, long-nose pliers, and crimping tools can pinch and cut. Use care in cutting wire since small pieces can become projectiles and hit another person in the face or eye.

Screwdrivers should be held properly so that they do not slip and puncture some part of the body. Do not use them as chisels or cutters.

A soldering iron should have a holder on which to place it. Care must be used not to burn the body or other materials. Be careful of hot solder, which can splash and cause severe burns, especially to the eyes and face.

A neat working area requires a careful and deliberate approach when setting it up. Test equipment and tools should be set out on the work-bench in a neat and orderly manner. Connecting wires from the test equipment to the circuit under test should be placed so as not to interfere with testing procedures.

Before power is applied to a circuit, the area around the circuit should be cleared of extra wires, components, hand tools, and debris (cut wire and insulation).

1-4-2 GENERAL PROCEDURES AND TEST EQUIPMENT TO USE

All power supplies should be turned off or not be connected to the test circuit when you are constructing, changing components, or disassembling the circuit. This prevents any surge currents from destroying the sensitive IC or damaging test equipment. Each circuit should be constructed and then double checked before applying power.

The power supply shown in the schematic diagrams is ±15 V; however, you may elect to use ±12 V or ±9 V with the same success. The power supply used can be similar to those shown in Section 1-1e but should have very good regulation. If you decide to use batteries (±12 V or ±9 V), be sure to bypass them to ground with 0.1-μF capacitors (see Figure 6-6). When checking the power-supply voltages, be sure that they are available at the corresponding pins of the IC.

A DC input voltage (signal) is required in several experiments. This signal can be supplied by 1.5-V cells, such as a fresh flashlight battery of size AA, C, or D.

Specifications and descriptions of the test equipment used in the experiments are as follows:

1. *Meters.* Voltmeters should have 20 kΩ/*V* or higher for measuring DC and be capable of measuring millivolts and microamperes. Electronic voltmeters, such as vacuum-tube, transistor, or FET, are the best to use and are an absolute must for measuring critical low values of voltage and current. A good-quality digital multimeter would be excellent for these experiments. The meters can be used to measure DC voltage and current as well as RMS values of AC voltage. An oscilloscope can be used to measure peak-to-peak voltages.

2. *Oscilloscope.* A basic oscilloscope can be used for most of the experiments; however, one having a voltage-calibrated vertical axis and a time-calibrated horizontal axis is easier to use and speeds up testing time. A dual-trace oscilloscope is even more advantageous, permitting you to look at input and output signals simultaneously.

3. *Signal generators.* The AC signals required for most of the experiments are sine waves or square waves within the audio-frequency range and can be supplied by an audio generator. An RF generator can be used for frequencies above this range, provided that it can produce a signal up to 1-V rms output. These generators should have low output impedance (the lower the better). A function generator is well suited for these experiments.

4. *Components.* Resistors can be or ¼ or ½ -W composition types with 5 percent or 10 percent tolerance. Capacitors are nonelectrolytic types, such as ceramic or Mylar, with a minimum 50-V rating. Potentiometers are standard composition type except where specified as wirewound (WW).

Since the same op amp, power-supply voltages, and test equipment are used throughout the experiments, only the components needed for a specific experiment will be given.

Figure 1-19 shows a typical set-up of equipment and components for performing the experiments. Notice how the power supply, signal generator, oscilloscope, and meter are situated. This set-up makes the experiment easier to perform and more efficient for data taking.

See Appendix B for a review of how to use basic test equipment.

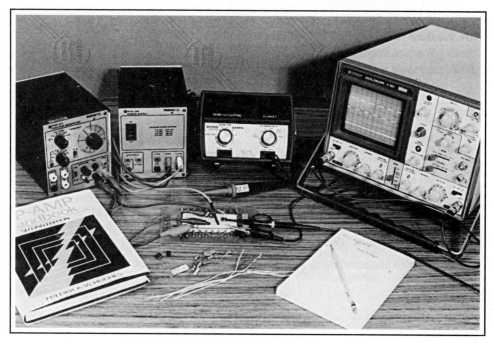

FIGURE 1-19 Equipment set-up for performing experiments.

EXPERIMENT 1-1 OUTPUT POLARITY

Objective:

To show how the op-amp output can swing positive and negative with respect to ground and is 180° out of phase with the input.

Introduction:

This experiment shows the phase relationship of input voltage to output voltage. In the first part of the experiment the inverting input is used to show the 180° out of phase voltage at the output. In the second part of the experiment, the non-inverting input is used to show the in phase relationship of input-to-output voltages. The output voltage reading should read approximately + or − 13.9 volts.

Required Components:

1 10-kΩ resistor (R_{in})

1 three-position switch (S_1)

Test Procedure:

1. With the power supply off, construct the circuit shown in Figure 1-20a.
2. Set the voltmeter to the next highest range above 15 V.
3. Turn the power supply on.
4. Record the V_{out} reading.(Meter may deflect due to offset.)
5. Place S_1 in position A.
6. Record V_{out}, indicating polarity.
7. Place S_1 in position B.
8. Record V_{out}, indicating polarity.
9. Turn the power supply off and remove the batteries.
10. Rearrange the circuit to that shown in Figure 1-20b. (Note the meter lead polarity.)

11. Repeat steps 3 through 9.

QUESTIONS FOR FIGURE 1-20

1. What is the V_{out} of Figure 1-20a when S_1 in position A? _____
2. What is the V_{out} of Figure 1-20a when S_1 is in position B? _____
3. What polarity will V_{out} be when V_{in} is positive for an inverting amplifier? _____
4. What polarity will V_{out} be when V_{in} is negative for an inverting amplifier? _____
5. What is the V_{out} of Figure 1-20b when S_1 is in position A? _____
6. What is the V_{out} of Figure 1-20b when S_1 is in position B? _____
7. What polarity will V_{out} be when V_{in} is positive for a noninverting amplifier? _____
8. What polarity will V_{out} be when V_{in} is negative for a noninverting amplifier? _____

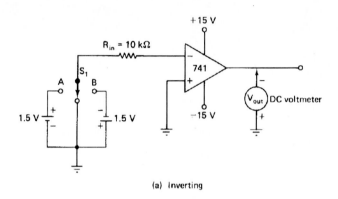

(a) Inverting

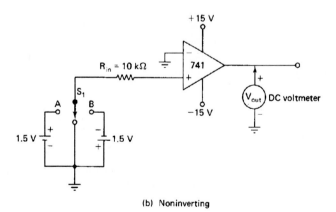

(b) Noninverting

FIGURE 1-20 Output polarity.

EXPERIMENT 1-2 CLOSED-LOOP DC VOLTAGE GAIN (INVERTING)

Objective:
To demonstrate how circuit voltage gain depends upon R_{in} and R_F.

Introduction:

The gain of this circuit is demonstrated by DC voltage measurements. The closed loop voltage gain of this circuit is determined by the resistance ratio of R_F/R_{in}. The circuit is configured as an inverting amplifier, therefore, the output voltage will be 180° out of phase with the input voltage. The actual output voltage will be the result of the resistance ratio and the amplitude of the input voltage, expressed by the formula:

$$V_{out} = -\left(\frac{R_F}{R_{in}}\right)(V_{in})$$

Required Components:

1 10-kΩ wirewound potentiometer (R_p)

1 10-kΩ resistor (R_{in})

1 100-kΩ resistor (R_F)

1 SPDT switch (S_1)

Test Procedure:

1. With the power supply off, construct the circuit shown in Figure 1-21.
2. Place S_1 to position A.
3. Turn on the power supply.
4. Adjust R_p for a V_{in} of +0.5 V.
5. Record V_{out}, indicating polarity.
6. Turn off the power supply.
7. Reverse the meter leads.
8. Place S_1 to position B.
9. Turn on the power supply.
10. Adjust R_p for a V_{in} of – 0.8 V.
11. Record V_{out}, indicating polarity.
12. Turn off the power supply and disconnect the batteries used for V_{in}.
13. Calculate the gain of the circuit from the formula

$$A = \frac{R_F}{R_{in}}$$

14. Calculate V_{out} from the formula

$$V_{out} = -\left(\frac{R_F}{R_{in}}\right)(V_{in})$$

15. Calculate the voltage gain from the formula

$$A_v = \frac{V_{out}}{V_{in}}$$

16. Repeat the experiment several times for different gains by changing the value of R_F.

QUESTIONS FOR FIGURE 1-21

1. What is V_{out} for a V_{in} of +0.5 V? (Remember polarity.) _____
2. What is V_{out} for a V_{in} of –0.8 V? (Remember polarity.) _____
3. What is the gain of the circuit? _____
4. What is the gain of the circuit if R_F = 120 kΩ? _____
5. What is V_{out} when R_F = 56 kΩ and V_{in} = +0.6 V? _____
6. What is V_{out} when R_F = 220 kΩ and V_{in} = –0.4 V? _____

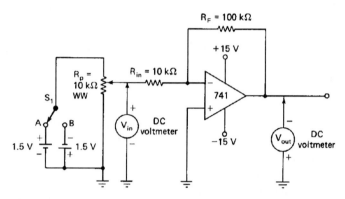

FIGURE 1-21 Closed loop DC voltage gain (inverting).

EXPERIMENT 1-3 CLOSED-LOOP DC VOLTAGE GAIN (NONINVERTING)

Objective:
To show how circuit gain is greater with the noninverting amplifier than with the inverting amplifier.

Introduction:
This circuit is a noninverting amplifier, therefore, the output voltage will be in phase with the input voltage. The closed loop voltage gain is also determined by the resistance ratio of R_F/R_{in} plus a factor of 1, expressed by the formula

$$A = \frac{R_F}{R_{in}} + 1$$

The actual output voltage will be the result of the resistance ratio plus 1 and the amplitude of the input voltage as expressed by the formula

$$V_{out} = \left(\frac{R_F}{R_{in}} + 1 \right)(V_{in})$$

Required Components:
1 10-kΩ wirewound potentiometer (R_p)

1 10-kΩ resistor (R_{in})
1 100-kΩ resistor (R_F)
1 SPDT switch (S_1)

Test Procedure:

1. With the power supply off, construct the circuit shown in Figure 1-22.
2. Place S_1 to position A.
3. Turn on the power supply.
4. Adjust R_p for a V_{in} of +0.5 V.
5. Record V_{out}, indicating polarity. _____
6. Place S_1 to position B.
7. Adjust R_p for a V_{in} of – 0.8 V.
8. Record V_{out}, indicating polarity. _____
9. Turn off the power supply and disconnect the batteries used for V_{in}.
10. Calculate the gain of the circuit from the formula

$$A = \frac{R_F}{R_{in}} + 1$$

11. Calculate V_{out} from the formula

$$V_{out} = \left(\frac{R_F}{R_{in}} + 1 \right)(V_{in})$$

12. Calculate the voltage gain from the formula

$$A_v = \frac{V_{out}}{V_{in}}$$

13. Repeat the experiment several times for different gains by changing the value of R_F

QUESTIONS FOR FIGURE 1-22

1. What is V_{out} for a V_{in} of +0.5 V? (Remember polarity.) _____
2. What is V_{out} for a V_{in} of –0.8 V? (Remember polarity.) _____
3. What is the gain of the circuit? _____
4. What is the gain of the circuit if $R_F = 120$ kΩ ? _____
5. What is V_{out} when $R_F = 56$ kΩ and $V_{in} = +0.6$ V? _____
6. What is V_{out} when $R_F = 220$ kΩ and $V_{in} = -0.4$ V? _____

EXPERIMENT 1-4 MAXIMUM DC OUTPUT-VOLTAGE RANGE

Objective:
To show the output voltage saturation of an op amp.
Introduction:
This experiment uses an inverting amplifier to demonstrate output voltage saturation. The

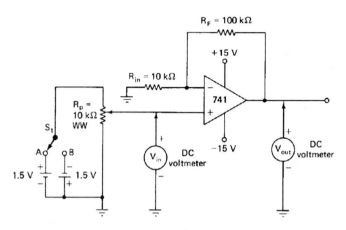

FIGURE 1-22 Closed loop DC voltage gain (noninverting).

input voltage is incremented in 0.2 volt steps while the output voltage is measured and recorded. Beyond 1.2 volts input voltage, the output will not increase, indicating output voltage saturation.

Required Components:
1 10-kΩ resistor (R_{in})
1 100-kΩ resistor (R_F)
1 10-kΩ wirewound potentiometer (R_p)
1 SPDT switch (S_1)

Test Procedure:
1. With the power supply off, construct the circuit shown in Figure 1-23
2. Place S_1 to position A.
3. Turn on the power supply.
4. Using data log-1, adjust R_p for the +V_{in} values shown and record each corresponding −V_{out} reading.
5. Turn off the power supply.
6. Place S_1 to position B.
7. Reverse the meter leads.
8. Turn on the power supply.
9. Using data log-2, adjust R_p for the −V_{in} values shown and record each corresponding +V_{out} reading.
10. Turn off the power supply and remove the batteries.
11. Observe the data logs.

The point where a further increase in V_{in} causes no change in V_{out} is called saturation. The lowest point at which +V_{out} and − V_{out} saturation occurs is the maximum DC output-voltage range.

QUESTIONS FOR FIGURE 1-23

1. What is the positive saturation voltage (+V_{sat})? _____

2. What is the negative saturation voltage $(-V_{sat})$? _____
3. What is the maximum DC output-voltage range? _____

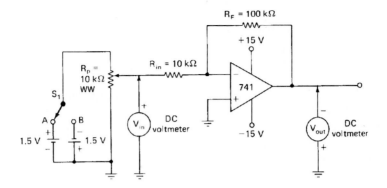

Data log 1	
$+V_{in}$	$-V_{out}$
0.2	
0.4	
0.6	
0.8	
1.0	
1.2	
1.4	
1.5	

Data log 2	
$-V_{in}$	$+V_{out}$
0.2	
0.4	
0.6	
0.8	
1.0	
1.2	
1.4	
1.5	

FIGURE 1-23 Maximum DC output-voltage range.

EXPERIMENT 1-5 MAXIMUM DC INPUT-VOLTAGE RANGE

Objective:
To demonstrate how input voltage causes output voltage saturation.
Introduction:
This experiment is a continuation of Experiment 1-4, dealing with output voltage saturation. There is a limit to the amount of input voltage amplitude that can be applied to an op amp. If this limit is exceeded, the output voltage will saturate. In this experiment, the maximum DC input voltage range will be found.
Required Components:
1 10-kΩ resistor (R_{in})
1 100-kΩ resistor (R_F)
1 10-kΩ wirewound potentiometer (R_p)
1 SPDT switch (S_1)
Test Procedure:

1. With the power supply off, construct the circuit shown in Figure 1-24.
2. Place S_1 to position A.
3. Turn on the power supply.
4. Adjust R_p until V_{out} reaches the value of $-V_{sat}$ from Experiment 1-4. Record the polarity and value of V_{in}. _____
5. Turn off the power supply.
6. Place S_1 to position B.
7. Reverse the meter leads.
8. Turn on the power supply.
9. Adjust R_p until V_{out} reaches the value of $+V_{sat}$ from Experiment 1-4. Record the polarity and value of V_{in}. _____
10. Turn off the power supply and remove the batteries.

QUESTIONS FOR FIGURE 1-24

1. What is the minimum V_{in} for $-V_{sat}$? _____
2. What is the minimum V_{in} for $+V_{sat}$? _____
3. What is the total (maximum) V_{in} DC range? _____

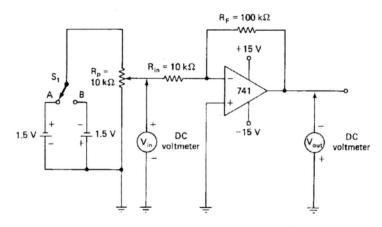

FIGURE 1-24 Maximum DC input-voltage range.

EXPERIMENT 1-6 INPUT IMPEDANCE

Objective:

A practical approach to finding op amp input impedance.

Introduction:

Resistor R_{in} is a major factor in determining the input impedance to an op amp circuit. Finding the actual input impedance of a particular op amp circuit is easily accomplished with the procedure in this experiment. A potentiometer is placed at the input of this inverting amplifier. The input signal is then adjusted for a nondistorted output. The input voltage is then adjusted for ½ of the amplitude by R_P. The power is removed from the circuit and the value of R_P is measured with an ohmmeter. This value represents the input impedance of the op amp circuit. An increase in input frequency will vary the input impedance of the circuit because of the capacitive reactance of the input stage of the op amp.

Required Components:

1 10-kΩ resistor (R_{in})
1 100-kΩ resistor (R_F)
1 50-kΩ wirewound potentiometer (R_p)
1 SPDT switch (S_1)

Test Procedure:

1. With the power supply off, construct the circuit shown in Figure 1-25. Place the wiper of R_p toward the generator.
2. Turn on the power supply.
3. Set the sine-wave generator to 1000 Hz.
4. Adjust the generator output amplitude for a maximum undistorted signal at v_{out}.
5. Record the peak-to-peak value of v_{in}. _____
6. Place S_1 to position B.
7. Adjust R_p until the peak-to-peak value of v_{in} is one-half the value recorded in step 5._____
8. Tum off the power supply.
9. Record the ohmic value of R_p from the wiper to the end connected to the generator. _____ This resistance value is equal to the input impedance of the op amp.
10. Repeat steps 2 through 9 for the following frequencies: 100 Hz, 10 kHz, 50 kHz, and 100 kHz.

QUESTIONS FOR FIGURE 1-25

1. What is the value of V_{in} in step 5? _____
2. What is this value divided by 2? _____
3. What is the ohmic reading of R_p from the wiper to the end connected to the generator? _____
4. What is the input impedance of the op amp? _____
5. Does the input impedance change with different input signal frequencies? _____ Why?

EXPERIMENT 1-7 OUTPUT IMPEDANCE

Objective:
A practical approach to finding op-amp output impedance.
Introduction:
The output impedance of an op amp circuit can be found with a similar procedure as was done for finding the input impedance in Experiment 1-6. The input signal voltage is adjusted for a nondistorted voltage output. Resistor R_P is then connected to the output. The output voltage should decrease as R_P loads down the circuit. Resistor R_P is then adjusted for the original output voltage. The power is removed from the circuit and R_P is measured with an ohmmeter. The measured value will be equal to the output impedance of the op amp circuit.
Required Components:
1 10-kΩ resistor (R_{in})
1 100-kΩ resistor (R_F)
1 1-kΩ wirewound potentiometer (R_p)
1 1-μF capacitor (nonpolarized) (C_1)
1 SPST switch (S_1)

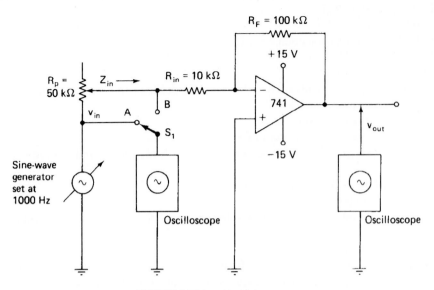

FIGURE 1-25 Input impedance.

Test Procedure:
1. With the power supply off, construct the circuit shown in Figure 1-26.
2. Set the sine-wave generator at 1000 Hz.
3. Turn on the power supply.
4. Adjust the generator output amplitude for a maximum undistorted signal at V_{out}.
5. Record the peak-to-peak value of V_{out}. _____
6. Close S_1. Observe that V_{out} is affected.
7. Adjust R_p so that V_{out} is the same as the original reading obtained in step 5.
8. Turn off the power supply.
9. Record the ohmic value of R_p from the end connected to S_1 and the wiper. _____
   This resistance value is equal to the output impedance of the op amp.
10. Repeat steps 2 through 9 for the following frequencies: 100 Hz, 10 kHz, 50 kHz, and 100 kHz.

QUESTIONS FOR FIGURE 1-26

1. What is the value of V_{out} in step 5? _____
2. What is the ohmic reading of R_p from the end connected to S_1 and the wiper?

   _____
3. What is the output impedance of the op amp? _____
4. Does the output impedance change with different input signal frequencies? _____
   Why?

EXPERIMENT 1-8 INPUT-OFFSET CURRENT

Objective:
To show how input-offset current affects output voltage.

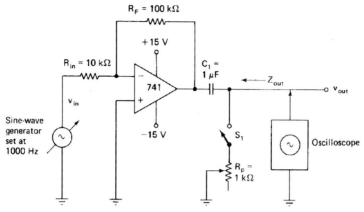

FIGURE 1-26 Output imedance.

Introduction:

The output voltage of an op amp should be zero when the input current is zero, however, because of the slight imbalance of internal components, the output voltage can not attain this ideal. In many actual circuits, an input current resistor or potentiometer is added to the circuit to be able to adjust the output voltage back to zero. In this experiment R_P is adjusted to cause the output to go to zero volts.

Required Components:

1 22-Ω resistor (R_1)

1 100-kΩ resistor (R_F)

1 10-kΩ wirewound potentiometer (R_p)

1 SPDT switch (S_1)

Test Procedure:

1. With the power supply off, construct the circuit shown in Figure 1-27.
2. Set the DC voltmeter at output to low range.
3. Turn on the power supply.
4. Record V_{out}. _____
5. Record I_{in}. _____
6. Close S_1 and adjust R_p until V_{out} is zero.
7. Record I_{in}. _____ This value of current is the input off-set current. An op amp may be offset-null-adjusted by this method.
8. Turn off the power supply and remove the battery.

QUESTIONS FOR FIGURE 1-27

1. What is V_{out} when S_1 is open? _____
2. What is the value of I_{in} when S_1 is closed and V_{out} is zero? _____
3. What is the value of input-offset current? _____

EXPERIMENT 1-9 INPUT-OFFSET VOLTAGE

Objective:

To show how input-offset voltage affects output voltage.

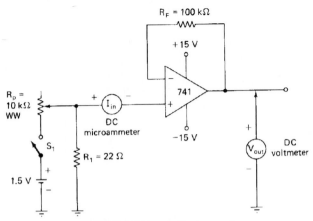

FIGURE 1-27 Input-offset current.

Introduction:

This experiment is a continuation of Experiment 1-8, except that the actual input offset voltage that produces the input-offset current is found.

Required Components:

1 22-Ω resistor (R_1)

1 100-kΩ resistor (R_F)

1 10-kΩ wirewound potentiometer (R_p)

1 SPST switch (S_1)

Test Procedure:

1. With the power supply off, construct the circuit shown in Figure 1-28.
2. Set the DC voltmeter to low range.
3. Turn on the power supply.
4. Record V_{out}. _____
5. Record V_{in}. _____
6. Close S_1 and adjust R_p until V_{out} is zero.
7. Record V_{in}. _____ This value of voltage is the input-offset voltage.
8. Turn off the power supply and remove the battery.

QUESTIONS FOR FIGURE 1-28

1. What is V_{out} when S_1 is open? _____
2. What is V_{in} when S_1 is open? _____
3. What is V_{in} when S_1 is closed and R_p is adjusted for a V_{out} of zero? _____
4. What is the value of input-offset voltage? _____

EXPERIMENT 1-10 OUTPUT-OFFSET VOLTAGE

Objective: To prove that output-offset voltage exists in an op amp.

Introduction:

This experiment is a continuation of Experiments 1-8 and 1-9, but shows the error voltage produced at the output when no input-offset adjusts are used. The circuit is a DC inverting

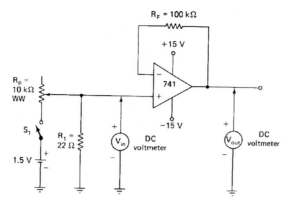

FIGURE 1-28 Input-offset voltage.

amplifier with a gain of 10. Theoretically, the voltage at the output should be zero as the circuit is shown.

Required Components:
1 10-kΩ resistor (R_{in})
1 100-kΩ resistor (R_F)

Test Procedure:
1. With the power supply off, construct the circuit shown in Figure 1-29
2. Set the DC voltmeter to low range.
3. Turn on the power supply.
4. Record V_{out} _____. This is the output offset voltage and may be either positive or negative, depending on the type of unbalance inside the op amp.
5. Turn off the power supply.

QUESTIONS FOR FIGURE 1-29

1. What is the value of V_{out}? _____
2. What is the value of output-offset voltage? _____

EXPERIMENT 1-11 OFFSET NULL ADJUSTMENT

Objective: To show a method of correcting offset voltage errors.
Introduction:
Experiments 1-8 and 1-9 showed how the ouput of an op amp circuit could be adjusted to zero volts using input resistors. Some op amps have extra pins for adjusting the ouput to zero referred to as offset null adjustment. The inverting amplifier shown in Figure 1-30 is adjusted with a 10K ohm potentiometer. See section 1-1-4-7 for more information.

Required Components:
1 10-kΩ resistor (R_{in})
1 10-kΩ resistor (R_F)
1 10-kΩ wirewound potentiometer (R_n)

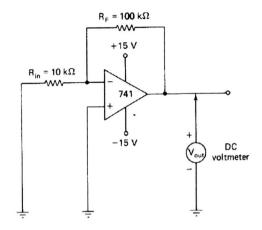

FIGURE 1-29 Output-offset voltage.

1 SPST switch (S_1)

Test Procedure:
1. With the power supply off, construct the circuit shown in Figure 1-30.
2. Set the DC voltmeter to low range.
3. Turn on the power supply.
4. Record V_{out}. _____
5. Close S_1 and adjust R_n for minimum V_{out} (hopefully zero). This method of offset null adjustment uses the internal connections of the op amp. Other methods of external offset null adjustment were shown in Experiments 1-8 and 1-9.
6. Turn off the power supply.

QUESTIONS FOR FIGURE 1-30

1. What is V_{out} when S_1 is open? _____
2. With S_1 closed and R_n properly adjusted, what is V_{out}? _____

EXPERIMENT 1-12 SLEW RATE

Objective: To demonstrate the limitations of the op amp due to slew rate.
Introduction:
Slew rate is simply how fast the output voltage amplitude of an op amp can change and is related to output distortion and frequency response. A square edge input signal may look distorted at the output of an op amp because of internal capacitance and propagation delay. This distortion usually resembles a slanting of the leading and trailing edges of the signal voltage. Various frequencies will cause more or less distortion . Carefully measure the changes shown in Figure 1-31 for accurate calculations. See section 1-1-4-10 for more information.
Required Components:
1 10-kΩ resistor (R_{in})
1 100-kΩ resistor (R_F)
Test Procedure:

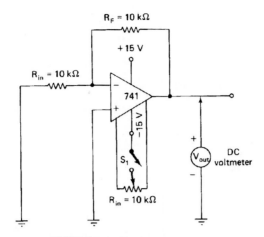

FIGURE 1-30 Offset null adjustment.

1. With the power supply off, construct the circuit shown in Figure 1-31.
2. Set the square-wave generator at 10 kHz.
3. Adjust the output amplitude of the generator to 1 V p-p.
4. Turn on the power supply.
5. Observe v_{in} and draw an accurate voltage waveform, indicating amplitude and time.
    _____
6. Observe v_{out} and draw an accurate voltage waveform, indicating amplitude and time.
    _____
7. Calculate the slew rate from the formula SR = $\Delta V/\Delta t$. _____
8. Repeat steps 2 through 7 for the following frequencies: 100 Hz, 1 kHz, 50 kHz, and 100 kHz.
9. Turn off the power supply.

QUESTIONS FOR FIGURE 1-31

1. What is the ΔV of the circuit at 10 kHz? _____
2. What is the Δt of the circuit at 10 kHz? _____
3. What is the slew rate of this circuit? _____
4. Does the slew rate increase, decrease, or remain the same when the input frequency decreases? _____
5. Does the slew rate increase, decrease, or remain the same when the input frequency increases? _____

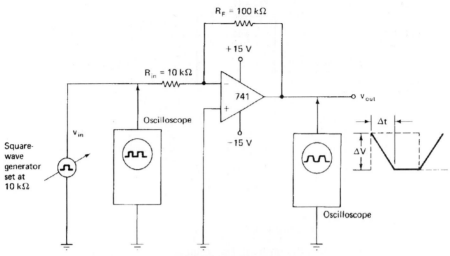

FIGURE 1-31 Slew rate.

EXPERIMENT 1-13 OPEN-LOOP FREQUENCY RESPONSE

Objective:

To show the limited frequency response and instability in the open-loop mode.

Introduction:

This experiment may be a little difficult to perform because of no feedback resistor and the resulting high gain. A variable signal generator is placed at the input to the circuit. The generator is adjusted both for frequency and amplitude to produce an undistorted output voltage of the op amp. The gain at higher frequencies should fall off to nearly zero.

Required Components:

None

Test Procedure:

1. With the power supply off, construct the circuit shown in Figure 1-32. Because the open-loop gain of the op amp is extremely high, the circuit is extremely sensitive and all leads should be kept as short as possible. Measurements will be difficult to perform and care should be taken to ensure accuracy.
2. Turn on the power supply.
3. Adjust the generator for an undistorted signal at the op-amp output. Use the various frequencies given in the data log and record v_{in} and v_{out}.
4. Turn off the power supply.
5. Calculate the voltage gain for each frequency given from the formula

$$A_v = \frac{v_{out}}{v_{in}}$$

Record the answer in the data log.

6. Calculate the dB gain for each frequency given from the formula

$$A_{dB} = 20\log\frac{v_{out}}{v_{in}}$$

Record the answers in the data log.
7. Sketch a graph of A_v versus frequency from the results shown in the data log. (Try to use semilog graph paper.)

QUESTIONS FOR FIGURE 1-32

1. What frequency had the highest gain? _____
2. What frequency had the lowest gain? _____
3. As frequency increases, what happens to A_v? _____
4. What is the dB loss from 1 to 10 kHz? _____

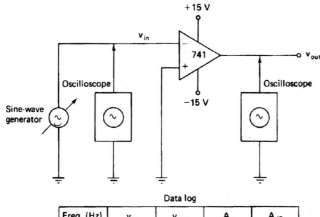

Data log

Freq. (Hz)	v_{in}	v_{out}	A_v	A_{dB}
50				
100				
500				
1 K				
5 K				
10 K				
100 K				
500 K				

FIGURE 1-32 Open-loop frequency response.

EXPERIMENT 1-14 UNITY-GAIN FREQUENCY

Objective:
To prove at what frequency v_{in} is equal to v_{out}.
Introduction:
The unity gain frequency is the maximum frequency that is passed by an op amp where its voltage gain is 1. The parameter helps extablish the frequency response of an op amp. For more information, see sections 1-1-4-.11 and 1-1-4-12.
Required Components:
None

Test Procedure:

1. With the power supply off, construct the circuit shown in Figure 1-33.
2. Turn on the power supply.
3. Set the generator to 100 Hz and adjust the amplitude of the generator to 100 mV or less, so as to produce an undistorted signal at the output of the op amp. A single generator capable of producing frequencies above 2 MHz should be used, or an audio generator and R_F generator will be needed. Since this circuit is in the open-loop mode, the same problems will be encountered as with the previous experiment.
4. While keeping v_{in} constant, run the generator through its frequencies until v_{out} is equal to v_{in}. This will mean monitoring both input and output simultaneously or taking measurements many times.
5. When v_{out} is equal to v_{in}, record the frequency setting of the generator. _____ This is the unity-gain frequency of the op amp.
6. Turn off the power supply.

QUESTIONS FOR FIGURE 1-33

1. At what frequency does A_v equal 1 ($v_{in} = v_{out}$)? _____
2. What is the unity-gain frequency of the op amp? _____

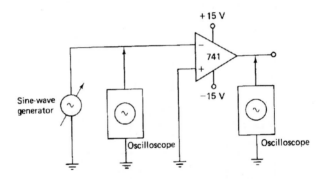

FIGURE 1-33 Unity-gain frequency.

EXPERIMENT 1-15 COMMON-MODE REJECTION

Objective:
To demonstrate the effectiveness of common-mode rejection.
Introduction:
Common-mode rejection is the ability of an op amp to reject unwanted signals at the inputs. For example, the standard electrical power frequency of 60 hertz may find its way to the inputs of an op amp. This 60 hertz will be in phase and induced at each input. An ideal op amp should not amplify this 60 hertz, while amplifying the normal input signal voltage. This circuit has the inputs connected together to establish the common mode situation. Each frequency setting requires two voltage measurements to be able to calculate the common mode rejection ratio. For more information, see section 1-1-4-14.
Required Components:
1 1-kΩ resistor (R_1)
1 1-μF capacitor (nonpolarized) (C_1)

Test Procedure:

1. With the power supply off, construct the circuit shown in Figure 1-34.
2. Turn on the power supply.
3. Set the generator for an undistorted output signal of 100 Hz.
4. Record v_{in_1}, and v_{out_1}, in the data log as a first reading for 100 Hz.
5. Reduce the generator amplitude and record v_{in_2} and v_{out_2} in the data log as a second reading for 100 Hz.
6. Repeat steps 3 through 5 for frequencies 1 kHz, 10 kHz, and 100 kHz, as shown in the data log.
7. Turn off the power supply.
8. Calculate the small change in $v_{in}(\Delta v_{in} = v_{in_1} - v_{in_2})$ for each frequency given.
9. Calculate the small change in $v_{out}(\Delta v_{out} = v_{out_1} - v_{out_2})$ for each frequency given.
10. Calculate the ratio $\Delta v_{in} / \Delta v_{out}$ for each frequency and record in the data log.
11. Convert this ratio to –dB for each frequency from the formula

$$-dB = 20\log\frac{\Delta v_{in}}{\Delta v_{out}}$$

Record the answers in the data log.

QUESTIONS FOR FIGURE 1-34

1. What is the –dB reading for 1 kHz? _____
2. What is the –dB reading for 10 kHz? _____
3. What happens to the common-mode rejection ratio when frequency increases? _____

SECTION 1-5 SUMMARY POINTS

1. Op amps have very high input impedance.
2. Op amps have very high open-loop gain.
3. Op amps have low output impedance.
4. Most op amps operate from dual (±) power supplies.
5. Controlled closed-loop gain is determined by the ratio of the feed-back resistor to the input resistor at the inverting input and is expressed $A_v = R_F/R_{in}$.
6. When the inverting input is more positive than the noninverting input, the output will be negative, and vice versa.
7. Input-offset voltage can be compensated by null adjusting (the output to zero) with external circuitry.
8. Op amps may be externally or internally frequency-compensated to prevent self-oscillation.
9. The slew rate is the maximum change in output voltage to the change in time, expressed $SR = \Delta V_{out\ (max)}/\Delta t$.
10. Op amps with high slew rates have wider bandwidths.
11. In the open-loop mode, gain falls off rapidly with frequency increase, resulting in a very

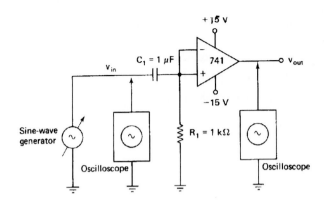

Data log

Freq. (Hz)	v_{in_1}	v_{in_2}	v_{out_1}	v_{out_2}	$\Delta v_{in}/\Delta v_{out}$	dB
100						
1 K						
10 K						
100 K						

FIGURE 1-34 Common-mode rejection.

     narrow bandwidth.

12. The greater the feedback in closed-loop mode, the wider the bandwidth.

13. The gain-bandwidth product is gain times bandwidth, which equals the unity-gain frequency: $GBP = G \times BW$.

14. Noise and temperature affect all electronic circuits and must also be taken into consideration when using op amps.

15. The common-mode rejection ratio (CMRR) is the ability of an op amp to amplify the differential input signal while rejecting the common-mode input signal, expressed $CMRR = A_D/A_{cm}$.

16. Op amps must be operated within their absolute maximum ratings to ensure circuit dependability.

17. There are five general groups of op amps: general purpose, DC and low-level performance, AC and high-level performance, high voltage and power, and unique or special devices.

18. Op amps come in four general packages: metal TO-group, flat pack, DIP, and mini-DIP.

19. An IC package may contain one, two, or four op amps.

20. The op amp is a versatile solid-state device, because it can be used in so many types of circuits.

SECTION 1-6 SELF-CHECKING QUIZ

Match each expression in column A with its best associated meaning or related expression in column B. (Some items in column A may have two answers.)

Column A		Column B
1. Open-loop mode has	a.	feedback
2. Closed-loop mode has	b.	gain × bandwidth
3. Controlled gain accomplished by	c.	narrow bandwidth
4. Input-offset voltage corrected by	d.	high
5. Self-oscillation eliminated by	e.	increases bandwidth
6. High slew rate	f.	wider bandwidth
7. Input impedance	g.	two inputs
8. Output impedance	h.	internal compensation
9. Differential amplifier has	i.	nulling
10. GBP	j.	low
	k.	controlled gain
	1.	high gain

True-or-False Questions

11. A positive voltage on the noninverting input will cause the output to swing negative.
12. The op amp consists basically of a differential amplifier, a high gain voltage amplifier, and a low impedance output amplifier.
13. The closed-loop-gain formula is $A_v = R_{in}/R_F$
14. Input-offset voltages can cause error in the output voltage.
15. An op amp has a unity-gain frequency of 4 MHz. For a gain of 50, its bandwidth is 80 kHz.
16. With a gain of 60 and a bandwidth of 100 kHz, the unity-gain frequency of a particular op amp is 6 MHz.
17. The formula for slew rate is $SR = \Delta V/\Delta t$.
18. Self-oscillations of an op amp can be reduced or stopped by offset nulling.
19. The higher the common-mode rejection ratio, the better the quality of an op amp.
20. Using a dual (±) power supply, the output of an op amp can swing positive and negative.
    (Answers at back of book)

CHAPTER 2

BASIC OP-AMP CIRCUITS

This chapter concentrates on the principles involved with basic op-amp circuits. Understanding these principles will provide you with the necessary foundation to use and test more complex op-amp circuits.

We will begin with a basic voltage comparator circuit that uses the open-loop gain of the op amp. This circuit configuration will show you how both inputs are actively used. It will then be shown how comparators are used for AC sensing and voltage-level detection.

More-in-depth information is given about amplification using the op amp and how the external resistors determine the gain for a particular circuit.

You will be able to understand how the op amp amplifies in the inverting and noninverting configurations. Easy-to-use formulas allow you to construct circuits that will perform to your expectations.

Special circuits, such as the summing amplifier and the difference amplifier, are presented to show you some of the versatility of op amps.

The popular 741 op amp is shown in most of the illustrations to enable you to construct these circuits right from the book.

2-1-1 VOLTAGE COMPARATOR

A voltage comparator compares the voltage on one input to the voltage on the other input. Figure 2-1 shows the basic voltage comparator. In this simplest circuit configuration, the open-loop mode, any minute difference between the two inputs will drive the op-amp output into saturation. The direction in which the output goes into saturation is determined by the polarity of the input signals. When the voltage on the inverting input is more positive than the voltage on the noninverting input, the output will swing to negative saturation ($-V_{sat}$) Similarly, when the voltage on the inverting input is more negative than the voltage on the noninverting input, the output will swing to positive saturation ($+V_{sat}$). Referring to the table in Figure 2-1, you can see that with +1 V on the inverting input and +2 V on the noninverting input, the former is 1 V negative with respect to the latter. Therefore, the output will go into positive saturation. When the input voltages are reversed (+2 V on –input and +1 V on +input), the inverting input is 1 V positive with respect to the noninverting input and the output goes into negative saturation. If the input voltages are the same amplitude and polarity, the output will be zero. Negative voltages applied to the inputs have the same effect on the output of the op amp as shown in the table.

Remember that the polarity relationship of the inverting input to the noninverting input will cause the output to be 180° out of phase.

2-1-1-1 Sensing a Sine Wave on the Inverting Input

A comparator can be used to detect a changing voltage on one input with a fixed reference voltage on the other input. In Figure 2-2, the inverting input is used to sense a sine-wave signal. A signal source is placed on the inverting input. Since the input impedance of the op amp could be considered infinite, resistor R_1 acts as the signal source load, which results in more

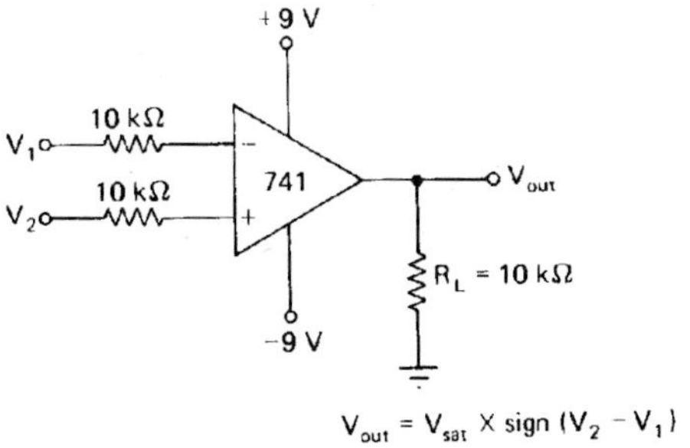

$$V_{out} = V_{sat} \times sign\ (V_2 - V_1)$$

(a) Schematic diagram

Input voltage		Output voltage
V_1	V_2	$\pm V_{sat}$
+1	+2	+8
+2	+1	−8
0	0	0
+1	−1	−8
−1	+1	+8
−1	−2	−8
−2	−1	+8

(b) Input/output voltage table

FIGURE 2-1 Voltage comparator: (a) schematic diagram; (b) input/output voltage table.

effective operation of the circuit. The noninverting input is grounded through resistor R_2. This resistor is used to balance the inputs for any input-offset current that might exist.

The noninverting input is at the reference voltage (O V). During the positive alternation of the input signal, the output is at $-V_{sat}$. At the point where the signal goes through zero to the negative alternation, the output swings to $+V_{sat}$. Notice that the output is 180° out of phase with the input.

2-1-1-2 Sensing a Sine Wave on the Noninverting Input

We can place the signal source on the noninverting input as shown in Figure 2-3. The inverting input is now the 0 V reference point. When the positive alternation of the signal is present, the output is at $+V_{sat}$. Similarly, when the signal goes through zero to the negative alternation, the output swings to $-V_{sat}$. With this circuit configuration, the output is in phase with the input.

These two circuits are sometimes referred to as zero detectors. Each time the input signal crosses zero, the output voltage swings to the opposite Polarity. It is also interesting to note how a square wave can be produced from a sine wave with these circuits.

2-1-1-3 Detecting Phase Difference

A comparator may be used to detect the phase difference of two signals with the same frequency as shown in Figure 2-4. Whenever the two signals are out of phase, there will be a differential voltage at the inputs and the output will be at $\pm V_{sat}$. When V_1 is more positive than V_2, the output will be at $\pm V_{sat}$, and vice versa. As the two signals become in phase, the output

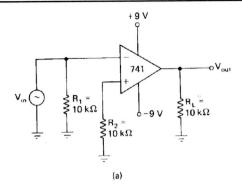

(a)

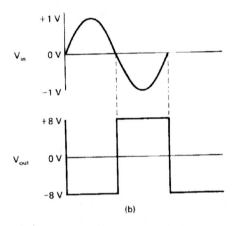

(b)

FIGURE 2-2 Comparator sensing a sine wave on the inverting input: (a) schematic diagram; (b) input/output voltage relationship.

goes to zero (the effect of common-mode rejection).

2-1-1-4 Positive-Voltage-Level Detector

A specific voltage level other than zero can be detected by a comparator, as shown in Figure 2-5. This positive-voltage-level detector uses the inverting input to sense the changing voltage, while a resistive voltage divider network establishes the reference voltage (V_{ref}) at the noninverting input. The resistive divider is connected between the +V supply and ground. The reference voltage can be determined by the ratio formula

$$V_{ref} = \frac{R_2}{R_2 + R_3}(+V)$$

By substituting the values of R_2, R_3, and +V in the formula, we have

$$V_{ref} = \frac{10k\,\Omega}{10k\,\Omega + 22k\,\Omega}(+9V) = 0.3125\,(+9V) = +2.8V$$

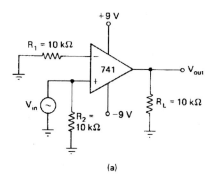

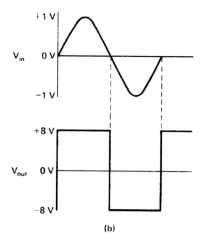

(b)

FIGURE 2-3 Comparator sensing a sine wave on the non-inverting input: (a) schematic diagram; (b) input/output voltage relationship

The noninverting input is +2.8 V above ground. As long as the changing voltage on the inverting input is below (negative to) +2.8 V, the output will be at $+V_{sat}$ ($\approx+8$ V). The instant that the voltage on the inverting input becomes greater (more positive) than +2.8 V, the output will swing to $-V_{sat}$ (≈-8 V), indicating that the comparator has detected a +2.8 V level. If this voltage on the inverting input falls below +2.8 V, the output will again swing to $+V_{sat}$.

2-1-1-5 Negative-Voltage-Level Detector

A negative-voltage-level detector can be constructed by connecting the resistive divider between $-V$ supply and ground, as shown in Figure 2-6. In this case, the V_{ref} is -2.8 V with reference to ground.If the changing voltage on the inverting input is more positive than the V_{ref}, the output will be at $-V_{sat}$. The instant detection occurs, the output will swing to $+V_{sat}$.

Voltage-level detectors can be designed with the noninverting input as the sensing input and the reference voltage applied to the inverting input. The output voltage will swing in opposite directions to the detectors that have been discussed.

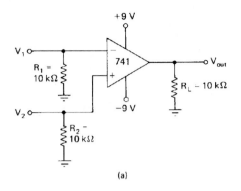

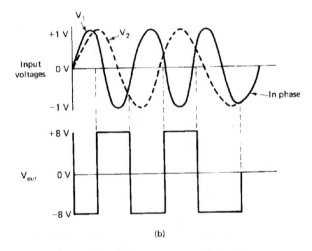

(b)

FIGURE 2-4 Comparator sensing an out-of-phase sine wave on both inputs: (a) schematic diagram; (b) input/output voltage relationship.

2-1-1-6 Determining Resistive Voltage Divider

One method of determining the resistive voltage divider for the reference voltage is illustrated in Figure 2-7. First, you would select or determine the V_{ref}. This is the same as the voltage drop V_2 across resistor R_2. Voltage V_1 is found by subtracting V_2 from V_{source}. Resistor R_2 is one input resistor to the op amp and is generally the same value as the other input resistor. Since we select V_{ref}, assume the value of R_2, and are able to find V_1, we only need to solve for R_1.

If the voltage drops and resistance are directly proportional:

$$\frac{V_1}{V_2} = \frac{R_1}{R_2}$$

then, rearranging the formula, we find

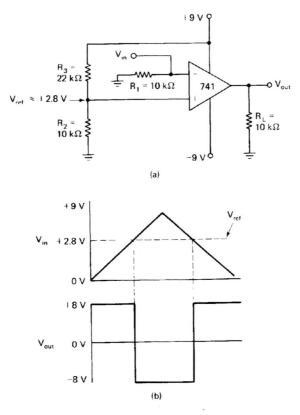

FIGURE 2-5 Positive voltage detector: (a) schematic diagram; (b) input/output voltage relationship.

$$R_1 = \frac{V_1 R_2}{V_2}$$

2-1-2 INVERTING AMPLIFIER

An amplifier accepts a small voltage or current at its input and produces a larger voltage or current at its output. An op-amp amplifier has relatively linear gain and the output is controlled as a function of the input. The basic op-amp inverting amplifier is shown in Figure 2-8.

In Chapter 1 you were introduced to the concept of closedloop mode of operation for the op amp. It was mentioned how the gain of the op amp can be controlled or determined by an external resistive ratio network in the closed loop mode.

A closed-loop arrangement of this type is called negative (degenerative) feedback. The out-of-phase voltage at the output is fed back to the inverting input, where it tends to cancel the original input voltage. The feedback voltage will greatly reduce the effects of the input voltage and keep the inverting input at nearly 0 V. Of course, the feedback voltage cannot

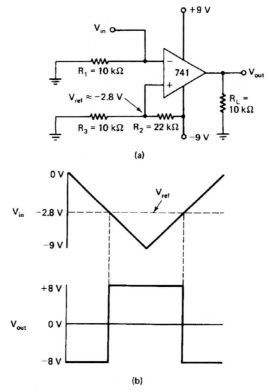

(a)

(b)

FIGURE 2-6 Negative voltage level detector: (a) schematic diagram; (b) input/output voltage relationship.

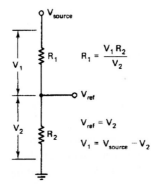

$$R_1 = \frac{V_1 R_2}{V_2}$$

$$V_{ref} = V_2$$

$$V_1 = V_{source} - V_2$$

FIGURE 2-7 Determining resistor divider for V_{REF}

completely cancel the input voltage or there would be no feedback. In other words, nothing at all would happen in the circuit. However, there is a slight change of perhaps a few microvolts at the inverting input. This change is amplified by the extremely high gain of the op amp to produce the voltage change at the output.

The voltage gain of a circuit is found by the formula

$$A_\upsilon = \frac{V_{out}}{V_{in}}$$

and the gain factor in the closed-loop mode for an inverting amplifier was given as

$$A_\upsilon = \frac{R_F}{R_{in}}$$

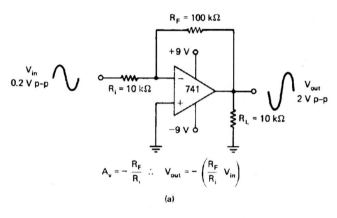

(a)

V_{in}	V_{out}
+0.3	−3
−0.3	+3
+0.52	−5.2
−0.52	+5.2

(b)

FIGURE 2-8 Inverting amplifier: (a) schematic diagram; (b) DC voltage table.

The output voltage can be determined if the known input voltage is multiplied by the gain factor:

$$V_{out} = -(A_\upsilon V_{in}) \text{ or } \left(\frac{R_F}{R_{in}} V_{in} \right)$$

The minus sign is disregarded in calculations and indicates only that the output is out of phase with the input.

As an example, referring to Figure 2-8, the gain is

$$-A_\upsilon = \frac{R_F}{R_{in}} = \frac{100k\Omega}{10k\Omega} = -10$$

and the output voltage is

$$V_{out} = -A_\upsilon V_{in} = -10 \times 0.2 \text{ V p-p} = -2 \text{ V p-p}$$

Also shown in Figure 2-8 is a sample DC voltage table. The input voltage is amplified by the gain factor of 10, and the output voltage indicates this gain together with the proper polarity for the inverting amplifier. This basic inverting amplifier circuit is the starting point for other more specific DC and AC amplifiers to be covered in subsequent chapters.

A closer analysis of this circuit will enable you to understand how the resistive ratio network (R_{in} and R_F) actually determine the closed-loop gain. Referring to Figure 2-9, you can see that a +1 V at the input will cause a current of 0.1 mA to flow by the formula

$$I_{in} = \frac{V_{in}}{R_{in}} = \frac{1V}{10k\Omega} = 0.1mA$$

(Electron flow is indicated for the examples in this book; however, conventional current flow can also be used depending on the reader's preference.)

Now, since the input impedance of an op amp is considered very high or even infinite, no current can now into or out of the input terminals for most practical purposes. Therefore, I_{in} must flow through R_F and is indicated by I_F (the feedback current). Since R_{in} and R_F are in series, then $I_{in} = I_F$. However, R_F is 10 times greater than R_{in}, and if the same current is supposed to flow through both resistors, then the voltage drop across R_F must be 10 times greater. The internal circuitry of the op amp adjusts accordingly and the output swings to − 10 V (notice that the polarity ensures that current will flow in the same direction). Because no current can flow into or out of the inverting input and R_{in} and R_F drop the total voltage from V_{in} to V_{out}, this point is at 0 V, commonly referred to as virtual ground. The output voltage (V_{out}) is across R_F, and I_F can be proven by the formula

$$I_F = \frac{V_{out}}{R_F}$$

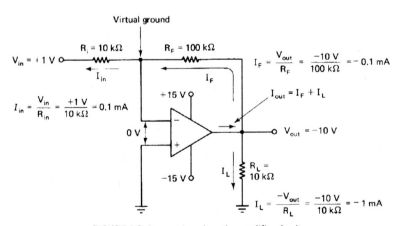

FIGURE 2-9 Currents in an inverting amplifier circuit.

If $I_{in} = I_F$, then

$$\frac{V_{in}}{R_{in}} = -\frac{V_{out}}{R_F}$$

Rearranging the equation, we obtain

$$-\frac{V_{\text{out}}}{V_{\text{in}}} = -\frac{R_F}{R_{\text{in}}}$$

You will recall that the voltage gain of any inverting amplifier stage can be expressed as

$$A_\upsilon = -\frac{V_{\text{out}}}{V_{\text{in}}}$$

Therefore,

$$A_\upsilon = -\frac{R_F}{R_{\text{in}}}$$

The op amp inverting-amplifier-stage gain factor is the ratio of the external resistors R_F and R_{in}.

The load current I_L flows out of the op amp toward ground and is determined by load resistor R_L, which can be found by the formula

$$I_L = -\frac{V_{\text{out}}}{R_L}$$

Therefore, the total current being supplied by the op amp can be expressed as

$$I_{\text{out}} = I_F + I_L$$

If the polarity of V_{in} is reversed (made negative), V_{out} would be positive and the current will flow into the op amp.

2-1-2-1 Virtual Ground

The concept of virtual ground may be understood better from Figure 2-10a. The two series-aiding batteries equal 20 V and the total circuit resistance equals 20 kΩ. Therefore, the current in the circuit is 1 mA. According to Ohm's law ($E = IR$), each resistor drops 10 V. The sum of the voltage drops of both resistors equals the total voltage. Point A will be 0 V with reference to ground and yet be isolated from ground. The same situation will occur for unequal voltages and proportionately unequal resistors, as shown in Figure 2-10b.

This circuit approximates the analogy of the op-amp inverting amplifier shown in Figure 2-10c. The fixed V_{in} will cause the op amp to adjust to the proper V_{out} according to the ratio of R_F to R_{in}. Thus, the inverting input will tend to be driven toward the same potential as the grounded noninverting input. It must be remembered that a wire short placed from point A to ground of the resistor networks shown in Figure 2-10a and b has little or no effect, while a wire short placed across the op-amp inputs of Figure 2-10c will affect the circuit, since the op amp is producing V_{out}.

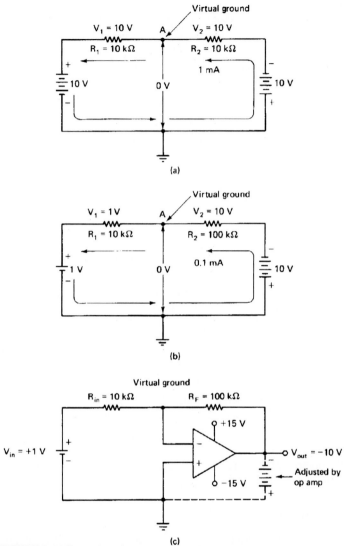

FIGURE 2-10 Examples of virtual ground: (a) equal resistors and voltages; (b) unequal resistors and voltages; (c) op-amp circuit.

2-1-2-2 Input Impedance

As mentioned earlier, the input impedance of an op amp is very high. But the input impedance of an inverting amplifier is determined by R_{in}. Therefore, the input impedance in Figure 2-8 is equal to 10 kΩ .

2-1-3 NONINVERTING AMPLIFIER

The op amp can be used as a noninverting amplifier shown in Figure 2-11. In this circuit configuration the feedback to control gain is still applied to the inverting input, while V_{in} is applied to the noninverting input. The output voltage will be in phase with the input voltage for this circuit.

Resistors R_F and R_{in} form a resistive ratio network to produce the feedback voltage (V_A) needed at the inverting input. Feedback voltage (V_A) is developed across R_{in}. Since the potential at the inverting input tends to be the same as the noninverting input (as pointed out with the description of virtual ground), for most practical purposes

$$V_{in} = V_A$$

Since $V_A = V_{in}$, the gain of the stage can be expressed

$$A_v = \frac{V_{out}}{V_A}$$

However, V_A is determined by the resistance ratio of R_{in} and R_F; thus,

$$V_A = \frac{R_{in}}{R_F + R_{in}} (V_{out})$$

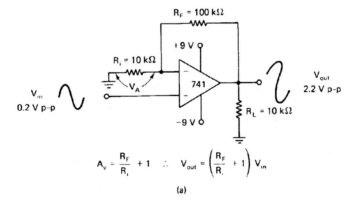

$$A_v = \frac{R_F}{R_i} + 1 \qquad \therefore \qquad V_{out} = \left(\frac{R_F}{R_i} + 1 \right) V_{in}$$

(a)

V_{in}	V_{out}
+0.3	+3.3
−0.3	−3.3
+0.52	+5.72
−0.52	−5.72

(b)

FIGURE 2-11 Noninverting amplifier: (a) schematic diagram; (b) DC voltage table.

If the equation is rearranged so that the voltages are on one side, the result is

$$\frac{V_A}{V_{\text{out}}} = \frac{R_{\text{in}}}{R_F + R_{\text{in}}}$$

Inverting the equation and simplifying, we obtain

$$\frac{V_{\text{out}}}{V_A} = \frac{R_F + R_{\text{in}}}{R_{\text{in}}}$$

$$\frac{V_{\text{out}}}{V_A} = \frac{R_F}{R_{\text{in}}} + \frac{R_{\text{in}}}{R_{\text{in}}}$$

$$\frac{V_{\text{out}}}{V_A} = \frac{R_F}{R_{\text{in}}} + 1$$

$$\frac{V_{\text{out}}}{V_A} = \frac{R_F}{R_{\text{in}}} + 1$$

The stage-gain formula is

$$A_\upsilon = \frac{V_{\text{out}}}{V_A}$$

Therefore,

$$A_\upsilon = \frac{R_F}{R_{\text{in}}} + 1$$

Finally, the output voltage can be found by

$$V_{\text{out}} = \left(\frac{R_F}{R_{\text{in}}} + 1\right) V_{\text{in}}$$

The output voltage of the circuit shown in Figure 2-11 can now be found:

$$V_{\text{out}} = \left(\frac{R_F}{R_{\text{in}}} + 1\right) V_{\text{in}} = \left(\frac{100\text{k}\Omega}{10\text{k}\Omega} + 1\right) 0.2\text{Vp-p} = 2.2\text{p-p}$$

The DC voltage table in Figure 2-11b shows some sample input voltage times a gain of 11. Notice that the input and output polarities are in phase.

2-1-4 VOLTAGE FOLLOWERS

Voltage followers are usually defined as circuits with a gain of 1 or less with the output voltage following the input voltage. There exists an impedance isolation between input and output. The op amp is particularly useful as a voltage follower, which is shown in Figure 2-12.

With the basic noninverting voltage follower (Figure 2-12a), the output is connected directly to the inverting input with the input voltage at the noninverting input. The feedback resistance equals 0; therefore, according to the stage gain for a noninverting amplifier,

$$A = \frac{R_F}{R_{in}} + 1 = \frac{0}{R_{in}} + 1 = 1$$

or the gain of the follower is 1. In other words, with 100 percent feedback, the output voltage follows the input voltage. Notice that the inverting input will always be the same potential as the noninverting input. Thus, the voltage difference between the two inputs will always be approximately zero.

The advantage of this circuit is an extremely high input impedance and a low output impedance, which is ideal for buffering or isolation between circuits.

If a particular application needed a voltage follower with phase inversion, the circuit in Figure 2-12b could be used. Since R_{in} equals R_F, the gain formula states

$$A_\upsilon = -\frac{R_F}{R_{in}} = \frac{10k\Omega}{10k\Omega} = -1$$

The limitations of this circuit would be a greatly reduced input impedance (since R_{in} equals the input impedance). Resistor R_x at the noninverting input is used to reduce input offset currents and is equal to the value of R_{in} in parallel with R_F: $R_x = R_{in} \parallel R_F$.

2-1-5 VOLTAGE SUMMING AMPLIFIER

By using the basic inverting amplifier circuit and adding another input resistor, we can create an inverting summing amplifier or analog adder, as shown in Figure 2-13. The output voltage is inverted and equals the algebraic sum of each input voltage times the ratio of its appropriate input resistor to the feedback resistor, which can be expressed

$$V_{out} = -\left(\frac{R_F}{R_1}V_1 + \frac{R_F}{R_2}V_2 + \ldots + \frac{R_F}{R_N}V_N\right)$$

The R_F/R_N (V_N) in the formula means that there can be more than two inputs. If all of the external resistors equal one another ($R_F = R_1 = R_2 = \ldots = R_N$), the output voltage can be found simply by algebraically adding up the input voltages and is expressed as

$$V_{out} = -(V_1 + V_2 + \ldots + V_N)$$

The input/output voltage table shows the results of various input voltages. Remember that the output will be inverted from the resulting polarity of the algebraic summation.

The virtual ground, described earlier, is referred to as the current summing point for this type of circuit. Understanding the concept of the summing point can be achieved by analyzing the currents in the summing amplifier as illustrated in Figure 2-14. Since the summing

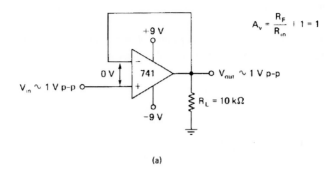

(a)

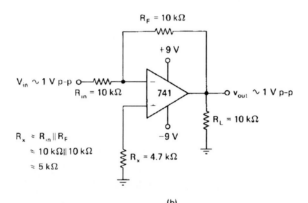

(b)

FIGURE 2-12 Voltage followers: (a) noninverting voltage follower; (b) inverting voltage follower.

point is the virtual ground, the voltage at this point will always be about the same as the non-inverting input (≈ 0 V).

With both input voltages positive, the current through each input resistor will flow in the same direction. In the case shown in Figure 2-14a, $I_1 = 0.1$ mA and $I_2 = 0.2$ mA. Therefore, I_F must equal 0.3 mA and the output will go to -3 V to accomplish this.

If one input voltage is positive and the other input voltage is negative, as shown in Figure 2-14b, one input current (0.3 mA) will flow toward the summing point, while the other input current (0.2 mA) will flow away from the summing point. Because the amount of current entering a point must be the same amount leaving that point, 0.1 mA must flow away from the summing point through R_F. The output voltage will go to $+1$ V in order to develop this needed current.

When both input voltages are negative, as shown in Figure 2-14c, both input currents will flow toward the summing point (0.1 mA and 0.2 mA). The current flowing through R_F must equal the sum of these two currents (0.3 mA). Again, the output voltage will go to $+3$ V to accomplish this.

2-1-5-1 Summing Amplifier with Gain

A summing amplifier may be constructed to provide a gain greater than 1, as shown in Figure 2-15. To accomplish this, R_F must be greater than the input resistors. The gain of each input is

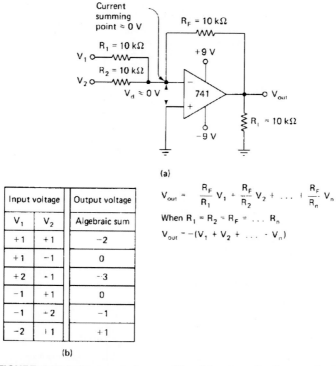

(a)

Input voltage		Output voltage
V_1	V_2	Algebraic sum
+1	+1	−2
+1	−1	0
+2	−1	−3
−1	+1	0
−1	−2	−1
−2	+1	+1

(b)

$$V_{out} = \frac{R_F}{R_1} V_1 + \frac{R_F}{R_2} V_2 + \ldots + \frac{R_F}{R_n} V_n$$

When $R_1 = R_2 = R_F = \ldots R_n$

$$V_{out} = -(V_1 + V_2 + \ldots - V_n)$$

FIGURE 2-13 Voltage summing amplifier: (a) schematic diagram; (b) input/output voltage table.

found and then summed to get the resulting output. For example:

$$V_{out} = -\left(\frac{R_F}{R_1} V_1 + \frac{R_F}{R_2} V_2 \right)$$

$$= -\left[(\frac{100k\Omega}{10k\Omega}) (0.1V) + (\frac{100k\Omega}{10k\Omega}) (0.2V) \right]$$

$$= -[(10)(0.1 \text{ V}) + (10)(0.2 \text{ V})]$$

$$= -(1 \text{ V} + 2 \text{ V})$$

$$= -3 \text{ V}$$

The V_{out} can also be expressed:

$$V_{out} = A_{v1} V_1 + A_{v2} V_2$$

where

$$A_{v1} = -\frac{R_F}{R_1}$$

$$A_{v2} = -\frac{R_F}{R_2}$$

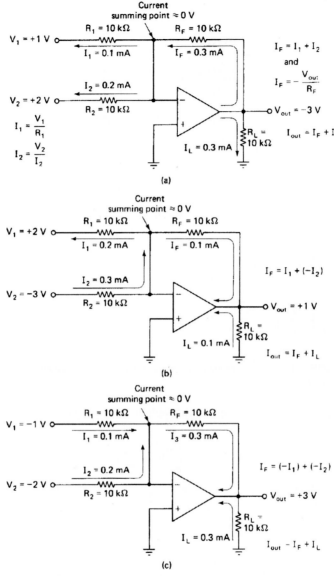

FIGURE 2-14 Currents in an inverting summing amplifier: (a) both inputs positive; (b) one input positive and one input negative; (c) both inputs negative.

2-1-5-2 Scaling Adder Amplifier

Some applications of a summing amplifier, may require one input to influence the output voltage more than another input. Different gains are then required for the various inputs.

Consequently, the input resistors will be of different values, as shown in Figure 2-16. This circuit is referred to as a scaling adder amplifier.

The same output voltage formula is used with this circuit as with the other summing amplifier circuits.

For example:

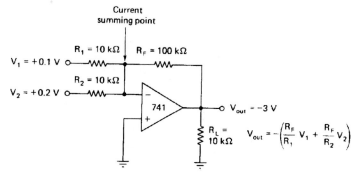

FIGURE 2-16 Scaling adder amplifier.

$$V_{out} = -\left(\frac{R_F}{R_1}V_1 + \frac{R_F}{R_2}V_2 + \frac{R_F}{R_3}V_3\right)$$

$$= -\left[\frac{10k\Omega}{10k\Omega}(3V) + \frac{10k\Omega}{4.7k\Omega}(2V) + \frac{10k\Omega}{2.2\Omega}(1V)\right]$$

$$= -[(1)(3\ V) + (2.13)(2\ V) + (4.5)(1\ V)]$$
$$= -(3\ V + 4.26\ V + 4.5\ V)$$
$$= -11.76\ V$$

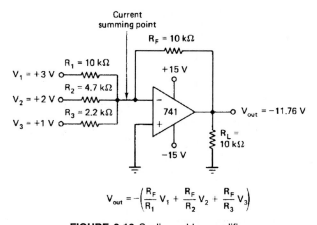

$$V_{out} = -\left(\frac{R_F}{R_1}V_1 + \frac{R_F}{R_2}V_2 + \frac{R_F}{R_3}V_3\right)$$

FIGURE 2-16 Scaling adder amplifier.

2-1-6 VOLTAGE DIFFERENCE AMPLIFIER

The voltage difference amplifier is similar to the comparator discussed in Section 2-1-1. Both inputs are used to sense a difference of potential between them, but the circuit utilizes the closed-loop mode, which results in a controlled and predictable output voltage. If all the external resistors are equal, the voltage difference amplifier functions as an analog mathematical circuit and is often called a voltage subtractor, as shown in Figure 2-17a. The output voltage is the inverted algebraic difference between the two input voltages and can be found by using the formula

$$V_{out} = -\frac{R_F}{R_1}V_1 + \left(\frac{R_g}{R_2+R_g}\right)\left(\frac{R_1+R_F}{R_1}\right)V_2$$

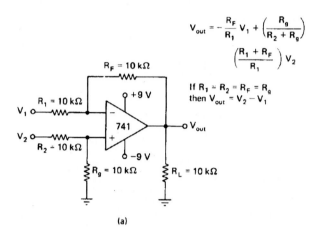

$$V_{out} = -\frac{R_F}{R_1}V_1 + \left(\frac{R_g}{R_2+R_g}\right)$$

$$\left(\frac{R_1+R_F}{R_1}\right)V_2$$

If $R_1 = R_2 = R_F = R_g$
then $V_{out} = V_2 - V_1$

(a)

Input/voltage		Output/voltage
V_1	V_2	Algebraic difference
+2	+4	+2
+4	+2	-2
+4	-2	-6
-2	+4	+6
-4	+2	+6
+2	-4	-6
-4	-2	+2
-2	-4	-2

(b)

FIGURE 2-17 Voltage difference amplifier: (a) schematic diagram; (b) input/output voltage table.

For example, referring to Figure 2-17, if $V_1 = +2$ V and $V_2 = +4$ V, then

$$V_{out} = -\frac{10k\Omega}{10k\Omega}(+2V) + \frac{10k\Omega}{10k\Omega + 10k\Omega}\frac{10k\Omega}{10k\Omega + 10k\Omega}(+4V)$$

$$= -1(+2V) + (\frac{10}{20})(\frac{20}{10})(+4'V)$$

$$= -1(+2V) + (10/20)(20/10)(+4V)$$

$$= -(+2V) + (0.5)(2)(+4V)$$

$$= -(+2) + 1(+4V)$$

$$= -2 + 4$$

$$= +2V$$

As with the comparator, the polarity of the output voltage will be positive if the voltage at the inverting input is more negative than the voltage at the noninverting input (as just proven with the formula), and vice versa.

The input/output voltage table of Figure 2-17b shows the proper polarity and algebraic difference output voltage for various input voltages.

2-1-6-1 Voltage Difference Amplifier with Gain

If the ratio of the resistors is changed (as shown in Figure 2-18), the voltage difference circuit can provide amplification.

The formula previously given can be used to find the output voltage. However, if the ratio of R_F to R_1 equals the ratio of R_g to R_2, which is normally the case, then the output voltage can easily be found by

$$V_{out} = \frac{R_F}{R_1}(V_2 - V_1)$$

Although this description deals primarily with an algebraic subtractor, a major advantage of a voltage difference amplifier is the ability to sense a small differential voltage buried within larger signal voltages. Unfortunately, the input impedance is very low and this type of circuit may require voltage followers for buffering or isolation.

SECTION 2-2 TERMINOLOGY EXERCISE

Write a brief definition for each of the following terms:

1. Voltage comparator
2. Voltage-level detector
3. Degenerative feedback
4. Feedback resistor
5. Inverting amplifier
6. Noninverting amplifier
7. Virtual ground
8. Voltage follower
9. Voltage summing amplifier
10. Scaling adder amplifier

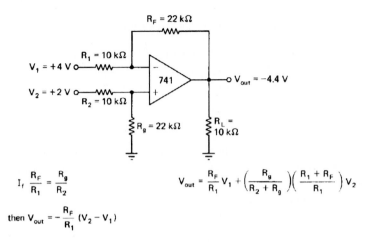

$$I_f \quad \frac{R_F}{R_1} = \frac{R_g}{R_2}$$

$$V_{out} = \frac{R_F}{R_1} V_1 + \left(\frac{R_g}{R_2 + R_g} \right) \left(\frac{R_1 + R_F}{R_1} \right) V_2$$

$$\text{then } V_{out} = - \frac{R_F}{R_1} (V_2 - V_1)$$

FIGURE 2-18 Voltage difference amplifier with gain.

11. Current summing point
12. Voltage difference amplifier

SECTION 2-3 PROBLEMS AND EXERCISES

1. Design two voltage-level detectors using ±15-V power supplies. Draw your circuits and show all values for the V_{ref} given.
   a. V_{ref} = +5 V
   b. V_{ref} = –3 V

2. Draw the output voltage waveform for the circuit shown in Figure 2-19. Make sure that the output follows the same time reference as the input.

3. Referring to Figure 2-20, find R_F, V_{out}, I_{in}, I_F, and I_L for an inverting amplifier with the various values of R_{in} gain and input voltage given. (Let $R_L = 10$ kΩ .)
   a. R_{in} = 4.7 kΩ
       A_{υ} = 10
       V_{in} = 1 V
       R_F = ?
       V_{out} = ?
       I_{in} = ?
       I_F = ?
       I_L = ?
   b. R_{in} = 1 kΩ
       A_{υ} = 22
       V_{in} = – 0.3 V
       R_F =?
       V_{out} =?
       I_{in} = ?
       I_F = ?

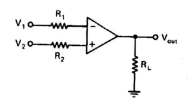

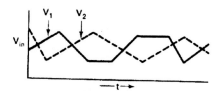

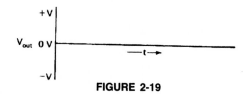

FIGURE 2-19

I_L = ?

c. R_{in} = 10 kΩ
    A_v = 100
    V_{in} = + 0.05 V
    R_F = ?
    V_{out} = ?
    I_{in} = ?
    I_F = ?
    I_L = ?

4. Referring to Figure 2-20, find R_{in}, V_{out}, I_{in}, I_F, and I_L for an inverting amplifier with the various values of R_F, gain, and input voltage given. (Let R_L= 47 kΩ.)

a. R_F = 100 kΩ
    A_v = 20
    V_{in} = – 0.6 V
    R_{in} = ?
    V_{out} = ?
    I_{in} = ?
    I_F = ?
    I_L = ?

b. R_F = 68 kΩ
    A_v = 10
    V_{in} = + 0.58 V
    R_{in} = ?
    V_{out} = ?
    I_{in} = ?

$$I_F \quad = ?$$
$$I_L \quad = ?$$

c. $R_F \quad = 10 \text{ k}\Omega$
$A_v \quad = 1$
$V_{in} \quad = -3 \text{ V}$
$R_{in} \quad = ?$
$V_{out} \quad = ?$
$I_{in} \quad = ?$
$I_F \quad = ?$
$I_L \quad = ?$

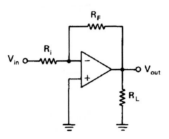

FIGURE 2-20

5. Calculate the gain and output voltage for the noninverting amplifier shown in Figure 2-21 for the various resistor values and input voltages given.

a. $R_{in} \quad = 10 \text{ k}\Omega$
$R_F \quad = 22 \text{ k}\Omega$
$R_L \quad = 10 \text{ k}\Omega$
$V_{in} \quad = +0.2 \text{ V}$
$A_v \quad = ?$
$V_{out} \quad = ?$

b. $R_{in} \quad = 4.7 \text{ k}\Omega$
$R_F \quad = 22 \text{ k}\Omega$
$R_L \quad = 100 \text{ k}\Omega$
$V_{in} \quad = -0.3 \text{ V}$
$A_v \quad = ?$
$V_{out} \quad = ?$

c. $R_{in} \quad = 100 \text{ k}\Omega$
$R_F \quad = 220 \text{ k}\Omega$
$R_L \quad = 47 \text{ k}\Omega$
$V_{in} \quad = +0.5 \text{ V}$
$A_v \quad = ?$
$V_{out} \quad = ?$

6. Draw the schematic diagram for a basic noninverting voltage follower.

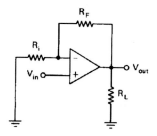

FIGURE 2-21

7. For a summing amplifier, where all resistors are equal, calculate the output voltage for the input voltages given. (See Figure 2-13.)

a.	V_1	$= + 3$ V
	V_2	$= + 2$ V
b.	V_1	$= + 5$ V
	V_2	$= - 2$ V
c.	V_1	$= - 4$ V
	V_2	$= + 3$ V
d.	V_1	$= - 5$ V
	V_2	$= + 2$ V
e.	V_1	$= + 2$ V
	V_2	$= + 5$ V
	V_3	$= - 4$ V
f.	V_1	$= 5$ V
	V_2	$= + 2$ V
	V_3	$= - 3$ V
	V_4	$= + 1$ V
g.	V_1	$= + 1.2$ V
	V_2	$= - 0.5$ V
	V_3	$= + 2.3$ V
	V_4	$= - 0.7$ V

8. Calculate the output voltage for the scaling adder shown in Figure 2-22 for the values given.

a.	R_1	$= 10$ kΩ
	R_2	$= 4.7$ kΩ
	R_3	$= 2.2$ kΩ
	R_F	$= 10$ kΩ
	V_1	$= + 1$ V
	V_2	$= + 2$ V
	V_3	$= + 0.5$ V
b.	R_1	$= 22$ kΩ
	R_2	$= 33$ kΩ
	R_3	$= 47$ kΩ

$$R_F \quad = 100 \text{ k}\Omega$$
$$V_1 \quad = +0.3 \text{ V}$$
$$V_2 \quad = -0.7 \text{ V}$$
$$V_3 \quad = +1.5 \text{ V}$$

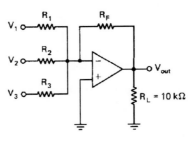

FIGURE 2-22

9. Find the output voltage of a difference amplifier where all resistors are equal, for the input voltages given. (See Figure 2-17.)

a.	V_1	$= +5$ V
	V_2	$= -3$ V
b.	V_1	$= -5$ V
	V_2	$= +3$ V
c.	V_1	$= 5$ V
	V_2	$= 3$ V
d.	V_1	$= +5$ V
	V_2	$= +3$ V

10. If each input equals +1.0 V and each op amp is considered ideal, what is the output voltage of each circuit shown in Figure 2-23? (*Hint*: Remember all formulas given in Chapter 2.)

SECTION 2-4 EXPERIMENTS

EXPERIMENT 2-1 BASIC OP-AMP COMPARATOR OPERATION

Objective:

To demonstrate the basic operation of an op amp and to understand a comparator circuit.

Introduction:

The polarity of the voltage at the output of an op amp depends on the relationship of the polarity between the voltages at the inputs. Remember that the inverting (–) input is referenced to the noninverting (+) input. When the – input is more positive than the + input, the output will be negative, and when the – input is more negative than the + input, the output will be positive. Without a feedback path, the output will either be at $+ V_{sat}$ or $- V_{sat}$.

Required Components:

2 10-kΩ linear potentiometers (R_1 and R_2)

3 10-kΩ resistors at 0.5 W (R_3, R_4 and R_L)

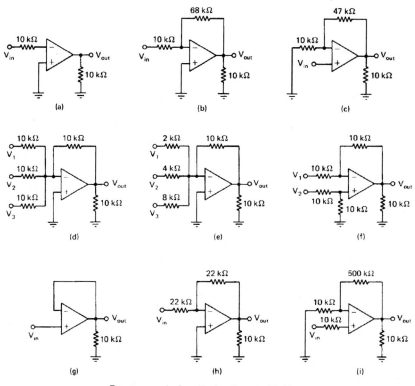

Power supply for all circuits = ± 15 V.

FIGURE 2-23

Test Procedure:
1. Construct the circuit shown in Figure 2-24a.
2. Set input voltages V_1 and V_2 according to the data table shown in Figure 2-24b.
3. Record V_{out} in the data table, indicating polarity.
4. Repeat steps 2 and 3 for the various values of V_1 and V_2.

QUESTIONS FOR FIGURE 2-24

1. Without feedback, the output of an op amp will be at either _____ or _____, depending on the polarity relationship of the input voltages.
2. The output of a comparator will be at _____ when the inverting input is more negative than the noninverting input.
3. If the output of a comparator is − V_{sat}, the inverting input voltage must be more _____ than the noninverting input voltage.

EXPERIMENT 2-2 SENSING SINE WAVES WITH AN OP AMP

Objective:
To show how an op amp comparator senses a sine wave as it crosses the zero reference point.
Introduction:

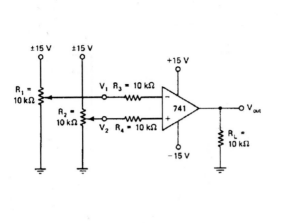

V_1 (V)	V_2 (V)	V_{out} (V)
+1	0	
−1	0	
0	+1	
0	−1	
+2	+1	
+1	+2	
+1	−1	
−1	+1	
−1	−2	
−2	−1	

(a)   (b)

FIGURE 2-24 Voltage comparator: (a) schematic diagram; (b) data table.

Taken from *Fundamental Electronic Devices: Concepts and Experimentation*, 2nd ed., Fredrick W. Hughes, Prentice Hall Inc., 1984, Figure 11-9, page 266.

This experiment has two parts. In the first part, the noninverting input is connected to ground (zero) point through resistor R_2 as shown in Figure 2-25a. The sine wave is applied to the inverting input, which is in parallel with R_1. When the signal voltage is positive with respect to ground, the output will be negative at $-V_{sat}$. As the signal crosses the zero point and goes negative, the output will switch to the positive direction and be at $+V_{sat}$.

In the second part of the experiment, the signal generator is connected to the noninverting input as shown in Figure 2-25b. In this case, when V_{in} is positive, V_{out} is also positive. Likewise, when the input signal is negative, V_{out} is negative.

Required Components:
3 10-kΩ resistors at 0.5 W (R_1, R_2, and R_L)

Test Procedure:
1. Construct the circuit shown in Figure 2-25a.
2. Place one channel of the oscilloscope across the signal generator.
3. Place other channel of the oscilloscope at V_{out}.
4. Turn on the power to the circuit.
5. Set the output of the signal generator for 1-kHz at 2 Vp-p.
6. Read the oscilloscope and draw the accurate voltage waveforms of V_{in} and V_{out} in the space provided. (see photo in Figure A-1a, Appendix A)
7. Turn off the power to the circuit.
8. Construct the circuit as shown in Figure 2-25b.
9. Apply power to the circuit.
10. Repeat steps 2 through 7. (see photo in Figure A-1b, Appendix A)

QUESTIONS FOR FIGURE 2-25

1. When the input signal to the inverting input goes negative, V_{out} goes _____ .
2. When the input signal to the noninverting input goes positive, V_{out} goes _____ .
3. Referring to Figure 2-25a, when the input signal crosses the zero point going positive, V_{out} switches _____ .

4. Referring to Figure 2-25b, when the input signal crosses the zero point going positive, V_{out} switches _____ .

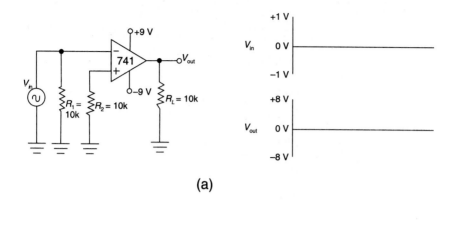

(a)

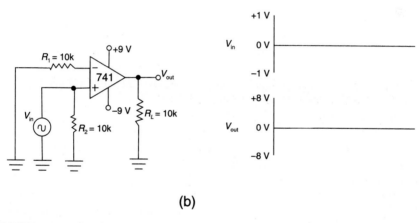

(b)

FIGURE 2-25 Sensing sine wave (a) inverting input signal; (b) noninverting input signal.

EXPERIMENT 2-3 OP-AMP VOLTAGE-LEVEL DETECTORS

Objective:

To demonstrate how an op amp can sense a specific voltage level, and how to calculate the reference voltage (V_{ref}).

Introduction:

An op-amp comparator can be used to detect a positive voltage level and give a negative output-voltage indication, as shown in Figure 2-26a. The reference voltage (V_{ref}) placed on the noninverting input is found by the formula

$$V_{ref} = \frac{R_3}{R_2 + R_3}(+V)$$

When the voltage at the inverting amplifier is below V_{ref}, the output is at $+ V_{sat}$. The instant the voltage at the inverting input increases above V_{ref}, the output swings to $- V_{sat}$.

When V_{ref} is at the inverting input as shown in Figure 2-26b, the output will swing from $- V_{out}$ to $+ V_{sat}$ the instant the voltage at the noninverting input is greater than V_{ref}.

If point A is moved to $- V$ power supply, the circuits will detect a negative voltage.

Required Components:

2 10-kΩ resistors at 0.5 W (R_3 and R_L)
1 22-kΩ resistor at 0.5 W (R_2)
1 10-kΩ linear potentiometer (R_1)

Test Procedure:

1. Construct the circuit shown in Figure 2-26a
2. Place the wiper of R_1 at ground (0 V).
3. Calculate V_{ref} and record here, using the formula

$$V_{ref} = \frac{R_3}{R_2 + R_3} (+V)$$

4. Using the voltmeter, measure V_{ref} and record it in the place provided in Figure 2-26a.
5. Using the voltmeter, measure V_{out} and record it in the place provided.
6. Adjust R_1 until V_{out} changes and record the new reading in the place provided.
7. Remove the wire at point A from the $+ V$ power supply and connect it to the $- V$ power supply.
8. Briefly repeat steps 2 through 6 to understand how a negative voltage is detected.
9. Construct the circuit shown in Figure 2-26b.
10. Place the wiper of R_1 at ground (O V).
11. Using the voltmeter, measure V_{ref} and record it in the place provided in Figure 2-26b.
12. Using the voltmeter, measure V_{out}, and record it in the place provided.
13. Adjust R_1 and V_{out} changes and record the new reading in the place provided.
14. Remove the wire at point A from the $+ V$ power supply and connect it to the $- V$ power supply.
15. Briefly repeat steps 10 through 13 to understand how a negative voltage is detected.

QUESTIONS FOR FIGURE 2-26

1. For an op-amp voltage-level detector, when V_{in} becomes greater than V_{ref}, the _____ voltage changes.
2. These circuits can detect _____ and _____ voltages.
3. Either input can be used for _____ and _____ .

EXPERIMENT 2-4 OP-AMP INVERTING AMPLIFIER

Objective:

To show the operation of an op-amp inverting amplifier with DC and AC voltages and be able to calculate the gain of the circuit.

Introduction:

The inverting amplifier shown in Figure 2-27a consists mainly of resistors R_{in}, R_F, R_n and R_L.

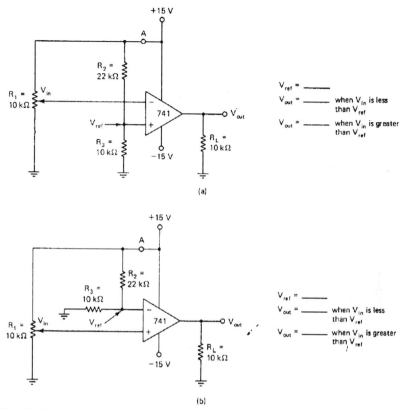

FIGURE 2-26 Op-amp voltage-level detectors: (a) inverting input sensor; (b) noninverting input sensor.

Taken from *Fundamental Electronic Devices: Concepts and Experimentation*, 2nd ed., Fredrick W. Hughes, Prentice Hall Inc., 1984, Figure 11-15, page 275.

Resistors R_1 R_2, and R_3 are used as a voltage divider to set the desired DC voltage at the inverting input. The gain of the circuit can be calculated by the formula $A_\upsilon = -R_F/R_{in}$ (where the minus sign indicates only that the polarity of the output voltage is opposite to the polarity of the input voltage), or can be found by $A_\upsilon = V_{out}/V_{in}$. Resistor R_n is used to reduce offset bias currents and is equal to the value of R_{in} and R_F in parallel ($R_n = R_{in}R_F/R_{in} + R_F$). The junction of R_{in} and R_F at the inverting input is about the same voltage as the noninverting input and is referred to as virtual ground. The input impedance is usually equal to R_{in}.

   When the inverting amplifier is used for AC signals, as shown in Figure 2-27c, capacitors are used to block any DC voltage from the circuit that might cause distortion. The frequency response of an op-amp circuit depends on its gain. The lower the gain, the wider the frequency response is.

Required Components:
1 4.7-kΩ resistor at 0.5 W (R_{in})
1 6.8-kΩ resistor at 0.5 W (R_n)
4 10-kΩ resistors at 0.5 W (R_1 R_3, R_{in}, and R_n)
1 22-kΩ resistor at 0.5 W (R_L)
1 47-kΩ resistor at 0.5 W (R_L)

1 100-kΩ resistor at 0.5 W (R_L)

110-kΩ linear potentiometers (R_2)

211-μF capacitors at 25 WV DC (C_{in}, C_{out})

Test Procedure:

1. Construct the circuit shown in Figure 2-27a using the value of R_{in} and R_F of the first line from the data table of Figure 2-27b.
2. Using the voltmeter, set V_{in} according to the data table.
3. Using the voltmeter, measure and record V_{out} in the data table.
4. Calculate the gain of the circuit from the formula $A_\upsilon = -R_F/R_{in}$, and record in the data table.
5. Calculate the gain of the circuit from the formula $A_\upsilon = V_{out}/V_{in}$ and record in the data table.
6. Repeat steps 2 through 5 for all values of R_{in} and R_F given in the data table.
7. Construct the circuit shown in Figure 2-27c using $R_F = 100$ kΩ.
8. Using the oscilloscope, set the signal generator for V_{in} to the frequency given in the first line of the data table shown in Figure 2-27d (maintain 1 V p-p)
9. Using the oscilloscope, measure and record V_{out} in the data table. (see photo in Figure A-2a of Appendix A)
10. Calculate the gain using the formula $A_\upsilon = \upsilon_{out}/\upsilon_{in}$ given in the datatable.
11. Repeat steps 9 and 10 for the various frequencies of υ_{in} given in the data table.
12. Change R_F to 47 kΩ and repeat steps 8 through 1 1.
13. Using the results of the data table shown in Figure 2-27d, draw the frequency-response curves for the two circuit gains in Figure 2-27e.

QUESTIONS FOR FIGURE 2-27

1. The gain of an op-amp inverting amplifier can be found by dividing _____ by _____ .
2. With the inverting amplifier, the output voltage is _____ degrees out of phase with the input voltage.
3. V_{out} can be found by multiplying _____ with A_υ.
4. Capacitors are used with an AC inverting amplifier to block _____ voltage.
5. An inverting amplifier with a lower gain has a wider _____ .

EXPERIMENT 2-5 OP-AMP NONINVERTING AMPLIFIER

Objective:

To demonstrate the operation of an op-amp noninverting amplifier with DC and AC voltages, and to learn how to calculate the gain of the circuit.

Introduction:

The noninverting amplifier shown in Figure 2-28a consists primarily of resistors R_{in}, R_F, R_n, and R_L. Resistors R_1, R_2, and R_3, are used as a voltage divider to set the desired DC voltage at the noninverting input. The gain of the circuit is calculated by the formula $A_\upsilon = R_F/R_{in} + 1$ or $A_\upsilon = V_{out}/V_{in}$.

When the noninverting amplifier is used for AC signals as shown in Figure 2-28c, capacitors are used to block any DC voltage from the circuit that might cause distortion. Even though the input voltage changes, an amplifier's gain remains the same. A noninverting amplifier is used for high input impedance, where R_{in}, cannot be made larger, because of

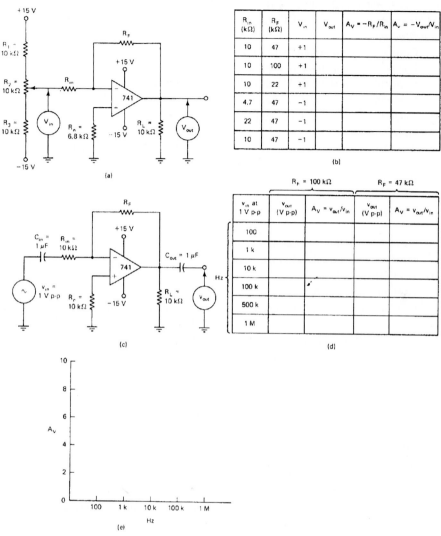

FIGURE 2-27 Op-amp inverting amplifier: (a) DC amplifier; (b) data table; (c) AC amplifier; (d) data table; (e) frequency response curve.

Taken from *Fundamental Electronic Devices: Concepts and Experimentation*, 2nd ed., Fredrick W. Hughes, Prentice Hall Inc., 1984, Figure 11-10, page 267.

affecting the gain of the circuit and creating more noise.

Required Components:

1 4.7-kΩ resistor at 0.5 W (R_{in})
1 6.8-kΩ resistor at 0.5 W (R_n)
4 10-kΩ resistors at 0.5 W (R_1, R_3, R_{in}, R_L, and R_n)
1 22-kΩ resistor at 0.5 W (R_{in}, R_F)
1 47-kΩ resistor at 0.5 W (R_F)
1 100-kΩ resistor at 0.5 W (R_F)

1 10-kΩ linear potentiometer (R_2)

2 1-μF capacitors at 25 WV DC (C_{in}, C_{out})

Test Procedure:

1. Construct the circuit shown in Figure 2-28a, using the values of R_{in}, and R_F of the first line from the data table of Figure 2-28b.
2. Using the voltmeter, set V_{in} according to the data table.
3. Using the voltmeter, measure and record V_{out}, in the data table.
4. Calculate the gain of the circuit from the formula $A_v = R_F/R_{in} + 1$ and record in the data table.
5. Calculate the gain of the circuit from the formula $A_v = V_{out}/V_{in}$ and record in the data table.
6. Repeat steps 2 through 5 for all values of R_{in} and R_F given in the data table.
7. Construct the circuit shown in Figure 2-28c.
8. Calculate the gain of the circuit using the formula $A_v = R_F/R_{in} + 1$ and record here:

    _____ .

9. Using the oscilloscope, set the signal generator for v_{in} (V p-p) given in the first line of the data table shown in Figure 2-28d.
10. Using the oscilloscope, measure and record v_{out} in the data table. (see photo in Figure A-2b of Appendix A.)
11. Calculate v_{out} using the formula $v_{out} = A_v v_{in}$ and record in the data table.
12. Repeat steps 10 and 11 for the various amplitudes of v_{in} given in the data table.
13. For the last measurement recorded in the data table of Figure 2-28d, explain why measured v_{out} was less than calculated v_{out} and why the signal was distorted

QUESTIONS FOR FIGURE 2-28

1. The gain of an op-amp noninverting amplifier can be found by dividing _____ by _____ and adding _____ .
2. With the noninverting amplifier, the output voltage is _____ phase with the input voltage.
3. V_{out} can be found by multiplying v_{in} with _____ .
4. Capacitors are used with an AC noninverting amplifier to _____ DC voltage.
5. The output signal of an amplifier may distort if the input signal is too _____ .

EXPERIMENT 2-6 TWO-STAGE OP-AMP AMPLIFIER

Objective:

To prove how the gain of one circuit is multiplied by the gain of another circuit and show signal phase relationships.

Introduction:

Both stages in Figure 2-29 are inverting amplifiers. The first stage has a voltage gain of 2.2 and the second stage has a voltage gain of 10. The output signal of the first stage is 180° out of phase with the input generator signal. The output signal of the second stage is 180° out of phase with its input, but in phase with the generator signal.

Required Components:

2 10-kΩ resistors (R_1, R_3)

1 22-kΩ resistor (R_2)

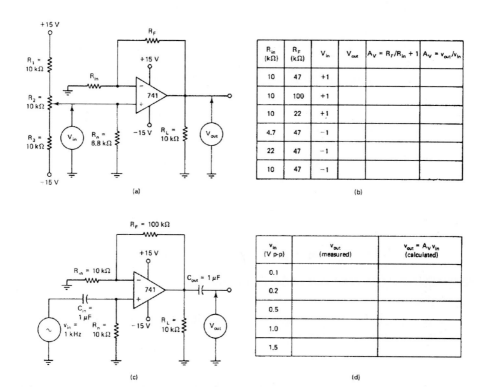

R_{in} (kΩ)	R_F (kΩ)	V_{in}	V_{out}	$A_V = R_F/R_{in} + 1$	$A_V = v_{out}/v_{in}$
10	47	+1			
10	100	+1			
10	22	+1			
4.7	47	-1			
22	47	-1			
10	47	-1			

(a)   (b)

V_{in} (V p-p)	V_{out} (measured)	$V_{out} = A_V V_{in}$ (calculated)
0.1		
0.2		
0.5		
1.0		
1.5		

(c)   (d)

FIGURE 2-28 Op-amp noninverting amplifier: (a) DC amplifier; (b) data table; (c) AC amplifier; (d) data table.

Taken from *Fundamental Electronic Devices: Concepts and Experimentation*, 2nd ed., Fredrick W. Hughes, Printice Hall Inc., 1984, Figure 11-11, page 269.

1 100-kΩ resistor (R_4)

Test Procedure:

1. With the power supply off, construct the circuit shown in Figure 2-29.
2. Turn on the power supply.
3. Set the sine-wave generator at 1000 Hz with an amplitude of 0.5 Vp-p.
4. Record the peak-to-peak voltage at the output of Op-1. _____
5. Record the peak-to-peak voltage at the output of Op-2. _____
6. Turn off the power supply.

QUESTIONS FOR FIGURE 2-29

1. What is the v_{out} of Op-1? _____
2. What is the A_v of Op-1? _____
3. What is the v_{out} of Op-2? _____
4. What is the A_v of Op-2? _____
5. What is the overall voltage gain of the circuit? _____

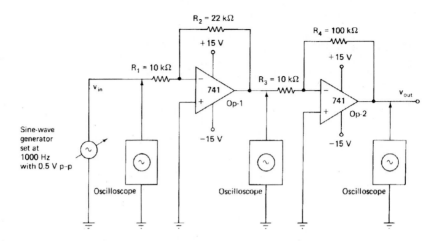

FIGURE 2-29 Two stage op-amp amplifier.

EXPERIMENT 2-7 OP-AMP VOLTAGE FOLLOWERS

Objective:

To demonstrate the operation of op-amp voltage followers, and to show differences between the inverting and noninverting types.

Introduction:

The noninverting voltage follower shown in Figure 2-30a has a gain of 1 because of the zero-resistance feedback loop. Its output voltage is in phase with the input voltage. The input impedance to this circuit can be made very high.

The inverting voltage follower shown in Figure 2-30b is similar to a standard inverting amplifier, except that its gain is 1 because R_{in}, and R_F are the same value ($A_v = -R_F/R_{in}$). Its output voltage is 180° out of phase with the input voltage. The input impedance to this circuit is usually lower, being limited by the value of R_{in}.

Voltage followers are used to match circuit impedances and act as buffer amplifiers, isolating one circuit from another.

Required Components:

1 4.7-kΩ resistor at 0.5 W (R_n)
3 10-kΩ resistors at 0.5 W (R_{in}, R_F, R_L)
1 100-kΩ resistor at 0.5 W (R_n)
2 1-μF capacitors at 25 WV dc (C_{in}, C_{out})
1 Breadboard for constructing circuit

Test Procedure:

1. Construct the circuit shown in Figure 2-30a.
2. Using the oscilloscope, set the signal generator for 1 kHz at 2 V p-p for v_{in}.
3. Using the oscilloscope, measure v_{out}.
4. Draw the output voltage waveform in the space provided, indicating the voltage peak to peak. (Assume that the input signal initially goes positive.)
5. Construct the circuit shown in Figure 2-30b.
6. Using the oscilloscope, set the signal generator for 1 kHz at 2 V p-p for v_{in}.
7. Using the oscilloscope, measure v_{out}.

8. Draw the output voltage waveform in the space provided, indicating the voltage peak to peak. (Assume that the input signal initially goes positive.)

QUESTIONS FOR FIGURE 2-30

1. Voltage followers are used for _____ matching and _____ .
2. An advantage of the noninverting voltage follower over the inverting type is that it has a higher _____ impedance.
3. The simplest voltage follower of the two types is the _____ .

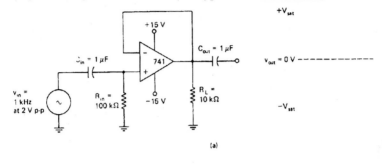

(a)

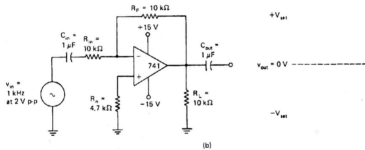

(b)

FIGURE 2-30 Op-amp voltage followers: (a) noninverting; (b) inverting.

Taken from *Fundamental Electronic Devices: Concepts and Experimentation*, 2nd ed., Fredrick W. Hughes, Prentice Hall Inc., 1984, Figure 11-12, page 271.

EXPERIMENT 2-8 SUMMING CURRENTS

Objective:
To show how input currents to an inverting amplifier are algebraically summed.
Introduction:
The input currents, I_1 and I_2, to the op amp shown in Figure 2-31 can be measured. These currents are algebraically summed and can be measured where I_F is indicated. Various polarity voltages can be placed on the inputs, resulting in various polarity currents through the op amp circuit. Some of these variations will be measured in this experiment.
Required Components:
3 10-kΩ resistors at 0.5 W (R_3, R_4, and R_L)
2 10-kΩ linear potentiometers (R_1, R_2)
Test Procedure:
1. Construct the circuit shown in Figure 2-31.

2. Apply power to the circuit.
3. Using the chart below, set the input voltages V_1 and V_2, accordingly.
4. Measure the input currents I_1 and I_2 and record their value in the chart. Remember to observe proper polarity when using the meter.
5. Measure the voltage at the inverting input of the op amp. This reading should be zero.
6. Measure I_F and record in the appropriate place in the chart.
7. Repeat steps 3 through 6. Changing the input current voltage and current polarity is accomplished by placing the ungrounded end of the potentiometers at either the + voltage or – voltage power supply source.

V_1	V_2	I_1	I_2	I_F
+ 1	+ 1	_____	_____	_____
+ 2	+ 1	_____	_____	_____
+ 2	– 1	_____	_____	_____
+ 3	– 2	_____	_____	_____
– 2	+ 3	_____	_____	_____
– 2	– 3	_____	_____	_____

QUESTIONS FOR FIGURE 2-31

1. The input currents to the circuit will algebraically equal the _____ current.
2. The voltage between the two inputs is _____ .
3. If $I_1 = + 0.2$ mA and $I_2 = + 0.3$ mA, then, I_F should equal _____ mA.
4. If $I_1 = – 0.2$ mA and $I_2 = + 0.3$ mA, then, I_F should equal _____ mA.
5. If $I_1 = – 0.4$ mA and $I_2 = – 0.3$ mA, then, I_F should equal _____ mA.

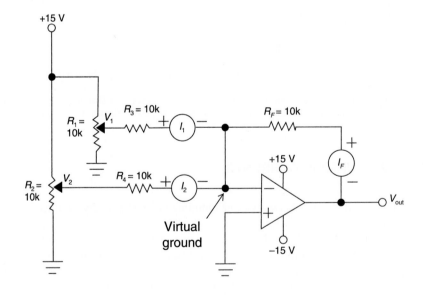

FIGURE 2-31 Summing currents.

EXPERIMENT 2-9 OP-AMP SUMMING AMPLIFIERS

Objective:

To demonstrate how an op amp can be used to sum algebraically various input voltages.

Introduction:

If more than one input is used on an inverting amplifier, it becomes a summing circuit or adder, as shown in Figure 2-32a and c. The output voltage is the algebraic sum of the inputs, but inverted, and can be found by the formula

$$V_{out} = -\left(\frac{R_F}{R_1}V_1 + \frac{R_F}{R_2}V_2 + \dots + \frac{R_F}{R_n}V_n\right)$$

where R_n and V_n are the number of input resistors and input voltages. If all the resistors are of the same value, the formula simplifies to $V_{out} = -(V_1 + V_2 + \dots + V_n)$. All input resistors may be of the same value, with R_F a larger value, resulting in a summing amplifier with gain. It may be required that some inputs influence the output voltages more than the others; therefore, different gains require various input resistor values. This type of circuit is called a *scaling adder*.

The input currents and current through R_F add up to zero at the inverting input, referred to as the *current summing point*. The summing amplifier can also be used as an audio signal mixer.

Resistors R_1 through R_6 are used to form two voltage dividers for setting the input voltages at V_1 and V_2.

Required Components:

1 4.7-kΩ resistor at 0.5 W (R_2)

7 10-kΩ resistors at 0.5 W (R_1, R_2, R_5, R_6, R_7, R_8, R_F)

1 22-kΩ resistor at 0.5 W (R_F)

2 10-kΩ linear potentiometers (R_3, R_4)

Test Procedure:

1. Construct the circuit shown in Figure 2-32a using all 10-kΩ resistors.
2. Using the voltmeter, adjust R_3 and R_4 for the voltage values of V_1 and V_2, respectively, given in the first line of the data table of Figure 2-32b.
3. Calculate and record in the data table V_{out} using the formula

$$V_{out} = -(V_1 + V_2)$$

4. Using the voltmeter, measure V_{out} and record it in the data table.
5. Repeat steps 3 and 4 for the remaining values of V_1 and V_2 given in the data table.
6. Change R_F to 22-kΩ.
7. Calculate and record in the data table V_{out} using the formula

$$V_{out} = -\left(\frac{R_F}{R_1}V_1 + \frac{R_F}{R_2}V_2\right)$$

8. Using the voltmeter, set V_1 and V_2 to the values shown on the first line of the data table.
9. Using the voltmeter, measure V_{out} and record it in the data table.
10. Repeat steps 7 through 9 for the remaining values of V_1 and V_2 given in the data table.

11. Construct the circuit shown in Figure 2-32c using the voltage-divider circuits of the first part of this experiment to set V_1 and V_2.
12. Using the voltmeter, set V_1 and V_2 to the values given in the first line of the data table of Figure 2-32d.
13. Calculate and record in the data table V_{out} using the formula

$$V_{out} = -\left(\frac{R_F}{R_1}V_1 + \frac{R_F}{R_2}V_2\right)$$

14. Using the voltmeter, measure V_{out} and record it in the data table.
15. Repeat steps 13 and 14 for the remaining values of V_1 and V_2 given in the data table.

QUESTIONS FOR FIGURE 2-32

1. An inverting op-amp adder _____ sums the voltages at the voltages at the inputs, but the output voltage is _____ .
2. If a summing amplifier has gain, R_F will be _____ than the other resistors in the circuit.
3. If all the resistors are the same value in an op-amp adder, the output-voltage formula is _____ .
4. A scaling adder has different-value _____ resistors.

EXPERIMENT 2-10 OP-AMP DIFFERENCE AMPLIFIER

Objective:
To show how an op amp can be used to find the algebraic differences between two input voltages.
Introduction:
Both inputs are used (or active) for a difference amplifier or subtractor, as shown in Figure 2-33a. The output voltage is found by the formula

$$V_{out} = -\left(\frac{R_F}{R_A}V_1\right) + \left(\frac{R_n}{R_B + R_n}\right)\left(\frac{R_A + R_F}{R_A}\right)V_2$$

If all resistors are equal, the formula simplifies to $V_{out} = V_2 - V_1$; however, the polarity of the output voltage depends on the relationship of the inverting and noninverting input polarities, similar to a comparator circuit.

A difference amplifier may have gain or use a scaling input arrangement where one input has more influence on the output. Resistors R_1 through R_6 are used for voltage dividers to set the input voltages V_1 and V_2.
Required Components:
9 10-kΩ resistors at 0.5 W (R_1, R_2, R_5, R_6, R_A, R_B, R_n, R_F, R_L)
2 10-kΩ linear potentiometers (R_3, R_4)
Test Procedure:
1. Construct the circuit shown in Figure 2-33a.
2. Using the voltmeter, set V_1, and V_2 to the values given in the first line of the data table

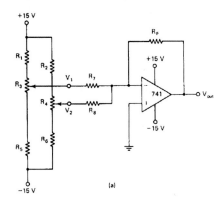

		$R_F = 10\ k\Omega$		$R_F = 22\ k\Omega$	
Input voltage		V_{out} algebraic sum (inverted)		V_{out} algebraic sum (inverted)	
V_1	V_2	Calculated	Measured	Calculated	Measured
+1	+2				
+1	−2				
+2	+1				
+2	−1				
−2	−2				

(a)   (b)

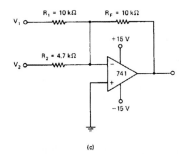

Input voltage		V_{out} algebraic sum (inverted)	
V_1	V_2	Calculated	Measured
+1	+2		
+1	−2		
+2	+1		
+2	−1		
−2	−2		

(c)   (d)

FIGURE 2-32 Op-amp summing amplifiers: (a) basic adder; (b) data table; (c) scaling adder; (d) data table.

Taken from *Fundamental Electronic Devices: Concepts and Experimentation*, 2nd ed., Fredrick W. Hughes, Prentice Hall Inc., 1984, Figure 11-13, page 272.

    shown in Figure 2-33b.

3.   Calculate and record in the data table V_{out} using the formula

$$V_{out} = - (V_2 - V_1)$$

(Remember to indicate the proper polarity.)

4.   Using the voltmeter, measure V_{out} and record it in the data table.

5.   Repeat steps 3 and 4 for the remaining values of V_1 and V_2 given in the data table.

QUESTIONS FOR FIGURE 2-33

1.   The output of an op-amp subtractor is the _____ difference at the inputs.

2.   If the voltage at the inverting input is more negative than the voltage at the noninverting input for an op-amp subtractor, the output will be _____ .

SECTION 2-5 SUMMARY POINTS

1.   A voltage comparator senses which input voltage is more positive (or negative) than the other, depending on which input is used as the reference voltage.

2.   A basic comparator output will be 0 V for 0 V between the inputs, or $+ V_{sat}$ (or $- V_{sat}$)

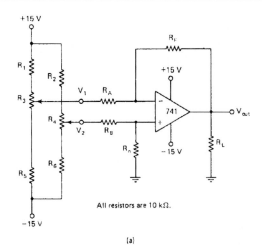

Input voltage		Output voltage algebraic difference (inverted)	
V_1	V_2	Calculated	Measured
+2	+4		
+4	+2		
+4	-2		
-2	+4		
-4	-2		

All resistors are 10 kΩ.

(a)   (b)

FIGURE 2-33 Op-amp voltage difference amplifier: (a) schematic diagram; (b) data table.

Taken from *Fundamental Electronic Devices: Concepts and Experimentation*, 2nd ed., Fredrick W. Hughes, Prentice Hall Inc., 1984, Figure 11-14, page 273.

for an input differential voltage.

3. The comparator output voltage polarity will be 180° out of phase with the inverting input voltage polarity in relation to the noninverting input voltage.
4. Comparators can be used as voltage-level detectors.
5. Degenerative (negative) feedback is used in a closed-loop mode to increase stability and bandwidth of an op amp.
6. An inverting amplifier inverts the signal 180°.
7. A virtual short exists between the two inputs of the op amp.
8. The inverting input of an op amp will tend to seek the same voltage potential as the non-inverting input.
9. Because of the high input impedance, for most practical purposes no current will flow into or out of the op-amp input terminals.
10. Current through the inverting input resistor (R_{in}) is the same as the current through the feedback resistor (R_F) for amplifier circuits.
11. A noninverting amplifier does not invert the signal.
12. Voltage followers have a gain of 1 and are used as isolating circuits.
13. An inverting summing amplifier will give an inverted algebraic summation output of the voltage at its inputs.
14. The summing amplifier may have gain if the feedback resistor is larger than the input resistors.
15. A scaling adder amplifies some inputs more than others, which depends on the various values of input resistors.
16. The virtual ground at the inverting input becomes the current summing point for a summing amplifier.
17. A voltage difference amplifier output provides the difference voltage between the inputs. The output may be algebraically proportional, include gain, or reflect a different gain for each input.

SECTION 2-6 SELF-CHECKING QUIZ

Match the names in column A with their proper schematic diagram in Figure 2-34.

Column A
1. Inverting amplifier
2. Summing amplifier
3. Comparator
4. Difference amplifier
5. Voltage follower
6. Noninverting amplifier

Multiple-Choice Questions

7. The output of a voltage comparator with + 2.5 V on the inverting input and + 2.7 V on the noninverting input will be:
   a. $+ V_{sat}$
   b. $-V_{sat}$
   c. + 0.2 V
   d. − 0.2 V
8. For a particular inverting amplifier, $R_{in} = 22$ kΩ , $R_F = 68$ kΩ, and $V_{in} = + 0.5$ V p-p. The output voltage will equal about:
   a. − 0.5V p-p
   b. + 15 V p-p
   c. − 1.5 V p-p
   d. 0 V
9. For a particular noninverting amplifier, $R_{in} = 10$ kΩ , $R_F = 120$ kΩ , and $V_{in} = + 0.6$ V p-p. The output voltage will equal about:
   a. + 7.8 V p-p
   b. − 7.2 V p-p
   c. − 8.2 V p-p
   d. + 8.8 V p-p
10. A noninverting voltage follower has an input voltage of +5.5 V p-p. Its output will be about:
   a. 0 V
   b. $+ V_{sat}$
   c. $- V_{sat}$
   d. + 5.5 V p-p
11. Referring to Figure 2-35, if $V_1 = + 2$ V, $V_2 = + 3$ V, and $V_3 = - 1$ V, V_{out} will be:
   a. + 4 V
   b. − 4 V
   c. + 6 V
   d. − 6 V

12. Referring to Figure 2-35, if $V_1 = - 3$ V, $V_2 = - 2$ V, and $V_3 = + 4$ V, V_{out} will be:
   a. + 1 V
   b. − 1 V
   c. + 9 V

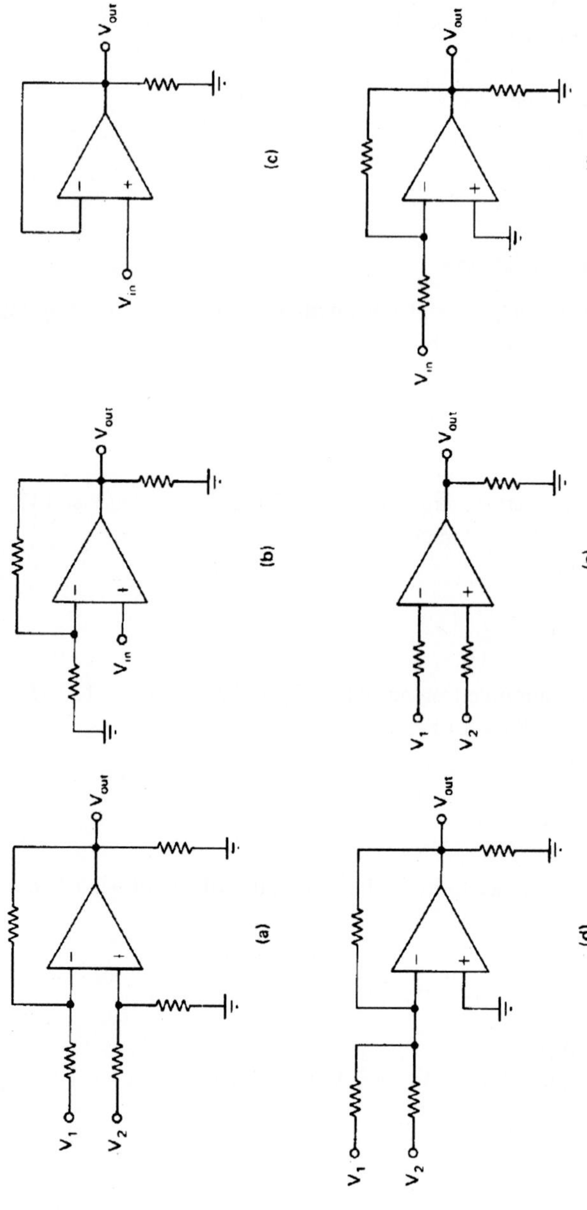

FIGURE 2-34

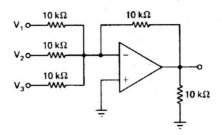

FIGURE 2-35

d.   − 9 V
13. Which of the following is *not* true for a voltage follower?
    a.   Low output impedance
    b.   Gain of 1
    c.   Low input impedance
    d.   Used as a buffer amplifier
14. The type of feedback used in the closed-loop mode to stabilize and increase bandwidth of an op-amp circuit is:
    a.   Positive
    b.   Negative
    c.   Regenerative
    d.   Degenerative
    e.   (b) and (c) are correct
    f.   (b) and (d) are correct
15. The value of V_{ref} in Figure 2-6 is about:
    a.   + 1.5 V
    b.   + 4.7 V
    c.   + 10.0 V
    d.   − 4.7 V

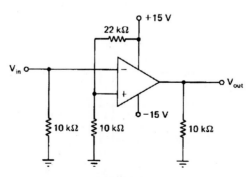

FIGURE 2-36

16. Referring to Figure 2-36, when $V_{in} = + 3$ V, the output will be about:
    a.   + 13.5 V
    b.   − 13.5 V
    c.   + 4.7 V

d.   − 4.7 V
17. Referring to Figure 2-37, when $V_1 = + 4$ V, and $V_2 = + 1$ V, V_{out} will equal:
    a.   + 3 V
    b.   − 3 V
    c.   + 5 V
    d.   − 5 V
18. Referring to Figure 2-37, when $V_1 = − 5$ V, and $V_2 = + 2$ V, V_{out} will equal:
    a.   + 3 V
    b.   − 3 V
    c.   + 7 V
    d.   − 7 V

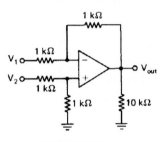

FIGURE 2-37

19. Virtual ground is also the:
    a.   Common ground
    b.   Summing point
    c.   Earth ground
20. Referring to Figure 2-38, the output voltage will be about:
    a.   + 1 V
    b.   − 1 V
    c.   + 4 V
    d.   − 4 V

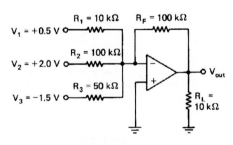

FIGURE 2-38

(Answers at back of book)

CHAPTER 3

SIGNAL PROCESSING WITH OP-AMPS

Signal processing involves the use of special circuits that change or modify given input signals. The output signals of these circuits can then be used to perform different functions. Wave-shaping circuits will actually change the signal's overall form, such as integration and differentiation. Other special circuits will attenuate the input signal at certain frequencies and are referred to as filters.

These signal-processing circuits can use passive components, such as resistors, capacitors, and inductors. With a passive circuit, there is a certain amount of signal lost or consumed, and they tend to be more bulky in size. Active circuits usually combine minimal passive components: resistors and capacitors, together with active devices such as transistors and other discrete solid-state amplifiers. These active circuits amplify or at least maintain the amplitude of the input signal.

In this chapter you will see how op amps are particularly suited for signal-processing circuits. In many areas, op-amp circuits are less expensive, easier to use, more efficient, require less external components, take less space, and are much lighter in weight, compared to circuits using discrete components.

3-1-1 INTEGRATOR CIRCUIT

An integrator circuit continuously adds up a quantity being measured over a period of time. The output waveform is proportional to the time interval of the input signal.

In a basic passive RC integrator circuit as seen in Figure 3-1, the output is taken across the capacitor. The voltage across the capacitor takes time to build up, depending on the RC time constant. Because the current decreases as the capacitor is charging, the voltage across the capacitor rises at an exponential rate, as indicated by the bending (or rounding-off) waveform. When the input pulse falls to 0 V, the capacitor discharges at an exponential rate also. Notice that the input voltage is divided across the resistor and capacitor. Hence, a loss is incurred and the output voltage amplitude is less than the input voltage. Integration occurs when the input pulse duration is much less than one time constant ($TC = RC$).

When an op amp is used in an integrator circuit, as shown in Figure 3-2, the capacitor becomes the feedback element. From the previous discussion in Chapter 2, remember that the feedback current must equal the input current. Therefore, the op amp provides a linear rising output voltage to keep the charging current constant. When the input pulse goes to 0 V, the falling output voltage is also linear. The resulting output voltage waveform is triangular. Since the inverting input is used, the output will be a negative-going waveform. This basic op-amp integrator is in the open-loop mode, and even when V_{in} is 0 V, the input bias current will cause the capacitor to charge. The capacitor will continue to charge until the output is at saturation and the circuit is unusable.

A large-value feedback resistor placed in parallel with the feedback capacitor, as shown in Figure 3-3, prevents output saturation and provides a practical integrator with reduced noise, less offset drift, and better stability. The gain can be set from 10 to 100, depending on the amount of output voltage needed. When V_{in} equals 0 V, V_{out} will equal 0 V. Remember that the capacitive reactance (X_c) varies with frequency. For lower frequencies, X_c increases, less signal is fed back, and the output voltage will increase. When the frequency is increased, X_c decreases, more signal is fed back, and the output voltage decreases. Because the X_c changes, the integrator circuit behaves like a low-pass filter.

As long as V_{in} is constant, the output voltage can be found with the expression

$$V_{out} = \frac{1}{R_{in} C_F} \int_0^t dV_{in}\, dt$$

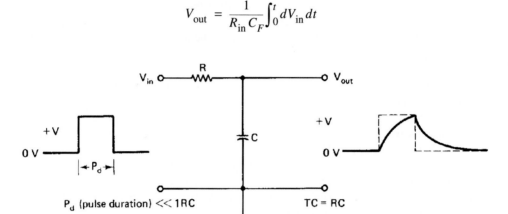

FIGURE 3-1 Simple passive integrator.

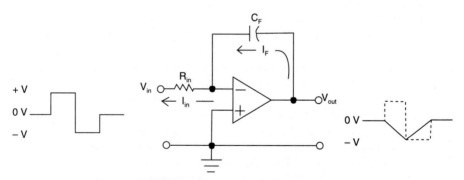

FIGURE 3-2 Basic op amp integrator.

The integral sign $\int_0^t$ indicates the period or limits of integration to be calculated, where V_{in} is constant and dt is the time or period of integration. For example, if the input signal of Figure 3-3 is symmetrical, the period of one cycle is 0.001 s. [Period (one cycle) = 1/F, where F is the frequency.] The pulse is at +0.5 V for half of the cycle, which is 0.0005 s. Now, substituting the values onto the formula, we obtain

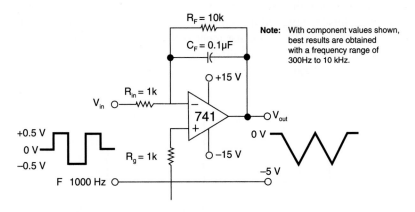

FIGURE 3-3 Practical op amp integrator.

$$V_{out} = -\frac{1}{(1\,k\Omega)\,(0.1\,\mu F)} \int_0^t (+5\,V)\,(0.0005s)\int_{t=0}^{t_1=0.0005}$$

$$= -10 \times 10^3\,(0.00025)$$

$$= -2.5\,V$$

The -0.5 input voltage of the second half of the cycle brings the output back to 0 V. The minus sign only indicates that the output is 180° out of phase with the input.

3-1-2 DIFFERENTIATOR CIRCUIT

The reverse concept of the integrator is the differentiator. The output of a differentiator circuit is proportional to the rate of change of the input signal. The output is taken across the resistor, as shown in the simple passive differentiator of Figure 3-4. Initially, when the leading edge of the pulse is applied to the input, maximum current flows. The I_R drop across the resistor (V_{out}) is also maximum at this time. As the voltage on the capacitor begins to build up, less current is required for the charging process. The V_{out} then drops off at an exponential rate. When the input pulse falls to 0 V, the capacitor discharges in the opposite direction and the same process occurs, but in the negative direction. Here again, the input voltage is divided across the capacitor and resistor, resulting in a loss at the output.

By using an op amp in the differentiator circuit shown in Figure 3-5, the output can be made equal to or larger than the input. The output voltage can be found by the expression

$$V_{out} = -2R_F C_{in}\frac{dV_{in}}{dt}$$

where dV_{in} is the change in input voltage and dt the change in time that it occurs. The minus sign only indicates phase inversion.

However, this input waveform is difficult to calculate because of the steep rise and fall times of the input pulse. The triangular input voltage shown in Figure 3-6 is easier to compute and shows the reverse effect of differentiation to that of integration. For example, with an input frequency of 1 kHz, the

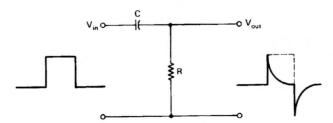

FIGURE 3-4 Simple passive differentiator.

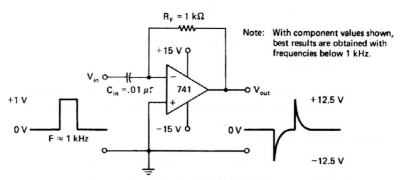

FIGURE 3-5 Basic op amp differentiator.

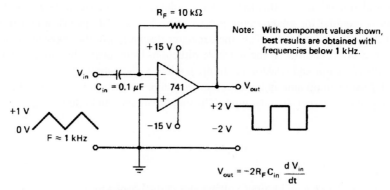

FIGURE 3-6 Practical op amp differentiator.

period of one cycle is 0.001 s. The change in time when the output voltage is either rising or falling is 0.0005 s. Substituting the values into the formula, we have

$$V_{out} = (-2)(10k\Omega)(0.1\mu F)(\frac{1V}{0.0005s})$$

$$= -0.002 \times 2000$$

$$= -4V$$

The differentiator circuit is useful in producing a sharp trigger pulse to drive other circuits. When the input signal increases in frequency, the X_C of the input capacitor decreases and the output signal increases. Therefore, the differentiator circuit serves as a basic high-pass filter.

3-1-3 ACTIVE LOW-PASS FILTER

A low-pass filter has a constant output voltage from DC up to a specific cutoff frequency (f_c). This cutoff frequency, f_c, is also called the 0.707 frequency, the –3-dB frequency, the corner frequency, or the "breakpoint" frequency. Frequencies above the f_c are attenuated (decreased). The range of frequencies below f_c are called the pass band, while the frequencies above f_c are known as the stop band. A low-pass-filter frequency-response curve is shown in Figure 3-7. The dashed line indicates an ideal cutoff. However, filters are usually not this efficient and tend to roll off or even peak and then roll off. The practical f_c occurs at the half-power point, or 70.7 percent of the maximum output voltage. This is also expressed in decibels (dB) and can be derived from the formula

$$dB = -20\log\frac{V_{out}}{V_{in}}$$

$$= -20\log\frac{0.707V}{1V}$$

$$= -20(0.15059)$$

$$= -3dB$$

Op-amp filters can be designed to have different roll-off characteristics, resulting in various slopes. A slope of – 20 dB/decade means that as the frequency increases by ten (×10) from f_c, the output voltage will decrease 20 dB. The more decibel loss per decade results in a steeper slope. Remember that it is desirable to have the largest dB loss per decade, since this represents a sharper cutoff filter.

A simple low-pass filter is shown in Figure 3-8. The circuit configuration is a voltage follower. Resistor R and capacitor C at the noninverting input form a voltage divider. For frequencies of V_{in} below f_c, the capacitor's X_C is large, and nearly all of V_{in} is dropped across C. With V_{in} being large, V_{out} is also large. The gain of the stage is maximum for these lower frequencies. When the frequencies of V_{in} increase above f_c, the capacitor's X_C decreases and most of V_{in} is dropped across the resistor. In effect, capacitor C shunts much of V_{in} to ground. With V_{in} small, V_{out} is also small; hence, the gain of the stage is less than maximum for higher frequencies.

The f_c for this circuit can be approximated by the formula

$$f_c \approx \frac{1}{2\pi RC}$$

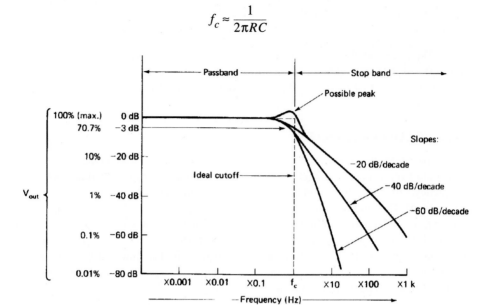

FIGURE 3-7 Low-pass filter frequency response curve.

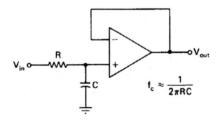

FIGURE 3-8 Simple low-pass filter.

For example, if $R = 10 \text{ k}\Omega$ and $C = 0.1 \text{ }\mu\text{F}$, then

$$f_c \approx \frac{1}{6.28 \, (10 \times 10^3) \, (0.1 \times 10^{-6})}$$

$$\approx \frac{1}{6.28 \, (0.001)}$$

$$\approx \frac{1}{0.00628}$$

$$\approx 159 \text{Hz}$$

This simple low-pass filter has a slope of approximately − 20 db/decade.

Because of the capacitors, filters do not have a constant phase angle (input-to-output phase) at f_c. A basic low-pass filter of − 20 db/decade has a phase angle of about − 45° at f_c. An increase of − 20 db/decade will cause the phase angle to increase by − 45°. For example, a − 40-dB/decade filter will have phase angle of − 90°.

A sharper cutoff low-pass filter with a slope of about − 40 db/decade is shown in Figure 3-9. Capacitor C_2 shunts current away from the input for frequencies above f_c. The X_c of capacitor C_1 is low for frequencies in this stop-band range and more negative feedback is applied at the input. Therefore, the gain is reduced drastically.

The corner frequency for this circuit can be approximated with the formula

$$f_c \approx \frac{1}{2\pi\sqrt{R_1 R_2 C_1 C_2}}$$

For example, let $R_1 = 10 \text{ k}\Omega$, $R_2 = 10 \text{ k}\Omega$, $C_1 = 0.1 \text{ μF}$, and $C_2 = 0.01\text{μF}$. Then

$$f_c \approx \frac{1}{6.28\sqrt{(10 \times 10^3)(10 \times 10^3)(0.1 \times 10^{-6})(0.1 \times 10^{-6})}}$$

$$\approx \frac{1}{6.28\sqrt{(100 \times 10^6)(0.001 \times 10^{-12})}}$$

$$\approx \frac{1}{6.28(0.316 \times 10^{-3})}$$

$$\approx 500\text{Hz}$$

This formula will be fairly accurate if $R_1 = R_2$ and C_1 is greater than C_2. Resistor R_3 is used for DC offset and should be equal to $R_1 + R_2$.

There are numerous types of filters for specific applications, involving complex calculations. These basic filters, with a few calculations, are presented in the sections of this chapter to acquaint you with the applications of op amps to these circuits.

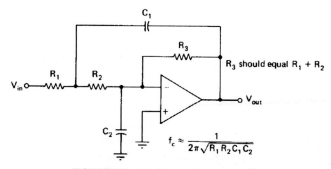

FIGURE 3-9 −40 dB/decade low-pass filter.

3-1-4 ACTIVE HIGH-PASS FILTER

A high-pass filter performs the opposite function from that of a low-pass filter. The high-pass filter attenuates all frequencies below a specific cutoff frequency f_c and passes all the frequencies above the f_c. Figure 3-10 shows a high-pass filter frequency-response curve. Similar to the low-pass filter, the practical f_c for a highpass filter also occurs at 70.7 percent of the maximum output voltage. A high-pass filter can have different slopes, depending on the design of the circuit.

By interchanging the R and C components of a low-pass filter, a high-pass filter can be created. A simple high-pass filter is shown in Figure 3-11. With V_{in} to the noninverting input, C and R form a voltage divider. When V_{in} is below f_c, the X_c of C is large and drops most of V_{in}. The voltage drop across R_1 is low and since the circuit is a follower, V_{out} is also low. When V_{in} increases above f_c, the X_c of C is low, allowing more V_{in} to be dropped across R; hence V_{out} is larger. This circuit has a slope of about -20 db/decade, and the same formula used to find f_c for a simple low-pass filter can also be used.

A more dependable high-pass filter with a slope of about -40 db/decade is shown in Figure 3-12. In this circuit, C_1 should equal C_2 and R_2 should be twice as large as R_1. Resistor R_3 should equal R_2 and is used for DC offset The X_c of C_1 and C_2 perform the same function as C with the simple high-pass filter of Figure 3-11. Feedback resistor R_1 connected to the junction of C_1 and C_2 provides a sort of double-filtering action.

The same formula can be used for this circuit to find f_c as that used for the low-pass filter of Figure 3-9.

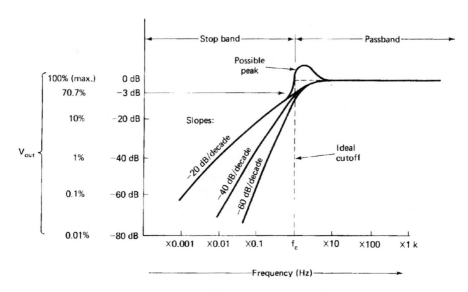

FIGURE 3-10 High-pass filter frequency response curve.

3-1-5 ACTIVE BANDPASS FILTER

A bandpass filter will pass a certain group of frequencies while rejecting all others. A typical frequency-response curve for a bandpass filter is shown in Figure 3-13a. The maximum output voltage of this type of filter will peak at one specific frequency known as the resonant frequency f_r. When the frequency varies from resonance, the output voltage decreases. The point

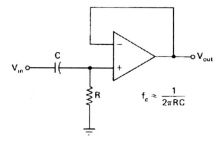

FIGURE 3-11 Simple high-pass filter.

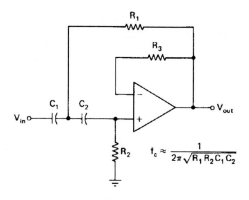

FIGURE 3-12 –40 dB/decade high-pass filter.

above and below f_r that V_{out} falls to 70.7 percent determines the bandwidth of the filter. The upper frequency that this point occurs can be designated f_H, while the lower frequency point can be f_L. The frequencies between f_L and f_H establish the bandwidth of the circuit (BW $= f_H - f_L$). If the bandwidth is less than 10 percent of f_r, the filter is considered as a narrow-bandpass filter, whereas greater than 10 percent would classify it as a widebandpass filter.

The narrower the bandwidth of a filter, the more selective it is said to be. The amount of selectivity is expressed as the quality factor, Q, of the circuit. The Q of a circuit can be determined by dividing the resonant frequency by its bandwidth,

$$Q = \frac{f_r}{BW}$$

The bandwidth of a circuit can be determined similarly:

$$BW = \frac{f_r}{Q}$$

A high-Q filter has a narrow bandwidth and tends to have a large V_{out}, while a low-Q

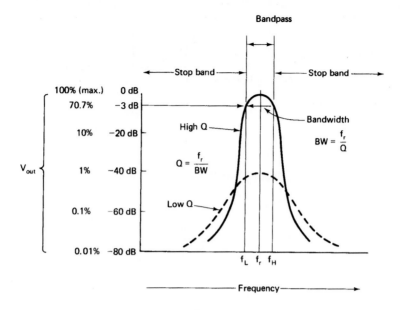

(a)

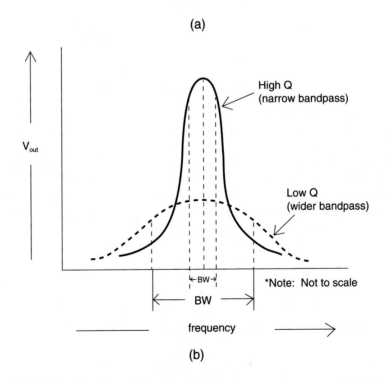

(b)

FIGURE 3-13 Bandpass: (a) bandpass filter frequency response curve; (b) comparison of high Q and low Q filters.

filter has a wider bandwidth and tends to have less V_{out}, as shown in Figure 3-13b. The dashed line in Figure 3-13b indicates a low-Q filter.

By combining low-pass and high-pass filtering circuits and selecting specific frequencies, a bandpass active filter can be constructed as shown in Figure 3-14. Components R_1 and C_2 provide low-pass filtering, while components C_1 and R_2 provide high-pass filtering. The f_r for this circuit is found with the formula

$$f_r \approx \frac{1}{2\pi\sqrt{R_pR_3C_1C_2}}$$

where R_p is the equivalent parallel resistance of R_1 and R_2, which is found thus:

$$R_p = \frac{R_1R_2}{R_1+R_2}$$

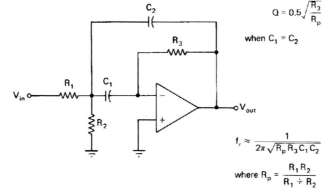

$$Q = 0.5\sqrt{\frac{R_3}{R_p}}$$

when $C_1 = C_2$

$$f_r \approx \frac{1}{2\pi\sqrt{R_pR_3C_1C_2}}$$

where $R_p = \dfrac{R_1R_2}{R_1 \div R_2}$

FIGURE 3-14 Active bandpass filter.

For simplification, the Q of this filter is found with the formula

$$Q = 0.5\sqrt{\frac{R_3}{R_p}}$$

when $C_1 = C_2$

Feedback resistor R_3 Plays an important part in this circuit. It not only establishes the gain of the circuit, but it affects the Q and f_r as well. When R_3 is relatively small, the f_r will be high and the Q low. But when R_3 is large, f_r is low and Q is high. For example, find the f_r, Q, and BW for the bandpass filter of Figure 3-14 when

$R_1 = 10\ k\Omega$	$C_1 = 0.01\ \mu F$
$R_2 = 10\ k\Omega$	$C_2 = 0.01\ \mu F$
$R_3 = 100\ k\Omega$	

$$R_p = \frac{R_1 R_2}{R_1 + R_2} = \frac{(10\text{k}\Omega)(10\text{k}\Omega)}{10\text{k}\Omega + 10\text{k}\Omega} = \frac{100\text{k}\Omega}{20\text{k}\Omega} = 5\text{k}\Omega$$

$$f_r = \frac{1}{2\pi\sqrt{R_p R_3 C_1 C_2}}$$

$$\approx \frac{1}{6.28\sqrt{(5\times10^3)(100\times10^3)(0.01\times10^{-6})(0.01\times10^{-6})}}$$

$$\approx \frac{1}{6.28\sqrt{0.05\times10^{-6}}}$$

$$\approx \frac{1}{6.28(0.224\times10^{-3})}$$

$$\approx \frac{1}{1.4\times10^{-3}}$$

$$\approx 714\text{Hz}$$

$$Q \approx 0.5\sqrt{\frac{R_3}{R_p}} \approx 0.5\sqrt{\frac{100\times10^3}{5\times10^3}}$$

$$\approx 0.5\sqrt{20}$$

$$\approx 0.5(4.5)$$

$$\approx 2.25$$

$$\text{BW} = \frac{f_r}{Q} = \frac{714}{2.25} = 317\text{Hz}$$

Therefore,

$$f_H = f_r + \frac{\text{BW}}{2} = 714 + \frac{317}{2} \approx 873\text{Hz}$$

$$f_L = f_r - \frac{\text{BW}}{2} = 714 - \frac{317}{2} \approx 556\text{Hz}$$

If R_3 is increased to 1 MΩ, the f_r is

$$f_r \approx \frac{1}{6.28\sqrt{(5 \times 10^3)\,(1 \times 10^6)\,(0.01 \times 10^{-6})\,(0.01 \times 10^{-6})}}$$

$$\approx \frac{1}{6.28\sqrt{0.5 \times 10^{-6}}}$$

$$\approx 225\,\text{Hz}$$

$$Q = 0.5 \qquad\qquad \frac{1 \times 10^6}{5 \times 10^3} = 7.07$$

$$\text{BW} = \frac{225}{7.07} \approx 32\,\text{Hz}$$

$$f_H = f_r + \frac{\text{BW}}{2} = 225 + \frac{32}{2} \approx 241\,\text{Hz}$$

$$f_L = f_r - \frac{\text{BW}}{2} = 225 - 16 \approx 209\,\text{Hz}$$

If it is desired to have a wide-bandpass filter with a fairly constant output during the bandwidth, a low-pass filter and a high-pass filter can be connected together. The frequency-response curve would resemble that of Figure 3-15. It makes no difference which filter comes first. The high-pass filter would have to be designed for an f_c at the low end of the bandwidth (f_L) and the low-pass filter would have to be designed for an f_c at the high end (f_H)

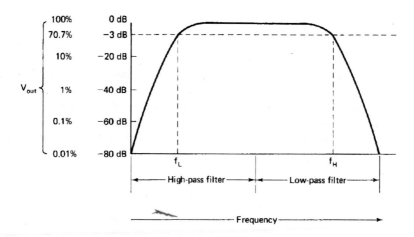

FIGURE 3-15 Wide-band pass frequency response curve using two filters.

3-1-6 ACTIVE NOTCH (BAND-REJECT) FILTER

A notch filter (formerly referred to as a band-reject filter) functions opposite to a bandpass filter. Figure 3-16 shows that this type of circuit passes all frequencies except a specific group. The output voltage will remain maximum until the applied frequency approaches f_r, where it is attenuated. The bandwidth occurs for amplitudes below 70.7 percent of V_{out}, and the same Q and BW formulas associated with the bandpass filter also apply to the notch filter. The notch filter is more highly selective than the older band-reject type and is used very often to reduce unwanted effects of specific frequencies, such as 60-Hz hum.

A basic active notch filter is shown in Figure 3-17. In this configuration, V_{in} is applied to both inputs. Components R_1, R_4, C_1, and C_2 form a frequency-selective feedback network. The ratio of the resistances to the reactances of the capacitors determine the f_r of the circuit and is expressed

$$f_r = \frac{1}{2\pi\sqrt{R_1 R_4 C_1 C_2}}$$

The Q of the circuit is determined by the ratio of R_1 to R_4 when C_1 equals C_2 and is given as

$$Q = 0.5\sqrt{\frac{R_4}{R_1}}$$

The slope of the notch is determined by the Q, whereas the depth of the notch is dependant on the Q and the percentage of R_3 to $R_2 + R_3$, and can be expressed

$$N(\text{slope'of'notch}) = \frac{\dfrac{1}{Q} - \dfrac{1-R_p}{R_p}(2Q)}{1/Q} \qquad\qquad R_p = \frac{R_3}{R_2 + R_3}$$

Resistor R_3 is typically 50 times greater than R_2.

The R_2 and R_3 voltage divider produces a differential voltage at the inputs of the op amp. For frequencies below fr, the X_c, of the capacitors is very high and there is little feedback; thus the output is maximum. When the frequency of V_{in} approaches fr, the reactances form the appropriate relationship and phase angle with the resistances to produce feedback, which decreases the output. As the frequency of V_{in} increases above f_r, the X_c of the capacitors decrease and the feedback factor approaches 1, or the gain of a voltage follower. As an example, let

$R_1 = 10\ k\Omega$ $C_1 = 0.0266\ \mu F$
$R_2 = 1\ k\Omega$ $C_2 = 0.0266\ \mu F$
$R_3 = 47\ k\Omega$ (*Hint*: Parallel one 0.02 μF with
$R_4 = 1\ M\Omega$ two 0.0033-uF capacitors.)

Then

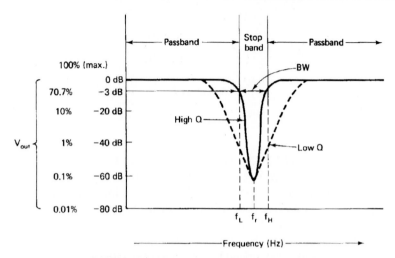

FIGURE 3-16 Notch filter frequency response curve.

and

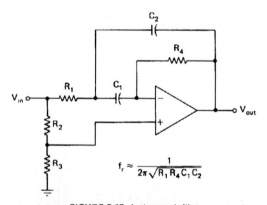

FIGURE 3-17 Active notch filter.

$$f_r = \frac{1}{6.28\sqrt{(10 \times 10^3)\,(1 \times 10^6)\,(0.0266 \times 10^{-6})\,(0.0266 \times 10^{-6})}}$$

$$= \frac{1}{6.28\sqrt{7.075 \times 10^{-6}}}$$

$$= \frac{1}{6.28\,(2.66 \times 10^{-3})}$$

$$\approx 60\text{Hz}$$

$$Q = 0.5 \sqrt{\frac{1 \times 10^6}{10 \times 10^3}}$$

$$= 0.5\sqrt{100}$$

$$= 5$$

Another popular notch filter is the twin-"T" notch filter shown in Figure 3-18. A basic twin-"T" notch filter (Figure 3-18a) simply consists of a double- or twin-"T" passive filter fed into an op-amp follower. This circuit usually has a very low Q (less than 1) and the op amp serves mainly as a buffer. The data notations indicate that R_3 is one-half the value of R_1 or R_2 and C_1 is twice the value Of C_2 or C_3.

An identical circuit, with a slight modification, is shown in Figure 3-18b. In this case, C_3 and R_3 are not returned to ground but are connected to the low-impedance output of the op amp. The Q of this circuit can reach up to 50, creating an extremely sharp notch. It also permits the use of high resistances and very low values of capacitances for f_r at low frequencies. The same formulas apply to both of the twin-"T" notch filters.

To minimize frequency shift with temperature, many op-amp filters use silver mica or polycarbonate capacitors with precision resistors.

SECTION 3-2 TERMINOLOGY EXERCISE

Write a brief definition for each of the following terms:
1. Integrator circuit
2. Differentiator circuit
3. Low-pass filter
4. High-pass filter
5. Bandpass filter
6. Band-reject filter
7. Notch filter
8. Cutoff frequency
9. Corner frequency
10. Resonant frequency
11. Frequency response curve
12. Slope (pertaining to a response curve)
13. Stop band
14. Bandpass
15. Bandwidth
16. Q of a circuit

SECTION 3-3 PROBLEMS AND EXERCISES

1. Referring to Figure 3-3, what is V_{out} when V_{in} is 2 Vp-p at 500 Hz?
2. Referring to Figure 3-6, what is V_{out} when V_{in} is + 2 V at 200 Hz?

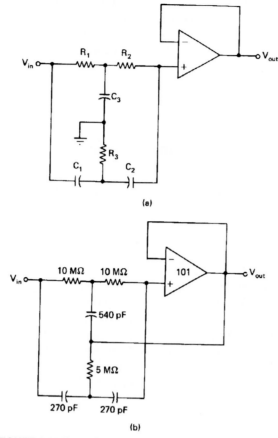

FIGURE 3-18 Twin "T" notch filters: (a) Basic twin "t" notch filter; (b) High Q notch filter.

$$f_r \approx \frac{1}{2\pi R_1 C_2} \qquad \text{where} \qquad R_1 = R_2 = 2R_3$$

$$C_2 = C_3 = \frac{C_3}{2}$$

3. What is the approximate f_c in Figure 3-8 when $R = 22$ kΩ and $C = 0.01$ μF?
4. What is the approximate f_c in Figure 3-9 when $R_1 = 22$ kΩ, $R_2 = 10$ kΩ, $C_1 = 0.01$ μF, and $C_2 = 0.01$ μF?
5. What is the approximate value of f_c in Figure 3-11 when $C = 0.016$ μF and $R = 10$ kΩ?
6. Find the approximate f_c in Figure 3-12 when $R_1 = 10$ kΩ, R_2 100 kΩ, $C_1 = 0.01$ μF, and $C_2 = 0.02$ μF.
7. What is the Q of a filter if its $f_r = 1$ kHz and its BW = 125 Hz? Find f_H and f_L for this circuit.
8. What is the BW of a filter if its $Q = 10$ and its $f_r = 400$ Hz? Find f_H and f_L for this circuit.
9. Find the f_r, Q, BW, f_H, and f_L of the filter shown in Figure 3-14 when $R_1 = 10$ kΩ, $R_2 = $

22 kΩ, $R_3 = 470$ kΩ, $C_1 = 0.1$ µF, and $C_2 = 0.1$ µF. If the input voltage is 2.5 V p-p, what is the voltage at the corner frequency $(f_H$ or $f_L)$?

10. Find the f_r, Q, BW, f_H, and f_L, of the filter shown in Figure 3-17 when $R_1 = 4.7$ kΩ, $R_2 = 1$ kΩ, $R_3 = 50$ kΩ, $R_4 = 2.2$ MΩ, $C_1 = 0.01$ µF, and $C_2 = 0.01$ µF.

SECTION 3-4 EXPERIMENTS

EXPERIMENT 3-1 PRACTICAL INTEGRATOR CIRCUIT

Objective:

To show how an op amp can be used as an integrator circuit and change the voltage waveform of an input voltage.

Introduction:

The integrator circuit shown in Figure 3-19 resembles an inverting amplifier circuit. The ratio of the resistors (R_F/R_{in}) indicates the circuit has a gain of 10. However, with the capacitor in parallel with R_F, changing frequencies at the input will cause the output voltage waveform to change. The RC time constant changes the shape of the voltage waveform. Increasing frequencies cause X_c to decrease, which in turn decreases the feedback impedance, thereby lowering the amplitude of the output voltage. Sine wave input signals will be amplified normally, but there will be about a 90° phase shift of input to output voltage waveforms. A square wave input tends to be changed to a triangle waveform. There are limitations to the input frequencies. With a reactive component such as the capacitor there is a frequency outoff (f_c) point. The circuit acts like a normal amplifier to frequencies below f_c and performs as an integrator with frequencies above f_c.

Required components:

1 100 kΩ resistor at 0.5 W (R_F)

2 10 kΩ resistor at 0.5 W $(R_{in}$ and $R_n)$

1 0.01 µF capacitor at 25 WVDC (C)

Test Procedure:

1. Construct the circuit shown in Figure 3-19a

2. Set the square wave generator for an amplitude of 2 Vp-p.

3. Using a dual trace oscilloscope, place channel 1 at the input and channel 2 at the output of the circuit. Adjust the oscilloscope to display four or five cycles.

4. Calculate the cutoff frequency of the circuit from the formula:

$$_c = \frac{1}{2\pi R_F C} = \underline{\hspace{3cm}}$$

5. Referring to the data table in Figure 3-19b, set the frequency of the square generator according to f_{in}.

6. Draw a simple sketch of the output voltage waveform on the table.

7. Measure the peak-to-peak voltage at the output and record the value in the data table.(-See photo in Figure A-3a of Appendix A.)

8. Repeat steps 4 through 6 for the remaining frequencies given in the table. The sweep frequency of the oscilloscope will have to be changed with each change of input frequency

in order to display four or five cycles.

QUESTIONS FOR FIGURE 3-19

1. The outoff frequency for the circuit is _____ .
2. Below f_c the circuit behaves like a(n) _____ .
3. Above f_c the circuit behaves like a(n) _____ .
4. With proper integration, a square wave at the input will produce a(n)_____ wave at the output.

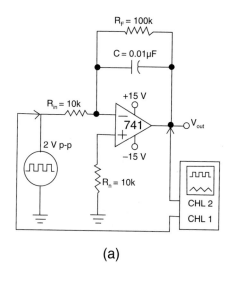

f_{in} (Hz)	Voltage Waveform	V_{out} p-p
100		
200		
500		
1k		
2k		
5k		

(a)

(b)

FIGURE 3-19 Practical integrator circuit: (a) schematic diagram; (b) data table.

EXPERIMENT 3-2 PRACTICAL DIFFERENTIATOR CIRCUIT

Objective:

To demonstrate how an op amp can be used as a differentiator circuit and to change the voltage waveform of an input voltage.

Introduction:

The differentiator circuit shown in Figure 3-20a is similar to the integrator circuit, except the capacitor is placed in series with the input. The function of the differentiator is different from that of the integrator. The output of the circuit is a function of the rate of change in amplitude of the input signal. However, there are limitations with the circuit. Below f_c the circuit performs as a differentiator, whereas above f_c the circuit operates as an amplifier.

Required Components:

1 10 kΩ resistor at 0.5W (R_{in})
1 22 kΩ resistor at 0.5 W (R_F)
1 0.005 μF capacitor at 25WVDC

Test Procedure:

1. Construct the circuit shown in Figure 3-20.a.

2. Set the square wave generator for an amplitude of 2 Vp-p.
3. Using a dual-trace oscilloscope, place channel 1 at the input and channel 2 at the output of the circuit. Adjust the oscilloscope to display four or five cycles.
4. Calculate the cutoff frequency of the circuit from the formula

$$f_c = \frac{1}{2\pi R_F C} = \underline{\hspace{2cm}}$$

5. Referring to the data table in Figure 3-20b, set the frequency of the square generator according to f_{in}.
6. Draw a simple sketch of the output voltage waveform on the table.
7. Measure the peak-to-peak voltage at the output and record the value in the data table. (see photo in Figure 3b of Appendix A.)
8. Repeat steps 4 through 6 for the remaining frequencies given in the table. The sweep frequency of the oscilloscope will have to be changed with each change of input frequency in order to display four or five cycles.

QUESTIONS FOR FIGURE 3-20

1. The cutoff frequency for the circuit is _____ .
2. Below f_c the circuit behaves like a(n) _____ .
3. Above f_c the circuit behaves like a(n) _____ .
4. With proper differentiation, a square wave at the input will produce a(n) _____ wave at the output.

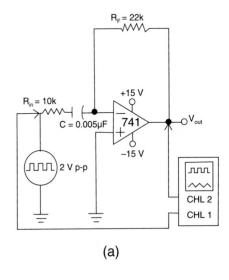

f_{in} (Hz)	Voltage Waveform	V_{out} p-p
100		
500		
1k		
2k		
5k		
10k		

(a)

(b)

FIGURE 3-20 Practical differentiator circuit: (a) schematic diagram; (b) data table.

EXPERIMENT 3-3 OP-AMP LOW-PASS FILTER

Objective:

To show how an op-amp low-pass filter will pass frequencies below the cutoff frequency (f_c) and attenuate the frequencies above this point.

Introduction:

A low-pass filter will pass or amplify the input signal to 70.7 percent or greater for all frequencies below the f_c. Frequencies above the f_c will be attenuated or not passed. Each time the input frequency is changed, the amplitude of the signal must be adjusted for the original value.

Required Components:

2 10 kΩ resistors (R_1 and R_2)

1 22 kΩ resistor (R_3)

2 0.01 µF capacitors (C_1 and C_2)

Test Procedure:

1. With the power supply off, construct the circuit shown in Figure 3-21a.
2. Turn on the power supply.
3. Adjust the sine-wave generator for the first frequency given in the data log shown in Figure 3-21b.
4. Set the sine-wave generator output amplitude for a 1 V p-p signal for each frequency given in the data log. Make sure this voltage level is maintained for each frequency setting.
5. Measure the V p-p of v_{out} and record its value in the data log.
6. Repeat steps 3, 4, and 5 for all frequencies given in the data log.
7. Turn off the power supply.
8. Calculate f_c from the formula:

$$f_c \approx \frac{1}{2\pi\sqrt{R_1 R_2 C_1 C_2}}$$

9. Draw a frequency response curve from the results shown in the data log (try to use semilog graph paper).

QUESTIONS FOR FIGURE 3-21

1. The f_c for the low-pass filter is about _____ .
2. Frequencies below f_c are _____ by this circuit.
3. Frequencies above f_c are _____ by this circuit.

EXPERIMENT 3-4 OP-AMP HIGH-PASS FILTER

Objective:

To demonstrate how an op-amp high-pass filter will block or attenuate frequencies below the cutoff frequency (f_c) and pass frequencies above this point.

Introduction:

A high-pass filter will pass or amplify the input signal to 70.7 percent or greater for all frequencies above the f_c. Frequencies below the f_c will be attenuated or not passed. Each time the input frequency is changed the amplitude of the signal must be adjusted for the original

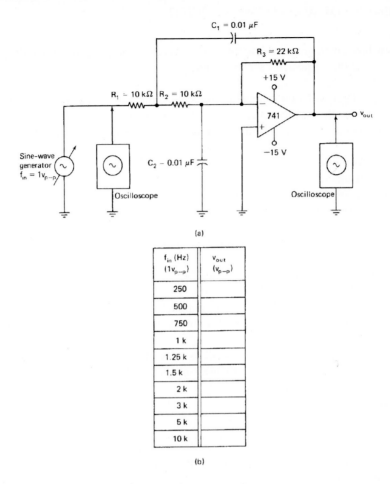

(a)

f_{in} (Hz) $(1v_{p-p})$	v_{out} (v_{p-p})
250	
500	
750	
1 k	
1.25 k	
1.5 k	
2 k	
3 k	
5 k	
10 k	

(b)

FIGURE 3-21 Low-pass filter.

value.

Required Components:

1 10-kΩ resistor (R_1)

2 22-kΩ resistors (R_2 and R_3)

2 0.01 µF capacitors (C_1 and C_2)

Test Procedure:

1. With the power supply off, construct the circuit shown in Figure 3-22a.
2. Turn on the power supply.
3. Adjust the sine-wave generator for the first frequency given in the data log shown in Figure 3-22b.
4. Set the sine-wave generator output amplitude for a 1 V p-p signal for each frequency given in the data log. Make sure this voltage level is maintained for each frequency setting.
5. Measure the V p-p of v_{out} and record its value in the data log.
6. Repeat steps 3, 4, and 5 for all frequencies given in the data log.
7. Turn off the power supply.

8. Calculate f_c from the formula: $f_c \approx \dfrac{1}{2\pi\sqrt{R_1 R_2 C_1 C_2}}$

9. Draw a frequency response curve from the results shown in the data log (try to use semilog graph paper).

QUESTIONS FOR FIGURE 3-22

1. The f_c for the high-pass filter is about _____ .
2. Frequencies below f_c are _____ by this circuit.
3. Frequencies above f_c are _____ by this circuit.

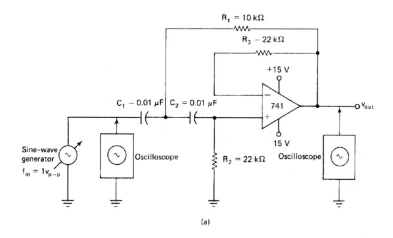

(a)

f_{in} (Hz) $(1v_{p-p})$	v_{out} (v_{p-p})
250	
500	
750	
1 k	
1.25 k	
1.5 k	
2 k	
3 k	
5 k	
10 k	

(b)

FIGURE 3-22 High-pass filter.

EXPERIMENT 3-5 OP-AMP BANDPASS FILTER

Objective:

To show how an op-amp bandpass filter will pass a certain group of frequencies and reject those above and below these limits.

Introduction:

A bandpass filter will pass or amplify the input signal to 70.7 percent or greater, all the frequencies below and above the resonant frequency, f_r. The bandwidth, BW, is those frequencies which are at least 70.7 percent of the maximum output voltage below and above f_r. Frequencies below the BW will be attenuated or not passed. Frequencies above the BW will also be attenuated. Each time the input frequency is changed the amplitude of the signal must be adjusted for the original value.

Required Components:

2	10 kΩ resistors (R_1 and R_2)
1	100 kΩ resistor (R_3)
2	0.01 μF capacitors (C_1 and C_2)

Test Procedure:

1. With the power supply off, construct the circuit shown in Figure 3-23a.
2. Turn on the power supply.
3. Adjust the sine-wave generator for the first frequency given in the data log shown in Figure 3-23b.
4. Set the sine-wave generator output amplitude for a 1 V p-p signal for each frequency given in data log. Make sure this voltage level is maintained for each frequency setting.
5. Measure the V p-p of v_{out} and record its value in the data log.
6. Repeat steps 3, 4, and 5 for all frequencies given in the data log.
7. Turn off the power supply.
8. Calculate f_r from the formula: $f_r \approx \dfrac{1}{2\pi\sqrt{R_p R_3 C_1 C_2}}$, where $R_p = \dfrac{R_1 R_2}{R_1 + R_2}$
9. Draw a frequency response curve from the results shown in the data log (try to use semilog graph paper).

QUESTIONS FOR FIGURE 3-23

1. The resonant frequency of the circuit is about _____ hertz.
2. The approximate bandwidth of the circuit is _____ hertz.
3. Frequencies below the bandpass are _____ .
4. Frequencies above the bandpass are _____ .

EXPERIMENT 3-6 OP-AMP NOTCH FILTER

Objective:

To demonstrate how an op-amp notch filter will pass all frequencies above and below a specific bandwidth while rejecting the frequencies within the bandwidth.

Introduction:

A band-reject or notch filter will pass or amplify the input signal to 70.7 percent or greater, all the frequencies below and above the bandwidth. The bandwidth, BW, is those frequencies which are less than 70.7 percent of the maximum output voltage below and above f_r. Frequencies below the BW will be amplified or passed. Frequencies above the BW will also be amplified. The bandwidth in this circuit is not amplified or passed, therefore the output voltage curve resembles that of a notch. Each time the input frequency is changed the amplitude of the signal must be adjusted for the original value.

Required Components:

1 1-kΩ resistor (R_2)

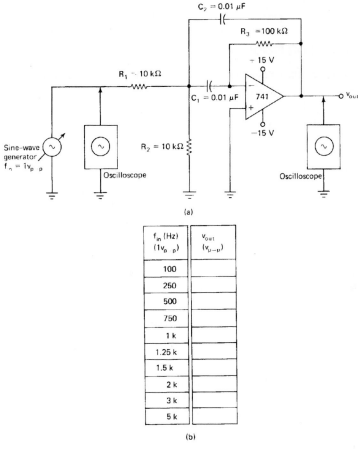

$C_2 = 0.01\ \mu F$

$R_3 = 100\ k\Omega$

$+ 15\ V$

$R_1 \sim 10\ k\Omega$

$C_1 = 0.01\ \mu F$ 741 V_{out}

$-15\ V$

Sine-wave generator
$f_n = 1v_{p\text{-}p}$

$R_2 = 10\ k\Omega$

Oscilloscope   Oscilloscope

(a)

f_{in} (Hz) $(1v_{p\text{-}p})$	v_{out} $(v_{p\text{-}p})$
100	
250	
500	
750	
1 k	
1.25 k	
1.5 k	
2 k	
3 k	
5 k	

(b)

FIGURE 3-23 Bandpass filter.

1 10-kΩ resistor (R_1)
1 47-kΩ resistor (R_3)
1 1-mΩ resistor (R_4)
2 0.01 μF capacitors (C_1 and C_2)

Test Procedure:

1. With the power supply off, construct the circuit shown in Figure 3-24a.
2. Turn on the power supply.
3. Adjust the sine-wave generator for the first frequency given in the data log shown in Figure 3-24b.
4. Set the sine-wave generator output amplitude for a 1 V p-p signal for each frequency given in the data log. Make sure this voltage level is maintained for each frequency setting.
5. Measure the V p-p of v_{out} and record its value in the data log.
6. Repeat steps 3, 4, and 5 for all frequencies given in the data log.
7. Turn off the power supply.
8. Calculate f_r from the formula: $f_r \approx \dfrac{1}{2\pi\sqrt{R_1 R_4 C_1 C_2}}$

9. Draw a frequency response curve from the results shown in the data log (try to use semilog graph paper).

QUESTIONS FOR FIGURE 3-24

1. The resonant frequency of the circuit is about _____ hertz.
2. The approximate bandwidth of the circuit is _____ hertz.
3. Frequencies below the notch are _____ .
4. Frequencies above the notch are _____ .

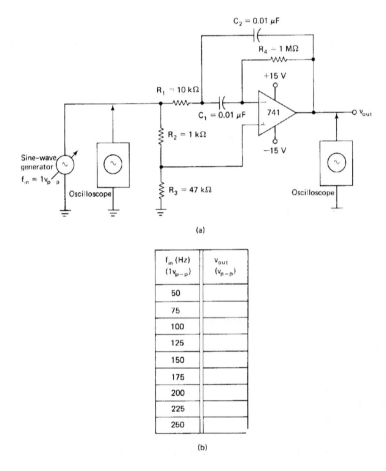

(a)

f_{in} (Hz) $(1v_{p-p})$	V_{out} (v_{p-p})
50	
75	
100	
125	
150	
175	
200	
225	
250	

(b)

FIGURE 3-24 Notch filter.

SECTION 3-5 SUMMARY POINTS

1. The capacitor is the major feedback element in an op-amp integrator.
2. An op-amp integrator produces a ramp output voltage for DC input voltage (a square wave produces a triangular wave).
3. An op-amp differentiator has a capacitor in series with the input.
4. An op-amp differentiator produces a sharp leading edge output for a ramp input voltage

(a triangular input voltage produces a square-wave output).

5. A practical op-amp low-pass filter shunts high frequencies to ground through a capacitor at the input and feeds back high frequencies through a capacitor to reduce gain.

6. A practical op-amp high-pass filter blocks low frequencies with series capacitors at its input.

7. An op-amp bandpass filter combines both low-pass and high-pass filtering elements so that the output voltage only peaks at f_r.

8. An op-amp notch filter uses both inputs, where a frequency-selective feedback network causes the output voltage to attenuate sharply at f_r.

9. The cutoff frequency, also called the comer frequency or break frequency, occurs at 70.7 percent of the output voltage (or -3 dB down from maximum output).

10. The bandwidth of a filter is the upper (f_H) and lower (f_L) frequencies, where 70.7 percent of the maximum output voltage occurs.

11. The Q of a filter determines how selective the circuit is to the resonant frequency, f_r.

12. Decibel loss per decade means the loss in decibels of a filter as the frequency increases by a factor of 10.

SELF-CHECKING QUIZ

Match each name in column A with its proper output frequency-response curve shown in Figure 3-25:

Column A
1. Integrator
2. Differentiator
3. Low-pass filter
4. High-pass filter
5. Bandpass filter
6. Notch filter

Match each name in column B with its proper schematic diagram shown in Figure 3-26 below:

Column B
7. Integrator
8. Differentiator
9. Low-pass filter
10. High-pass filter
11. Bandpass filter
12. Notch filter

True-or-False Questions

13. A low-pass filter and a high-pass filter can be connected to produce a bandpass filter.

14. A notch filter passes the frequencies in its bandwidth.

15. A differentiator will produce a triangular output wave when a square wave is applied to the input.

16. The bandwidth of a filter can be found by dividing f_r by Q.

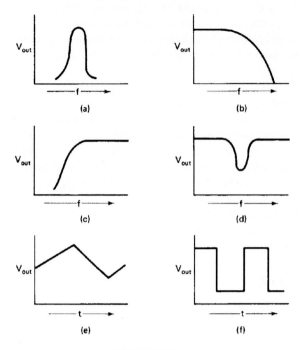

FIGURE 3-25

17. The depth of the notch in a notch filter is determined by Q.
18. An op-amp integrator will transform a square-wave input to a triangular-wave output.
19. A high-Q bandpass filter will have a wider bandwidth than a low-Q bandpass filter.
20. A voltage decrease from 8 V to 5.7 V is the same as a $-$ 3-dB loss.
    (Answers at back of book)

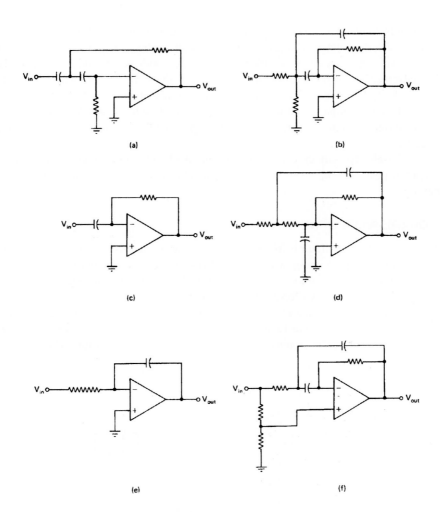

FIGURE 3-26 Continued

CHAPTER 4

OP-AMP OSCILLATORS

Oscillators convert DC voltage into AC voltage or pulsating DC voltage. The cycles per second at which the voltage changes is called the oscillator frequency. There are four basic oscillator waveforms: square wave, triangle wave, sawtooth wave, and sine wave. The term "signal generator" is often used interchangeably with oscillator. A signal generator is classified by the type of waveform it generates. The stability of an oscillator indicates how well it will maintain its output amplitude and remain on or close to the desired frequency for which it was designed. Signal generators are used to provide the signal source for other electronic circuits.

This chapter will show how op amps are applied to signal generators. Using op amps and a few passive components can produce signal generators that are fairly stable and easy to build.

4-1-1 SQUARE-WAVE GENERATOR

The square-wave generator belongs to that family of oscillators known as multivibrators. It is referred to as a free-running or astable multivibrator, since its output is constantly changing states (high and low) without any input signal. A basic square-wave generator is shown in Figure 4-1. There are two feedback paths for this circuit. One goes from the output to the inverting input and contains a feedback resistor and a capacitor connected to ground. This RC combination determines the fundamental operating frequency of the generator. The other feedback path goes to the noninverting input and contains two resistors. These resistors form

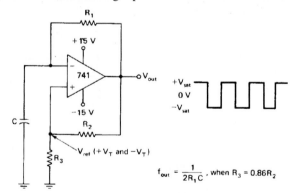

FIGURE 4-1 Basic square wave generator.

a voltage divider that produces a reference voltage (V_{ref}) at the noninverting input. If these resistors are selected so that R_3 is 86 percent of the value of R_2, the approximate frequency of the generator can be found by the simple expression

$$f_{out} = \frac{1}{2R_1C}$$

124

With the R_2 and R_3 voltage divider providing the V_{ref} at the noninverting input, the circuit behaves like a voltage-level detector.

For instance, when power is applied to the circuit, the capacitor begins to charge up through R_1 to the value of V_{out}. The op-amp output will be at $+V_{sat}$, and V_{ref} at the noninverting input will be at the positive threshold voltage, $+V_T$. When the voltage across the capacitor increases above $+V_T$, the op amp switches states and V_{out} goes in the negative direction to $-V_{sat}$. The V_{ref} at the noninverting input is now at the negative threshold voltage, $-V_T$. The capacitor now changes its charging direction and begins to charge toward $-V_{sat}$. The instant the voltage on the capacitor increases below $-V_T$, the op amp switches back to the original state and V_{out} goes to $+V_{sat}$. A cycle has now been completed and the process is repeated. Figure 4-2 illustrates the action of the capacitor voltage, V_c, and the op-amp output voltage, V_{out}.

Threshold voltages $+V_T$ and $-V_T$ are determined by the resistor voltage divider of R_2 and R_3 and is expressed as

$$+V_T = \frac{R_3}{R_3 + R_2}(+V_{sat}) = 0.46\,(+V_{sat})$$

and

$$-V_T = \frac{R_3}{R_3 + R_2}(-V_{sat}) = 0.46\,(-V_{sat})$$

To build a signal generator with a 1-kHz test signal, let $R_1 = 10\ \text{k}\Omega$, $C = 0.05\ \mu\text{F}$, $R_2 = 100\ \text{k}\Omega$, and $R_3 = 86\ \text{k}\Omega$.

To verify the output frequency,

$$f_{out} = \frac{1}{2\,(10 \times 10^3)\,(0.05 \times 10^{-6})}$$

$$= \frac{1}{2\,(0.5 \times 10^{-3})}$$

$$= \frac{1}{1 \times 10^{-3}}$$

$$= 1\,\text{kHz}$$

If $+V_{sat}$ and $-V_{sat}$ equal +13.5 V and –13.5 V, respectively, the threshold voltage amplitudes can be found:

$$+V = 0.46\,(+13.5\ \text{V})$$

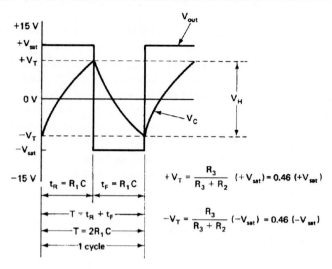

FIGURE 4-2 Capacitor voltage versus output voltage.

$$= + 6.21 \text{ V}$$

and

$$- V_T = 0.46(- 13.5 \text{ V})$$
$$= - 6.21 \text{ V}$$

Therefore, the peak-to-peak threshold voltage V_H is

$$V_{H(p-p)} = (+ V_T) - (- V_T)$$
$$= + 6.21 - (- 6.21)$$
$$= 12.42 \text{ V}$$

or, in other words, the V_H is twice $+ V_T$ or twice $- V_T$:

$$V_{H(p-p)} = 2 (+ V_T) \text{ or } 2 (- V_T)$$

4-1-2 SAWTOOTH-WAVE GENERATOR

A sawtooth-wave generator, or a ramp-voltage generator as it is sometimes called, is shown in Figure 4-3a. Notice that it resembles an op-amp integrator circuit. If a − 1 V is placed at the active (inverting) input, the capacitor will begin to charge up at a linear rate in a positive direction. It will continue to charge until + V_{sat} is reached. If the switch is momentarily closed before + V_{sat} is reached, the capacitor will discharge rapidly. When the switch is again open, the process will be repeated, as shown in Figure 4-3b. The output voltage is determined by

$$V_{out} = V_{in} \left(\frac{1}{R_{in} C_f} \right) \times t$$

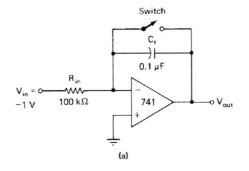

(a)

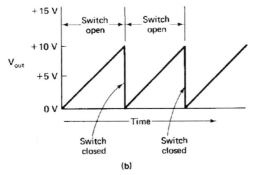

(b)

FIGURE 4-3 Basic sawtooth wave generator with manual control: (a) schematic diagram; (b) sawtooth waveform voltage output.

where t is the time in seconds that the switch is open. The slope is determined by V_{in}, R_{in}, and C_f. If a negative ramp voltage is needed, V_{in} should be positive.

Manual operation of this circuit, of course, results in an extremely low output frequency. Therefore, an electronic switch is used in place of the manual switch in order to produce a useful sawtooth-wave generator, as shown in Figure 4-4.

A programmable unijunction transistor (PUT) is used as the active switch. The PUT belongs to the thyristor family of electronic devices and resembles a silicon-controlled rectifier (SCR) in operation, the difference being that it is triggered on by a negative-going pulse. However, as shown, if the gate voltage is set at a determined positive voltage V_p (peak voltage) by R_4 and R_5 resistor voltage dividers and the anode (A) to cathode (K) voltage (V_{AK}) goes more positive than V_p, the PUT will fire (turn on). This is the same effect as a negative pulse to the gate. The PUT will remain on until the current through it falls below its minimum holding current value. It then turns off and becomes like an open switch.

Component values and variable resistors are given in Figure 4-4 so that you can change the frequency of the generator and verify the formula that will be given. Voltage dividers R_1 and R_2 are used to develop V_{ref}. Diodes D_1 and D_2 help to stabilize the voltage across R_2 when it is adjusted to vary the frequency. The V_{out} amplitude is determined by R_4, which in turn affects the frequency.

Let us say that we set V_{ref} to -1 V and V_p to $+4$ V. The capacitor begins charging up linearly toward $+V_{sat}$. At some point just greater than V_p, the PUT fires, the capacitor discharges, and V_{out} goes to minimum. The current through the PUT falls below the minimum holding current, the PUT turns off, and the process begins again. When the PUT is on, it does not act like a normal closed switch because it has a forward voltage drop (V_F) of a few tenths of a volt up to 1 V, depending on the particular PUT used. We can, however, approximate the output frequency with the expression

$$f_{out} = \frac{V_{ref}}{R_3 C_f} \left(\frac{1}{V_P - 0.5V} \right)$$

For instance, with the voltages given above and $R_3 = 100$ kΩ and $C_f = 0.1$ µF,

$$f_{out} = \frac{1}{(100 \times 10^3)(0.1 \times 10^{-6})} \left(\frac{1}{4 - 0.5} \right)$$

$$= \frac{1}{0.01} \left(\frac{1}{3.5} \right)$$

$$= (100)(0.286)$$

$$= 29 \text{Hz}$$

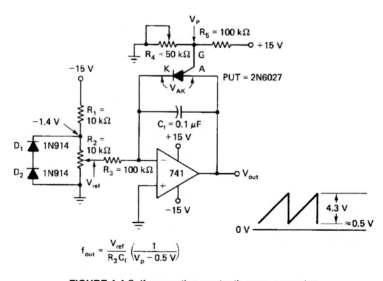

$$f_{out} = \frac{V_{ref}}{R_3 C_f} \left(\frac{1}{V_p - 0.5 \text{ V}} \right)$$

FIGURE 4-4 Self-generating sawtooth wave generator.

The peak amplitude of f_{out} will be a few tenths of a volt greater than V_P (in this case about +0.3 V).

This equation shows how the amplitude of V_{ref} and V_P along with R_3 and C_f affect the f_{out} of the generator. How fast V_{out}, rises is determined by V_{ref} and R 3 and C_f, as that part of the equation $V_{ref}/R_3\ C_f$, while $(V_p - 0.5)$ sets the value to which V_{out} can rise before the capacitor discharges. Since the voltage plays a part in f_{out}, a circuit like this is sometimes referred to as a voltage-to-frequency converter or a voltage-controlled oscillator.

4-1-3 TRIANGLE-WAVE GENERATOR

The triangle-wave generator usually requires at least two op amps to operate. A basic circuit is a square-wave generator connected to an integrator, as shown in Figure 4-5a. From the discussions on the op-amp integrator (Section 3-1a) and the sawtooth generator (Section 4-1a), it was shown that the V_{out} of the integrator can ramp up or ramp down. For this reason it is often called a ramp generator.

When the output of the square-wave generator goes positive, the output of the ramp generator ramps negative. Similarly, when the output of the square-wave generator goes negative, the output of the ramp generator ramps positive. This action is illustrated in Figure 4-5b, which produces the triangle-wave output (V_{tri}). There is also a square-wave output (V_{squ}). A signal generator such as this, which produces two or more different waveforms, is referred to as a function generator.

The frequency of the triangle-wave output is the same as the frequency of the square-wave generator, which can be determined from Section 4-1. It is desirable to have the RC time constant of R_4 and C_2 be twice as large as the time constant of R_1 and C_1 to prevent distortion of the triangle waveform. The amplitude of the square will be nearly $\pm V_{sat}$, while the amplitude of the triangle wave can be determined from the integrator circuit discussed in Section 3-1.

4-1-3-1 Positive Feedback

Another very popular triangle-wave generator uses a ramp generator combined with a voltage-sensing comparator. To understand the action of this type of triangle-wave generator, it will be of value to analyze an op amp with positive feedback. An op-amp circuit with positive feedback is shown in Figure 4-6. Notice that the inverting input is connected to ground while the noninverting input is placed above it. It is advisable to scrutinize a schematic diagram using op amps, since this arrangement is used very often. Realizing that a circuit contains this type configuration will aid you in analyzing the operation of a particular circuit.

When power is initially applied to the circuit, a slight differential voltage at the inputs or the offset voltage will cause V_{out} to saturate in either the positive or negative direction. This is because the regenerative action of positive feedback increases the voltage at the input, therefore driving the op amp harder in the direction in which its output is going. In Figure 4-6a, V_{out} is at $+V_{sat}$ and will remain in this state until V_{in} drops to the negative threshold voltage ($-V_T$), at which time V_{out} will be driven to $-V_{sat}$. Remember from Section 2-1 on voltage comparators that each time the voltage on the active input crossed the zero reference

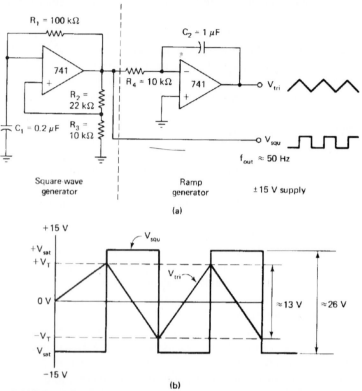

FIGURE 4-5 Simple triangle wave generator; (a) combination of two basic circuits; (b) output waveforms.

point, V_{out} would swing to the opposite saturation voltage. At this time of changing states, the differential voltage V_d at the inputs is nearly 0 V. We can understand this better by analyzing the current path through the resistors. If $V_{in} = 0$ V and $V_{out} = +13.5$ V, then by Ohm's law ($I_{in} = I_F = V_{out}/R_{in} + R_F$), the current through R_{in} and $R_F = 0.123$ mA (the current is the same since both resistors are in series). Therefore, $V_d = R_{in} \times I_{in} = +1.23$ V. As V_{in} is made more negative, V_d decreases, because of the algebraic summation of voltages of unlike polarities. When V_d reaches 0 V, V_{out} swings to $-V_{sat}$.

When V_{out} is at $-V_{sat}$ (Figure 4-6b), V_d will be -1.23 V. The same process given above must occur to force V_{out} to $+V_{sat}$, except that V_{in} must equal $+V_T$.

The threshold voltages, $+V_T$ and $-V_T$, are dependent on the ratio of R_{in} and R_f, as shown by the expressions

$$+V_T = \frac{+V_{sat}}{(R_F/R_{in})} \qquad \text{and} \qquad -V_T = -\frac{V_{sat}}{(R_F/R_{in})}$$

This type of comparator is used with a ramp generator to produce the triangle-wave generator shown in Figure 4-7a. The output of the ramp generator is connected to the input of the comparator, while its output is fed back to the input of the ramp generator. Each time the ramp voltage reaches the threshold voltage, the comparator changes states, as shown in Figure 4-7b. Therefore, oscillation is sustained by the circuit.

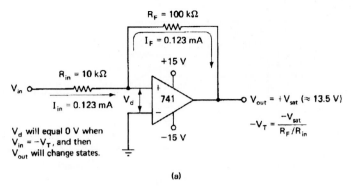

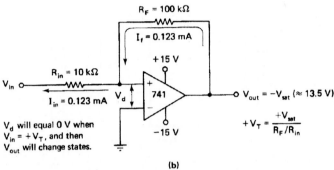

FIGURE 4-6 Op amp positive feedback: (a) in the $+V_{sat}$ state; (b) in the $-V_{sat}$ state.

The output frequency for this circuit can be determined by finding the rise time t_R and the fall time t_F of the triangle wave, which constitutes one cycle T, and then solve for the reciprocal. The rise and fall times can be found by the expression

$$t_R = \frac{V_H}{-V_{sat}}(R_1 C) \qquad \text{and} \qquad t_F = \frac{V_H}{+V_{sat}}(R_1 C)$$

where V_H, the hysteris voltage as it is called, is the difference between $+V_T$ and $-V_T$; thus,

$$V_H = +V_T - (-V_T)$$

or twice the value of either threshold voltage.

One cycle or T, then, is

$$T = t_R + t_F$$

and the output frequency f_{out} is

$$f_{out} = \frac{1}{T}$$

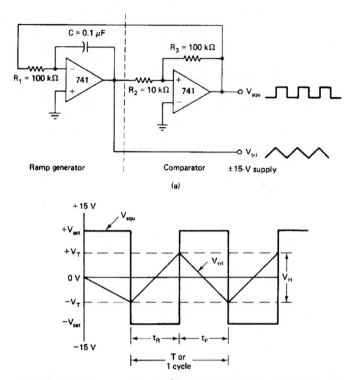

FIGURE 4-7 Basic Triangle wave generator (with less components): (a) combination of basic circuits; (b) output waveforms.

For example, using the values shown in Figure 4-7a,

$$+V_T = \frac{+13.5}{10} = +1.35\text{V} \qquad \text{and} \qquad -V_T = \frac{-13.5}{10} = -1.35\text{V}$$

$$V_H = +1.35\text{V} - (-1.35\text{V}) = 2.7\text{V}$$

$$t_R = \frac{2.7\text{V}}{-13.5\text{V}}(100 \times 10^3)(0.1 \times 10^{-6}) = 0.002\text{s}$$

$$t_F = \frac{2.7\text{V}}{+13.5\text{V}}(100 \times 10^3)(0.1 \times 10^{-6}) = 0.002\text{s}$$

$$T = 0.002\text{s} + 0.002\text{s} = 0.004\text{s}$$

$$f_{\text{out}} = \frac{1}{0.004\text{s}} = 250\text{Hz}$$

The amplitude of the triangle-wave output will be $\pm V_T$ or V_H. The amplitude of the square-wave output will be $\pm V_{\text{sat}}$.

4-1-4 SINE-WAVE OSCILLATOR

A sine-wave oscillator can generate a single sine wave using a frequency-selective network similar to a narrow bandpass filter. One of the oldest types of sine-wave generators is the Wien bridge oscillator. An application of a Wien bridge oscillator using an op amp is shown in Figure 4-8.

Feedback is applied to both inputs of the op amp. The frequency-selective network consisting of R_1, C_1 and R_2, C_2 provides positive feedback to the noninverting input. Negative feedback is provided to the inverting input via R_3, R_4, and R_5. The positive feedback

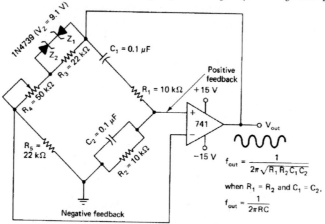

FIGURE 4-8 Wien-bridge oscillator.

must be greater than the negative feedback in order to sustain oscillations. Potentiometer R_4 is used to accomplish this by reducing the negative feedback. In effect, it is set to start the circuit oscillating. The frequency-selective network controls the amount of positive feedback, depending upon the frequency. After R_4 is adjusted to start oscillations, the ratio of reactances and resistances determines the proper positive feedback at the noninverting input. If the frequency begins to decrease, the reactance of C_1 becomes greater and the positive feedback decreases. Likewise, if frequency begins to increase, the reactance of C_2 decreases and more positive feedback is shunted to ground. Therefore, the oscillator is forced to operate at the resonant frequency by this network.

Positive feedback causes the output voltage to increase until the op amp locks into saturation. To prevent saturation and have a useful circuit, two zener diodes face to face (or back to back, as it matters very little) are connected across R_3. When the output voltage rises above the zener voltage point, one or the other zener diode conducts, depending on the polarity of the output. The conducting zener diode shunts R_3, Causing the resistance of the negative feedback circuit to decrease. More negative feedback is applied to the op amp and the output voltage is controlled at a certain level.

The output frequency can be determined by the formula

$$f_{out} = \frac{1}{2\pi\sqrt{R_1 R_2 C_1 C_2}}$$

or, if $R_1 = R_2$ and $C_1 = C_2$, then

$$f_{out} = \frac{1}{2\pi R_1 C_1}$$

The f_{out} for Figure 4-8 with the components shown is about 160 Hz.

Another type of sine-wave oscillator using two op amps can be produced as shown in Figure 4-9. This circuit consists of a bandpass filter and comparator. One way of generating sine waves is to filter a square wave, which results in the fundamental sine wave at the output. The comparator is fed with a sine wave from the bandpass filter to obtain a square-wave output. The square wave is fed back to the input of the bandpass filter to cause oscillation.

The f_{out} is determined by R_1, R_3, R_4, C_1, and C_2 by the expression

$$f_{out} = \frac{1}{2\pi \sqrt{R_p R_4 C_1 C_2}}$$

where

$$R_p = \frac{R_1 R_3}{R_1 + R_3}$$

Resistor R_2 can be considered part of R_1, but is negligible, because of its extremely small value. It is used only to keep from shorting the feedback to ground.

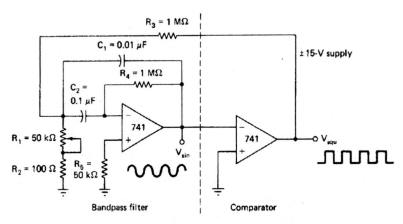

FIGURE 4-9 Two op amp sine wave oscillator.

Since R_1 is variable, the frequency of the oscillator can be changed. The frequency range of the oscillator with the component values shown is about 20 to 500 Hz. Other ranges within the audio band can be obtained easily by changing C_1 and C_2

Two outputs are provided by this circuit, a sine wave (V_{sin}) from the bandpass filter and a square wave (V_{squ}) from the comparator.

4-1-5 QUADRATURE OSCILLATOR

Sometimes in electronic systems it is necessary to have two sine waves, 90° out of phase, termed quadrature. Figure 4-10 shows a quadrature oscillator, where the outputs are labeled sine and cosine. Basically, the circuit consists of two integrators with positive feedback. The sine output comes from Op-1 and the cosine output comes from Op-2. Since the phase shift of an integrator is 90°, the cosine output is 90° out of phase with the sine output.

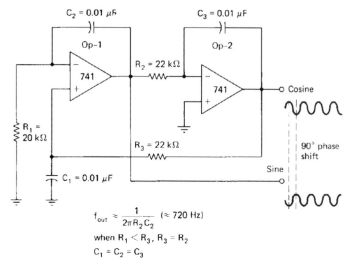

$$f_{out} \approx \frac{1}{2\pi R_2 C_2} \quad (\approx 720 \text{ Hz})$$

when $R_1 < R_3$, $R_3 = R_2$

$C_1 = C_2 = C_3$

FIGURE 4-10 Basic quadrature oscillator.

Resistor R_1 is usually slightly less in value than R_3 to ensure that the circuit oscillates. If R_1 is too small in value, the outputs will be clipped and resemble square waves. A potentiometer may be used to adjust for minimum distortion of the output voltages. The output voltages may also reach op-amp saturation. If this situation prevails, two zener diodes may be connected face to face across C_3 to limit the output.

If $R_2 = R_3$ with $R_1 < R_3$ and $C_1 = C_2 = C_3$, then f_{out} can be easily found by the expression

$$f_{out} = \frac{1}{2\pi R_2 C_2}$$

4-1-6 FUNCTION GENERATOR

As mentioned before, a function generator is any signal generator that has two or more different waveform outputs. Various basic circuits can be combined to produce a function generator, as shown in Figure 4-11. A basic sine/square-wave generator (Figure 4-9) is used to establish f_{out} and the sine-wave and square-wave outputs. The output from the comparator is fed to a voltage follower (Figure 2-12a) to prevent loading down the basic oscillator. This also helps to prevent any change in the oscillator's frequency due to loading. The output of the follower is then fed to an integrator (Figure 3-3) to produce the triangle-wave output. Since three outputs are available, the circuit could be called a trifunction generator.

This circuit can be built from a single 14-pin DIP 324 (quad op amp) IC. The pin identification is shown to facilitate construction. A ±15-V supply is used. The amplitudes of the output voltages are about as follows:

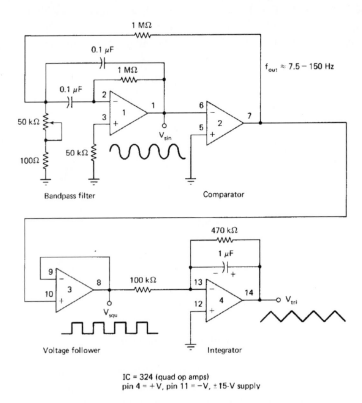

FIGURE 4-11 Basic low frequency tri-function generator.

square wave   =   26 V p-p
sine wave   =   16 V p-p
triangle wave   =   0.3 – 6 V p-p (depending on f_{out})

By adjusting the 50-kΩ potentiometer, f_{out} can vary from about 7.5 to 150 Hz. Decreasing the value of the two capacitors in the bandpass amplifier will increase f_{out}. It is a good practice to keep their values equal, and it also simplifies calculating f_{out} from the formula given with this circuit in Section 4-1d.

SECTION 4-2 TERMINOLOGY EXERCISE

Write a brief definition for each of the following terms:
1. Square-wave voltage
2. Sawtooth-wave voltage
3. Triangle-wave voltage
4. Sine-wave voltage
5. Regenerative feedback
6. Quadrature oscillator
7. Threshold voltages
8. Astable multivibrator
9. Frequency

10. Function generator

SECTION 4-3 PROBLEMS AND EXERCISES

1. Referring to Figure 4-1, find the f_{out} when $R_1 = 47$ kΩ , $R_2 = 100$ kΩ , $R_3 = 86$ kΩ , and $C = 0.002$ μF.
2. If the saturation voltages in problem 1 are ± 10.8 V, what is $+ V_T$ and $- V_T$?
3. What is the f_{out} of Figure 4-4 when $V_{ref} = 0.5$ V, $R_3 = 47$ kΩ , $C_f = 0.01$ μF, and $V_p = 3.5$ V?
4. What is the approximate peak voltage amplitude of the output waveform in problem 3?
5. What is $+ V_T$ and $- V_T$ of Figure 4-6 when $R_{in} = 22$ kΩ and $R_F = 180$ kΩ ?
6. What is the f_{out} and voltage amplitude of the triangle-wave output of Figure 4-7 when $R_2 = 22$ kΩ and $R_3 = 150$ kΩ ? ($\pm V_{sat} = \pm 13.5$ V.)
7. What is the f_{out} and voltage amplitude for the square-wave output of problem 6?
8. Find the f_{out} for the Wien bridge oscillator of Figure 4-8 when $R_1 = R_2 = 100$ kΩ and $C_1 = C_2 = 0.01$ μF.
9. What is the approximate f_{out} of Figure 4-9 when $R_1 = 100$ kΩ , $R_2 = 100$ Ω , $R_3 = 2.2$ MΩ , $R_4 = 1$ MΩ , and $C_1 = C_2 = 0.02$ μF?
10. Find the f_{out} of Figure 4-10 when $R_2 = R_3 = 47$ kΩ and $C_1 = C_2 = C3 = 0.1$$\mu$F.

SECTION 4-4 EXPERIMENTS

EXPERIMENT 4-1 OP-AMP SQUARE-WAVE GENERATOR

Objective:
To show how an op amp can be used as a square-wave generator, and how to calculate its output frequency.

Introduction:
An op amp can be constructed to produce a square-wave generator as shown in Figure 4-12. Resistors R_2 and R_3 form a voltage divider from the output of the op amp to ground and determine the $\pm V_{ref}$. Assume, initially, that V_{out} is at $+ V_{sat}$. Capacitor C_1 begins to charge up through R_1 to $+ V_{sat}$. The instant the voltage on the capacitor is greater than $+ V_{ref}$ at the non-inverting input, the output switches to $- V_{out}$. The capacitor now charges toward $- V_{sat}$, and the instant V_{C1}, is greater than $- V_{ref}$, the output switches back to $+ V_{sat}$ and the process begins again. The square-wave output at V_{out} is $\pm V_{sat}$ in amplitude. The amplitude of V_{C1} is $\pm V_{ref}$ and can be found by the formula

$$+ V_{ref} = \frac{R_3}{R_2 + R_3} (+ V_{sat}) \qquad \text{and} \qquad - V_{ref} = \frac{R_3}{R_2 + R_3} (- V_{sat})$$

If R_3 is 86 percent of R_2, the approximate output frequency can be found by the formula

$$f_{out} = \frac{1}{2R_1 C_1}$$

Required Components:

1 4.7-kΩ resistor at 0.5 W (R_1)
1 10-kΩ resistor at 0.5 W (R_1)
1 22-kΩ resistor at 0.5 W (R_1)
1 86-kΩ resistor at 0.5 W (R_3)
1 100-kΩ resistor at 0.5 W (R_2)
1 0.02-uF capacitor at 25 WV DC (C_1)
1 0.05-uF capacitor at 25 WV DC (C_1)
1 0.1-uF capacitor at 25 WV DC (C_1)
1 breadboard for constructing circuit

Test Procedure:

1. Construct the circuit shown in Figure 4-12a using the values given in the first line of the data table of Figure 4-12b for R_1 and C_1.
2. Calculate $\pm V_{ref}$ using the formulas

$$+V_{ref} = \frac{R_3}{R_2 + R_3}(+V_{sat}) = \underline{\hspace{2cm}}$$

and

$$-V_{ref} = \frac{R_3}{R_2 + R_3}(-V_{sat}) = \underline{\hspace{2cm}}$$

3. Using the oscilloscope, measure $+V_{sat}$, $-V_{sat}$, $+V_{ref}$ and $-V_{ref}$ and record on the figure.
4. Calculate the frequency of the generator and record in the data table using the formula

$$f_{out} = \frac{1}{2R_1 C_1}$$

5. Measure the f_{out} with the oscilloscope and record it in the data table.
6. Repeat steps 4 and 5 for the remaining values of R_1 and C_1 given in the data table.

QUESTIONS FOR FIGURE 4-12

1. The amplitude of the square-wave output of the op-amp generator is _____ .
2. The voltage waveform across the capacitor is a(n) _____ .
3. The formula for calculating f_{out} = _____ .
4. When R_1 or C_1 increases, the f_{out} _____ .
5. When R_1 or C_1 decreases, the f_{out} _____ .

EXPERIMENT 4-2 SQUARE/TRIANGLE WAVE GENERATOR

Objective:

To demonstrate how two op amps can function as a square/triangle-wave generator in a simple circuit as shown in Figure 4-13a.

Introduction:

In the first circuit, OP-1 serves as a basic integrator with the output giving a triangle voltage

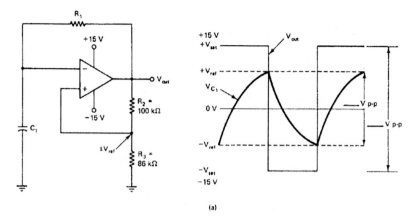

(a)

R_1 (kΩ)	C_1 (μF)	f_{out} (Hz)	
		Calculated	Measured
10	0.05		
22	0.05		
4.7	0.05		
10	0.02		
10	0.1		

(b)

FIGURE 4-12 Op-amp square-wave generator: (a) schematic diagram; (b) data table.

Taken from *Fundamental Electronic Devices: Concepts and Experimentation*, 2nd ed., Fredrick W. Hughes, PrenticeHall Inc., 1990, Figure 11-16, page 276.

waveform. Its output is fed into the noninverting input of Op-2, which acts as a comparator whose output swings between $+ V_{sat}$ and $- V_{sat}$, producing a square voltage waveform. The frequency of the generator can be approximated by the formula:

$$ f_o = \frac{1}{4R_1 C_1} \left(\frac{R_3}{R_2} \right) $$

This experiment varies the components to show how the output frequency can be changed.
Required Components:
2 10-kΩ resistors at 0.5 W
2 100-kΩ resistors at 0.5 W
1 22-kΩ resistor at 0.5 W
1 0.1-μF capacitor at 25 WVDC
1 0.01-μF capacitor at 25 WVDC

Test data for each circuit:

Test #1	Test #2	Test #3	Test #4
$R_1 = 100 \text{ k}\Omega$	$R_1 = 10 \text{ k}\Omega$	$R_1 = 10 \text{ k}\Omega$	$R_1 = 10 \text{ k}\Omega$
$R_2 = 10 \text{ k}\Omega$	$R_2 = 10 \text{ k}\Omega$	$R_2 = 10 \text{ k}\Omega$	$R_2 = 10 \text{ k}\Omega$
$R_3 = 100 \text{ k}\Omega$	$R_3 = 100 \text{ k}\Omega$	$R_3 = 22 \text{ k}\Omega$	$R_3 = 22 \text{ k}\Omega$
$C_1 = 0.1 \text{ μF}$	$C_1 = 0.1 \text{ μF}$	$C_1 = 0.1 \text{ μF}$	$C_1 = 0.01 \text{ μF}$
$f_o(\text{cal.}) =$ ____	$f_o(\text{cal.}) =$ ____	$f_o(\text{cal.}) =$ ____	$f_o(\text{cal.}) =$ ____
$f_o(\text{mea.}) =$ ____	$f_o(\text{mea.}) =$ ____	$f_o(\text{mea.}) =$ ____	$f_o(\text{mea.}) =$ ____

Test Procedure:
1. Construct the circuit shown in Figure 4-13a using the data given in Test #1.
2. Calculate the output frequency with the data given and record answer at $f_o(\text{cal.})$.
3. Place a dual-trace oscilloscope at the square wave output and the triangle wave output.
4. Measure the output frequency and record answer at $f_o(\text{mea.})$.
5. Draw the output voltage waveforms for the square wave and the triangle wave in Figure 4-13b. Indicate V p-p for each waveform voltage. (See photo in Figure A-4a. of Appendix A.)
6. Perform steps 1 through 4 for the remaining test circuits #2, #3, and #4.

QUESTIONS FOR FIGURE 4-13.

1. The square wave voltage output is from _____ to _____ .
2. The threshold voltages at which OP-2 switches is dependent on the ratio of resistors _____ and _____ .
3. If components R_1 or C_1 decrease in value, the output frequency _____ .
4. Resistors R_2 and R_3 also have an effect on _____, because they determine the threshold _____ .
5. As the frequency increases, the amplitude of the triangle wave voltage _____, whereas, the amplitude of the square wave voltage _____ .

EXPERIMENT 4-3 TWO OP-AMP SINE-WAVE OSCILLATOR

Objective:
To show how a simple circuit can be constructed using two op amps to produce a sine wave voltage output.

Introduction:
A voltage square wave contains many harmonies of the original frequency. The square wave can be filtered to produce the desired sine wave. The comparator Op-2, shown in Figure 4-14a, feeds a square wave to the input of the bandpass filter, Op-1. The bandpass filter resonates at the desired frequency and feeds a sine wave to the input of the comparator, which keeps it producing the square wave output. With the components given in this experiment the oscillator has a range of 200 – 1.7 kHz.

Required Components:
1 100-Ω resistor at 0.5 W
1 47-kΩ resistor at 0. 5 W
2 1-MΩ resistors at 0.5 W
1 10-kΩ linear taper potentiometer
2 0.01 μF capacitors at 25 WVDC

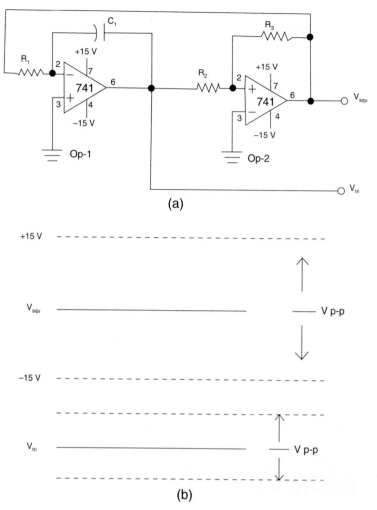

(a)

(b)

FIGURE 4-13 Square/triangle wave generator: (a) schematic diagram; (b) output voltage waveforms.

Test Procedure:

1. Construct the circuit shown in Figure 4-14a, using the parts indicated below:
    $R_1 = 10$ kΩ , $R_2 = 100$ Ω , $R_3 = 47$ kΩ , $R_4 = 1$ MΩ , $R_5 = 1$ MΩ , $C_1, C_2 = 0.01$ μF
2. Connect a dual-trace oscilloscope to the V_{sine} and V_{squ} outputs.
3. Adjust R_1 to obtain a frequency of approximately 1 kHz.
4. Draw the output voltage waveforms in their proper place in the waveform graph of Figure 4-14b. Indicate the voltage amplitude for each signal. (See photo in Figure A-4b of Appendix A.)
5. Vary R_1 from one extreme to the other and measure the frequency at the outputs. Notice the amplitude of the sine wave when the frequency is varied. The frequency range of the oscillator can be changed by using other component values. The output frequency can be determined by the formula

$$f_{ut} = \frac{1}{2\pi\sqrt{R_p R_4 C_1 C_2}} \qquad \text{where,} \qquad R_p = \frac{R_1 R_3}{R_1 + R_3}$$

QUESTIONS FOR FIGURE 4-14

1. The sine wave output is obtained by filtering a _____ wave with the bandpass filter circuit.
2. Referring to the formula, it is obvious that if any of the component values increase, the output frequency will _____ .
3. When the frequency of the oscillator increases, the amplitude of the sine wave output _____ .
4. When the frequency of the oscillator is varied, the amplitude of the square wave output _____ the _____ .

Experiment 4-4 BASIC QUADRATURE OSCILLATOR

Objective:
To demonstrate how two op amps can be connected to produce a double sine wave voltage output which is 90° out of phase.

Introduction:
The connection of the two op amp circuits, which are basic integrators as shown in Figure 4-15a, keeps the circuit oscillating. Resistor R_3 provides positive feedback from OP-2 to OP-1 to sustain the oscillation. In this circuit $R_2 = R_3$, and R_1 should be equal to or slightly less than R_2 to initiate oscillation. A dual-trace oscilloscope connected to the outputs will show a phase shift between the two output signals of approximately 90.

Required Components:
3 16-kΩ resistors at 0.5 W
3 0.01-μF capacitors at 25 WVDC

Test Procedure:
1. Construct the circuit shown in Figure 4-15a, using the parts indicated below:
    R_1, R_2 and $R_3 = 16$ kΩ , C_1, C_2, and $C_3 = 0.01$ μF
2. Calculate the output frequency using the formula

$$f_{out} = \frac{1}{2\pi R_2 C_2} \qquad\qquad f_{out} = \underline{\hspace{2cm}}$$

3. Connect a dual-trace oscilloscope to the V_{sine} and V_{cosine} outputs.
4. Draw the output voltage waveforms in the proper place in Figure 4-15b. Note the difference in phase between the two signals. Indicate the voltage amplitude for each signal. (See photo in Figure A-5 of Appendix A.)

QUESTIONS FOR FIGURE 4-15

1. The quadrature oscillator produces _____ output voltage waveforms.
2. The output voltage waveforms are approximately _____ degrees out of phase.

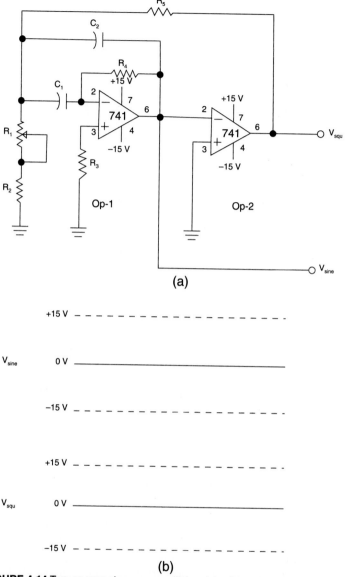

(a)

(b)

FIGURE 4-14 Two op amp sine wave oscillator: (a) schematic diagram; (b) output voltage waveforms.

EXPERIMENT 4-5 TRI-FUNCTION GENERATOR

Objective:

To show how four op amps can be combined from basic circuits to produce a three-output waveform generator.

Introduction:

The tri-function generator consists of basic circuits which you have already constructed as shown in Figure 4-16. The bandpass filter develops the sine wave output. The comparator cir-

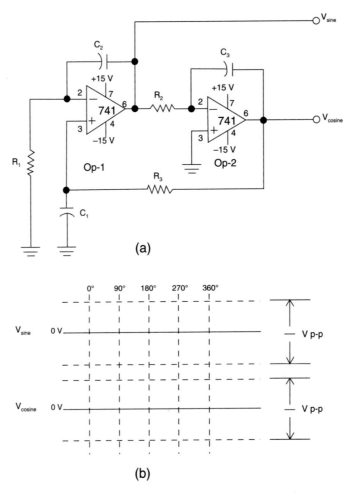

(a)

(b)

FIGURE 4-15 Basic quadrature oscillator: (a) schematic diagram; (b) output voltage waveforms

cuit, which sustains the oscillations of the entire circuit, has a square wave output which is fed to a noninverting voltage follower. The follower acts as a buffer and produces the square wave output for the circuit. This square wave is fed to an integrator circuit, which develops the triangular waveform output. The output frequency is determined by the bandpass filter circuit (See experiment 4-3).

Required components:
1 100-Ω resistor at 0.5 w
1 47-kΩ resistor at 0.5 w
1 100-kΩ resistor at 0.5 w
1 470-kΩ resistor at 0.5 w
2 1-MΩ resistors at 0.5 w
3 0.01-μF capacitors at 25 WVDC

Test Procedure:
1. Construct the circuit shown in Figure 4-16.
2. Connect a dual-trace oscilloscope to the V_{sin} and V_{tri} outputs. Set the time base of the

oscilloscope at 1 ms/cm.

3. Adjust R_1 for an output frequency of about 1 kHz. One cycle should be 1 cm long on the face of the oscilloscope.

4. Measure the amplitude of each output and place the value in the space provided on Figure 4-16.

5. Vary R_1 and notice how the period of the voltage waveform increases and decreases. Also notice how the amplitude of each output changes with a change in frequency. Basically, the integrator circuit is an inverting amplifier. When the frequency increases, the X_C of the feedback capacitor decreases, which decreases the gain of the stage.

QUESTIONS FOR FIGURE 4-16

1. When f_{out} is 1 kHz, the amplitude of the outputs is: V_{sin} = _____V p-p, V_{squ} = _____ V p-p, V_{tri} = _____ V p-p.

2. When the frequency increases, the amplitude of V_{tri} _____ .

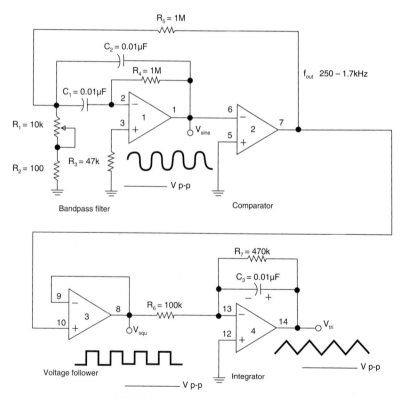

FIGURE 4-16 Tri-function generator.

SECTION 4-5 SUMMARY POINTS

1. Oscillators convert DC voltage to AC voltage or other time-varying DC voltages.

2. Four basic waveforms are the square wave, triangle wave, sawtooth wave, and sine wave.

3. Positive feedback is required for oscillation.

4. The output frequency for op-amp oscillators depends on RC time constants.
5. A square-wave generator belongs to the multivibrator family.
6. An integrator is the basic component used in a ramp-voltage generator.
7. A sawtooth-wave generator uses an electronic switch to discharge the capacitor.
8. The switching of some op-amp oscillators is established by threshold voltages.
9. The ratio of the resistors (R_F/R_{in}) used with positive feedback in an op-amp circuit establishes the $\pm$ threshold voltages.
10. A function generator provides two or more different output waveforms.
11. Bandpass filters are used to select the fundamental sine wave from a square wave in some types of op-amp sine-wave generators.
12. A quadrature oscillator has two outputs 90° out of phase.

SECTION 4-6 SELF-CHECKING QUIZ

Match each oscillator (generator) in column A with its proper schematic diagram in Figure 4-17.

> *Column A*
>   1.   Square-wave generator
>   2.   Triangle-wave generator
>   3.   Sawtooth-wave generator
>   4.   Wien bridge oscillator
>   5.   Quadrature oscillator

True-or-False Questions

6. The output of an op-amp square-wave generator goes positive and negative with reference to ground.
7. If the rise time (t_R) of a sawtooth-wave generator output is 0.02 ms, its frequency is 50 kHz.
8. A quadrature oscillator produces four output waveforms.
9. A Wien bridge oscillator uses both positive and negative feedback.
10. If the rise time (t_R) of the output voltage from a symmetrical triangle wave generator is 0.025 s, its frequency is 40 Hz.
(Answers at back of book)

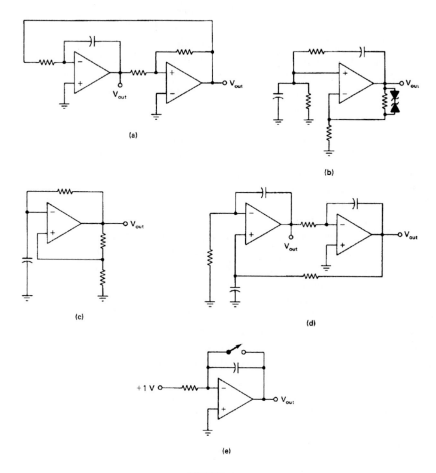

FIGURE 4-17

C H A P T E R 5

OP-AMP APPLICATIONS TO AUDIO CIRCUITS

Modern semiconductor technology, especially integrated circuits, has made it possible for all of the marvelous consumer products (miniature portable radios, portable color TV sets, cassette tape recorders, CDs, etc.) available today. All of these products use audio circuits. The IC op amp has many advantages when employed in audio circuits: small size, lower power consumption (a must for portable devices), minimum associated components, and reliable performance at low cost. Not only is it easier for the engineer to design complex audio systems, but the home experimenter and hobbyist can easily design and construct various audio circuits using IC op amps.

Audio circuits are a specialized area that places unique requirements upon op-amp parameters. The op amp must be able to process complex AC signals in the frequency range 20 Hz to 20 kHz whose amplitudes vary from a few hundred microvolts to several volts. These waveforms are characterized by steep complex wavefronts of a transient nature separated by incalculable periods of absolute silence. The op amp must process these complex AC signals with a minimum of distortion of any kind, either harmonic, amplitude, or phase, and it has to be done as noiselessly as possible. Figure 5-1 illustrates a typical audio waveform. Referencing this figure to musical and voice reproduction, low sustaining frequencies, such as those associated with the string bass, have larger periods of time; medium sustaining frequencies, associated with voice or instruments (trumpet, saxophone, piano, guitar, etc.), have medium periods of time; and high sustaining frequencies, associated with the higher range of the instruments already listed as well as flute, piccolo, and violins, have narrow periods of time. Percussion instruments, particularly drums and cymbals, have sharp rise times and relatively fast decays. The combinations of these waveforms are, of course, endless, depending on the type of material being produced and the mode of performance.

A word about noise. Noise is particularly objectionable to audio circuits because its effects can be heard in the speaker. As mentioned in Chapter 1, there are two categories of noise, external and internal. External noise originates from operating electrical equipment such as motors, switches, and lights. This type of noise can be minimized in audio circuits by using shielded cables, shielding various parts of a circuit, proper component layout, and noise decoupling techniques. Internal noise results from offset voltages and currents, charge carriers crossing junctions, and thermal noise in passive resistive elements. Proper biasing and input-offset compensation can reduce offset voltage and current noise. Thermal noise can be kept to a minimum by using low-resistance-value resistors, especially in that part of an op-amp circuit that determines gain.

Noise can range from 0.01 Hz to megahertz, and determining its approximate frequency can sometimes be useful in reducing or eliminating it. Low-frequency noise, such as 60 or 120 Hz, comes from AC lines or power supplies, and simple low-pass filters can often reduce these effects. Medium and high-frequency noise can also be reduced by appropriate filtering.

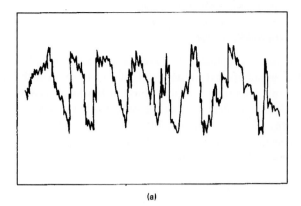

(a)

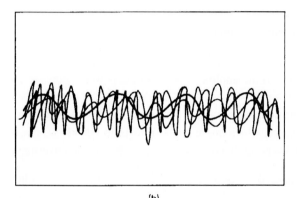

(b)

FIGURE 5-1 Oscilloscope display of typical audio signal: (a) horizontal scan set at about 100 hertz; (b) expanded view.

A capacitor of a few picofarads connected across the feedback resistor in an op-amp amplifier can reduce the gain of high-frequency noise.

General-purpose op amps are suitable for limited audio work in noncritical applications. However, solid-state manufacturers have developed special op amps to meet the stringent requirements of audio work. These op amps will have one or more of the following features that are ideal for audio use:

1. High slew rate.
2. High gain-bandwidth product.
3. High input resistance or impedance.
4. High-voltage and/or-power operation.
5. Low-distortion operation.
6. Very low input (voltage and/or current) noise.
7. Very low input current.
8. Easily used with single power-supply source.

This chapter will acquaint you with basic audio circuits using op amps and provide some practical audio circuits, which you may want to construct.

5-1-1 THE INVERTING AMPLIFIER

An inverting amplifier as applied to audio use is shown in Figure 5-2. It is the same basic circuit used for DC amplifiers, except with capacitor C_i in series with the inverting input. This capacitor serves two important functions. First, it blocks any DC from a previous stage or device that could be amplified, causing the output to go to some unwanted DC level other than zero. This may cause amplifier saturation and distortion when the audio signal is applied to the input. Second, the capacitor helps to block any low-frequency noise from getting to the input of the amplifier. The low-frequency cutoff is determined by C_i and R_i with the formula

$$f_c = \frac{1}{2\pi R_i C_i}$$

The stage gain is found the same way as with the inverting amplifier in Chapter 2. $A_v = -R_F/R_i$ and the input resistance (R_{in}) is the same as R_i.

Single power-supply inverting amplifier. In some instances it may be desirable to operate an op-amp inverting amplifier from a single power supply, as shown in Figure 5-3. The output should be operated at one-half the voltage supply in the quiescent state (V_q) in order to obtain maximum undistorted output. This is accomplished by making biasing resistors R_3 and R_4 equal resistances, which might range from 10 to 100 kΩ . Capacitor C_3 helps to filter out (or decouple) power-supply noise from getting into the noninverting input. Capacitor C_2 will most likely be needed to block the DC output ($\frac{1}{2}$ + V) from the following stages. All capacitors are electrolytic and polarity should be observed when connecting them into the circuit. Values for C_2 and R_L depend upon the input impedance of the following stage.

Although a positive voltage supply is used with the circuit in Figure 5-3, the circuit

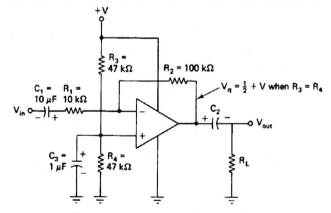

FIGURE 5-3 Inverting amplifier using single power supply.

could operate as well from a negative voltage supply. Resistor R_3 and the positive supply terminal of the op amp would have to be grounded while the bottom of R_4 and the negative supply terminal of the op amp would be connected to the negative voltage supply (– V). Also, remember that all capacitors must be reversed to operate with the proper voltage polarity.

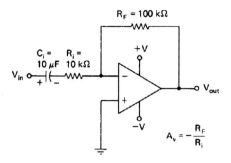

FIGURE 5-2 Inverting AC amplifier.

Some special audio op amps can be used with single or dual power supplies without the need for special biasing resistors.

5-1-2 THE NONINVERTING AMPLIFIER

Since the input impedance of the inverting amplifier equals R_1, matching a high-impedance source (such as a microphone) may present a formidable problem. The noninverting AC amplifier shown in Figure 5-4 is often used in audio circuits to overcome this problem.

Components C_i, R_i, and R_F serve the same function as with the inverting amplifier in Figure 5-2. The noninverting input offers an exceptionally high input impedance and can be matched to the source impedance more readily with the use of C_g and R_g (Fig. 5-4). The rolloff frequency is found the same for C_g and R_g, as it is for C_i and R_i. The rolloff frequency at the noninverting input may be up to 10 times lower than the rolloff frequency at the inverting input.

The gain of the AC noninverting amplifier is the same as its DC counterpart. Input impedance is approximately equal to R_g. The rolloff frequencies are found in the same way as with the inverting amplifier.

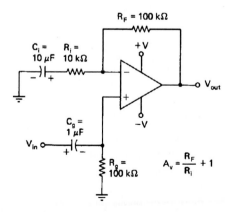

FIGURE 5-4 Noninverting AC amplifier.

Single power-supply noninverting amplifier. The noninverting amplifier may also be used with a single power supply, as shown in Figure 5-5. All components function the same way as with the inverting amplifier of Figure 5-3. However, a noise decoupling capacitor cannot be connected directly to the noninverting input, since this would bypass the signal as well as the noise to ground. An additional circuit for noise decoupling can be inserted at points a and b, if needed. The 47-kΩ resistor tends to isolate R_3 and R_4 from V_{in}, while the power-supply noise is bypassed to ground by the 1-μF capacitor without affecting the input signal.

Negative power-supply operation is also possible with this circuit by grounding R_3 and the positive supply terminal of the op amp while connecting the bottom of R_4 and the negative supply terminal of the op amp to the negative voltage supply.

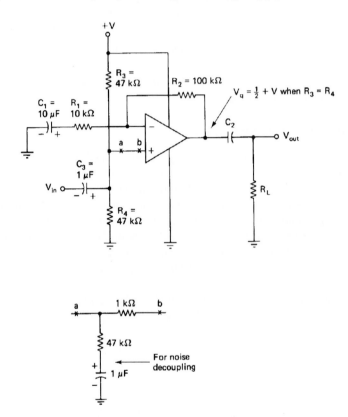

FIGURE 5-5 Noninverting amplifier using single power supply.

5-1-3 SIMPLE AUDIO-VOLTAGE-AMPLIFIER APPLICATIONS

Four examples of audio voltage amplifiers are given in the following figures. These are simple, noncritical circuits that perform rather satisfactorily. Each circuit has a voltage gain of 100 (40 dB gain) and any op amp can be used. However, the higher the quality of the op amp, the better the performance.

A high-impedance input microphone preamplifier is shown in Figure 5-6. The rolloff frequency is about 1.5 Hz. By making R_F adjustable, the gain of the circuit can be varied. Resistor R_g might also be made variable, to match the impedance of the microphone. The microphone should have an impedance larger than 600 Ω.

A low-impedance-input differential microphone preamplifier is shown in Figure 5-7.

Unbalanced microphone lines are susceptible to common-mode noise signals coupled into the cable. The differential input arrangement of this circuit helps to minimize such induced noise. Matched 1.0 percent resistors also improve the degree of common-mode rejection. Performance of the circuit is best when used with microphones with impedances of less than 600 Ω (the lower the better).

A single standard op amp can very effectively drive a set of headphones, as shown in Figure 5-8. The headphones should not be lower than 150 Ω. Other headphone sets can be placed in parallel as long as the total load impedance is above 150 Ω. A low-impedance headphone set or speaker can be used if it is coupled by an impedance matching transformer, as shown by the dashed lines. Resistor R_3 serves as a volume control. Components C_3 and R_4 help to bypass high-frequency noise and improve the sound quality at the output.

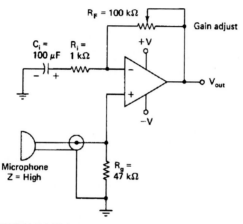

FIGURE 5-6 High-impedance input microphone preamplifier.

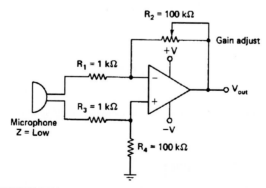

FIGURE 5-7 Low-impedance input, differential microphone preamplifier.

Special power op amps with up to a few watts of output can be used to drive headphones and speakers for certain applications. If, however, you need only about twice as much current to drive a load efficiently, you could use the circuit shown in Figure 5-9. The voltage amplifier is connected to two voltage followers in parallel, which in effect doubles the current available to the load. With the dual and quad op-amp ICs now commonly available, it may be advantageous to use one of these packages in a circuit, which would not be considered using single devices.

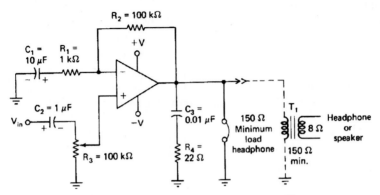

FIGURE 5-8 Basic headphone driver amplifier.

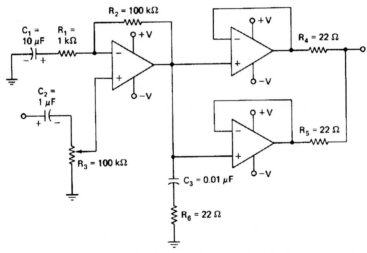

FIGURE 5-9 Amplifier with followers to increase output load current requirements.

5-1-4 EQUALIZATION PREAMPLIFIERS

5-1-4-1 RIAA Equalization Preamplifier

Producing a phonograph record, commonly called "cutting a record," is a highly complex and technically exacting procedure which is beyond the scope of this book. Basically, however, the grooves of a typical stereo record are cut by a chisel-shaped cutting stylus which vibrates mechanically from side to side. This "lateral cut," as it is termed, is in accordance with the audio signal placed on the cutting-stylus mechanism. This lateral cut is known as groove modulation. The amplitude of the audio signal translates to groove modulation, while the frequency of the audio signal determines the rate of change of the groove modulation. Normally, the groove modulation is set to cut one groove at 1 kHz without affecting adjacent grooves. Lower frequencies produced by musical instruments have larger amplitudes which will drive the cutting stylus beyond its fixed limit into adjacent grooves. Higher frequencies from the instruments have smaller amplitudes, which will not drive the stylus sufficiently and result in a poor signal-to-noise ratio when the record is played back. Therefore, an electronic procedure known as equalization attenuates the amplitude of the lower frequencies and amplifies the amplitude of the higher frequencies during the recording process.

When a record is played back, the preamplifier of the audio system must reverse the equalization process, as illustrated by the Record Industry Association of America (RIAA) curve shown in Figure 5-10. The turnover frequencies indicate the frequency ranges that need playback equalization. For instance, the preamplifier must have a higher gain for the frequencies from 50 to 500 Hz, since these were attenuated during the recording process, whereas the preamplifier must have less gain for the frequencies from 2 to 20 kHz, since these were amplified in the original recording.

Some phonograph cartridges (playback stylus and device) such as ceramic and crystal produce from 100 MV to 2 V of output and do not require a preamplifier. These outputs are generally fed to a passive tone network and then directly to a power amplifier, as found in most lo-fi or mid-fi systems. On the other hand, magnetic cartridges produce from 3 to 10 MV output and require a preamplifier with gain. These cartridges are used with hi-fi systems. A preamplifier should have a gain of at least 100, to amplify a signal of, say, 5 MV from a magnetic cartridge to drive the other circuits in a system.

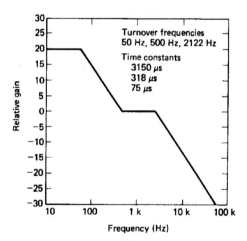

FIGURE 5-10 Standard RIAA equalization curve. (Permission to reprint granted by Signetics Corporation, a subsidiary of U.S. Philips Corp., 811 E. Arques Avenue, Sunnyvale, CA 94086.

A typical RIAA preamplifier is shown in Figure 5-11. The 47-kΩ resistor sets the preamplifier input resistance to match the internal resistance of the magnetic cartridge. The 100-kΩ resistor from the inverting input to ground and the 1.2-MΩ feedback resistor set the DC bias. The 180-Ω resistor and the 100-kΩ feedback resistor establish the reference gain for frequencies 500 Hz to 2 kHz (in this case, about 560). At frequencies below 500 Hz, the

X_c, of the 0.003-μF capacitor is large, causing the feedback impedance to be larger, which results in higher gain for these frequencies. At frequencies above 2 kHz, the X_c of the 0.003-μF capacitor and the 0.001-μF capacitor is low, causing the feedback impedance to be

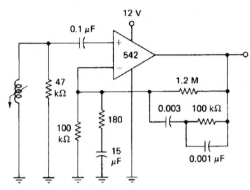

All resistor values are in ohms.

FIGURE 5-11 Typical RIAA preamplifier. (Permission to reprint granted by Signetics Corporation, a subsidiary of U.S. Philips Corp., 811 E. Arques, Avenue, Sunnyvale, CA 94086.)

smaller, and the gain falls off for these frequencies.

5-1-4-2 NAB Equalization Preamplifier

Tape recorder playback preamplifiers require a different type of equalization since the recording process has its own inherent problems with relation to frequencies. The tape head (recording or playback) is an inductive device whose impedance varies directly with frequency (X_L becomes larger when frequency increases). Therefore, the higher the frequency, the larger the impedance, and a larger amplitude is produced. Information recorded on the magnetic tape then has low amplitudes for low frequencies and high amplitude for high frequencies. However, because of the amount of magnetic material on the tape, tape magnetic saturation, the speed of the tape, and the width of the tape-head gap, the amplitude of the audio signal can fall off anywhere from 2 to 20 kHz. Nevertheless, a standard tape playback equalization curve does exist, given by the National Association of Broadcasters (NAB), and is shown in Figure 5-12.

The playback preamplifier must be able to amplify low frequencies and attenuate high frequencies. Tape speed also affects the gain, as indicated by the two standard speeds of $7\frac{1}{2}$ ips and $3\frac{3}{4}$ ips.

A typical NAB tape playback preamplifier is shown in Figure 5-13. Similar to the RIAA preamplifier, resistors R_4 and R_5 set the DC bias. The reference gain of the circuit is set by R_6 and R_7. High-frequency attenuation is determined by X_{C4} and R_7, while low-frequency rolloff is determined by X_{C2} and R_6. The tape head (indicated by the iron-core inductor symbol) is fed through a 1-μF capacitor to the noninverting input.

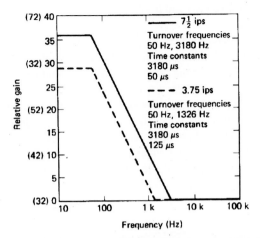

FIGURE 5-12 Standard NAB equalization curve. (Permission to reprint granted by signetics Corporation, a subsidiary of U.S. Philips Corp., 811 E. Arques Avenue, Sunnyvale, CA 94086.)

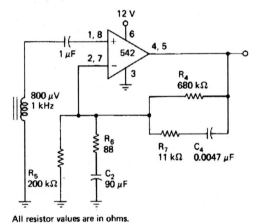

FIGURE 5-13 NAB response amplifier. (Permission to reprint granted by signetics Corporation, a subsidiary of U.S. Philips Corp., 811 E. Arques Avenue, Sunnyvale, CA 94086.)

5-1-5 Active-Tone-Control Circuits

Many precautions are taken to record music exactly as it is produced, and equalization preamplifiers are designed to reproduce the material exactly (or "flat") as the original. Then why would the user of audio equipment want to alter the frequency response of the material being played? There are several reasons. The output of the amplifier can be affected by speaker response, room acoustics, and other factors, but probably most important is the listener's personal taste. Some persons prefer "bassy" music while others prefer it "trebley." A basic discussion on passive bass and treble tone controls will aid you in understanding active tone controls.

A typical passive bass tone control is shown in Figure 5-14. The term "bass" refers to low frequencies or low audible sounds; therefore, this circuit controls low-frequency amplification or attenuation. Passive tone controls require "audio taper" (logarithmic) potentiometers, since our hearing ability is also logarithmic. When the wiper is set at the halfway point of rotation, the total resistive element is split into two portions, with 90 percent above the wiper and 10 percent below the wiper. Basically, when the wiper is placed toward R_1 (bass boost), capacitor C_1 is shorted and there is more resistance from V_{out} to ground, which produces a larger amplitude. When the wiper is moved toward R_3 (bass cut), there is less resistance between V_{out} and ground and the lower frequencies are allowed to pass through C_1 and C_2 to R_3. Therefore, the amplitude is less.

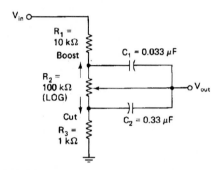

FIGURE 5-14 Typical passive bass tone control.

A typical passive treble tonecontrol is shown in Figure 5-15. The term "treble" refers to high frequencies or high audible sounds; therefore, this circuit controls high-frequency amplification or attenuation. Essentially, the components of the bass circuit have been rearranged for the treble circuit except that the values of the capacitors are changed, since this circuit deals with high frequency. When the wiper of R_2 is placed toward C_1 (boost), there is a larger impedance to ground and more V_{out} is produced. When the wiper is moved toward C_2 (cut), there is less resistance and the signal is shunted to ground.

A passive bass and treble tone control can be combined into a single circuit, as shown in Figure 5-16. Resistor R_4 helps to isolate the two controls and minimizes interaction.

Passive tone controls consume power in the resistors and capacitors used and are referred to as insertion losses. Additional amplification is required to build up the overall signal amplitude to meet the audio system requirements.

The use of an op amp with tone control circuits keeps the output at the overall level of the input or may even result in some gain. This type of circuit is referred to as an active-tone-control circuit, as shown in Figure 5-17.

The addition of a midrange control, which acts to boost or cut the midrange frequencies in a manner similar to the bass and treble controls, offers greater flexibility in tone control. A three-band active tone control is shown in Figure 5-18. The circuit is for the left channel of a stereo amplifier. The input op amp serves as a follower-buffer. If the bass control is a low--

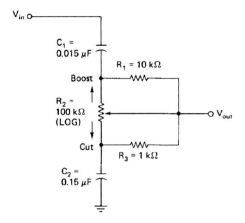

FIGURE 5-15 Typical passive treble tone control.

pass filter and the treble control is a high-pass filter, the midrange control is a combination of both, or a bandpass filter.

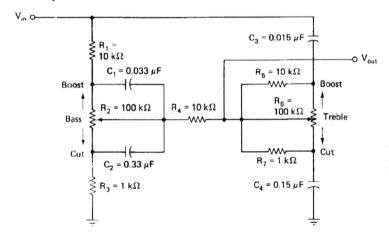

FIGURE 5-16 Complete passive bass and treble tone control.

It may be desirable to add more tone-control sections; however, three paralleled sections appear to be the realistic limit as to what can be expected from a single op amp. More tone-control circuits can be used in an audio system, and this is discussed in Section 5-1-7-4.

5-1-6 AUDIO MIXERS

Audio mixers are basically the same as summing amplifiers, discussed in Section 2-1-5. With a basic audio mixer as shown in Figure 5-19a, each input resistor is made variable. This allows variable gain for each input, in a similar manner as a scaling adder. However, the input resistance to the op amp is constantly changing, which may prove detrimental to circuit efficiency. An improved audio mixer is shown in Figure 5-19b. In this circuit the potentiometers are used as independent input volume controls. Here the gain for each input is constant and the potentiometers adjust the voltage to each input.

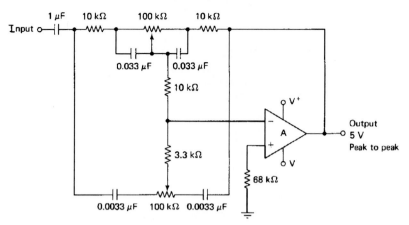

All resistor values are in ohms.

Notes:
1. Amplifier A may be NE531 or 301. Frequency compensation, as for unity-gain noninverting amplifiers, must be used.
2. Turnover frequency — 1 kHz.
3. Bass boost +20 dB at 20 Hz, bass cut −20 dB at 20 Hz, treble boost +19 dB at 20 kHz, treble cut −19 dB at 20 kHz.

FIGURE 5-17 Tone control circuit for operational amplifiers. (Permission to reprint granted by signetics Corporation, a subsidiary of U.S. Philips Corp., 811 E. Arques Avenue, Sunnyvale, CA 94086.)

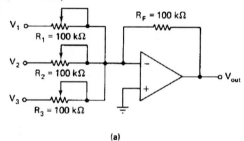

(a)

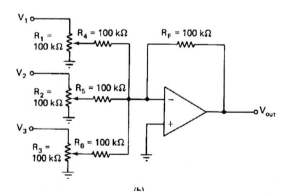

(b)

FIGURE 5-19 Audio mixers: (a) basic circuit; (b) improved circuit.

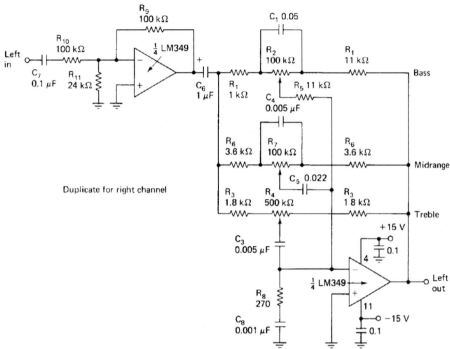

FIGURE 5-18 Three band active tone control—bass, midrange and treble. (Courtesy National Semiconductor Corp.)

5-1-7 MISCELLANEOUS AUDIO CIRCUITS

5-1-7-1 Scratch Filter

A scratch filter is a low-pass filter used to roll off excess high-frequency noise appearing as hiss, ticks, and pops from worn records. The circuit shown in Figure 5-20 has a comer frequency of 10 kHz with a slope of – 12 dB octave.

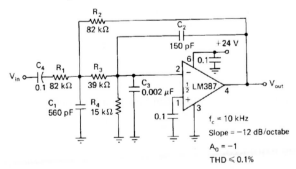

FIGURE 5-20 Scratch filter. (courtesy National Semiconductor Corp.)

5-1-7-2 Rumble Filter

A rumble filter is a high-pass filter used to roll off low-frequency noise associated with worn turntable and tape transport mechanisms. Figure 5-21 shows such a circuit with a corner frequency of 50 Hz with a slope of – 12 dB/octave.

5-1-7-3 Speech Filter

In some audio applications only voice is required, where the frequency range is from 300 Hz to 3 kHz. Frequencies above and below this are not needed and are attenuated so that the voice information is as distortionless as possible. The speech filter shown in Figure 5-22 consists of a high-pass filter in cascade with a low-pass filter to produce the necessary bandpass filter. The corner frequencies are 300 Hz and 3 kHz with a rolloff of – 40 dB/decade.

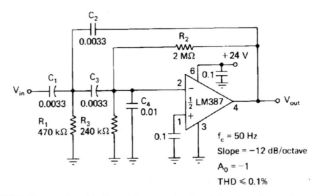

FIGURE 5-21 Rumble filter. (Courtesy National Semiconductor Corp.)

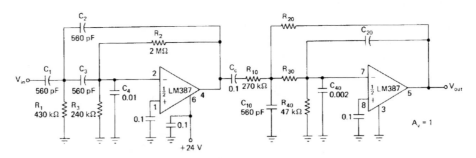

FIGURE 5-22 Speech filter, 300 Hz - 3 kHz bandpass. (Courtesy National Semiconductor Corp.)

5-1-7-4 Octave Equalizer

Musically speaking, an octave is a note or group of notes that can be twice the frequency or half the frequency of a particular reference note or group of reference notes. Optimum results can be realized in an audio system if the frequency response of each octave can be controlled separately throughout the entire audio-frequency range.

The basic octave equalizer as shown in Figure 5-23 is a simple tone-control circuit. The values of C_1 and C_2 determine the frequency range or octave, which is affected by the circuit. It is designed to compensate for any unwanted amplitude-frequency or phase-frequency characteristics of an audio system.

The basic octave equalizer can be duplicated to produce a 10-section octave equalizer, as shown in Figure 5-24. By using quad op-amp ICs, the entire circuit consists of only three IC packages. The input buffer amplifier provides a low source impedance to drive the equalizer while presenting a high input impedance for the preamplifier. Resistor R_8 is used to stabilize the circuit while retaining its fast slew rate of 2 V/μs. A unity-gain output summing amplifier is used to add each equalized octave of frequencies together again. Resistor R_{20} is

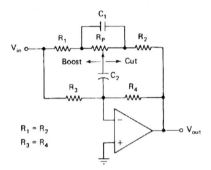

FIGURE 5-23 Typical octave equalizer section.

scaled such that its in-phase signal is actually subtracted from the inverted (out-of-phase) signals, coming from each equalizer to maintain an overall gain of 1. Capacitor C_3 minimizes the possibility of large DC offset voltages from appearing at the output. Capacitor C_4 in each equalizer section provides more stability. Also, an input and output capacitor may be needed if DC voltages are present.

Table 5-1: Values of C_1 and C_2 for appropriate octave. (Courtesy National Semiconductor.)

f_0	C_1	C_2
32 Hz	0.18 μF	0.018 μF
64 Hz	0.1 μF	0.01 μF
125 Hz	0.047 μF	0.0047 μF
250 Hz	0.022 μF	0.0022 μF
500 Hz	0.012 μF	0.00 12 μF
1 kHz	0.0056 μF	560 pF
2 kHz	0.0027 μF	270 pF
4 kHz	0.0015 μF	150 pF

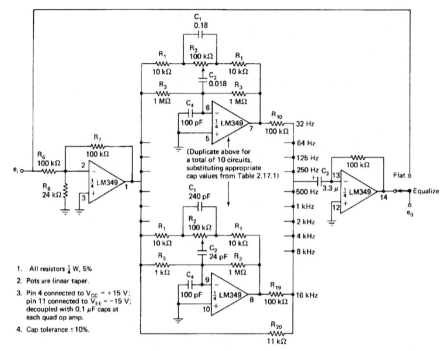

FIGURE 5-24 Complete 10-section octave equalizer. (Courtesy National Semiconductor Corp.)

Table 5-1: Values of C_1 and C_2 for appropriate octave. (Courtesy National Semiconductor.)

f_0	C_1	C_2
8 kHz	680 pF	68 pF
16 kHz	240 pF	24 pF

Table 5-1 lists the values of C_1 and C_2 for each given octave within the audio range.

5-1-7-5 Active Crossover Network

To achieve maximum speaker efficiency, only high frequencies should be applied to the smaller tweeter speaker, while low frequencies are applied to the larger woofer speaker. Such a circuit to accomplish this is known as a crossover network. An op-amp crossover network is shown in Figure 5-25. The circuit basically uses a high-pass filter for driving the tweeter power amplifier and a low-pass filter to drive the woofer power amplifier. This circuit uses a quad op-amp IC and shows the left channel of a stereo system, leaving two other op amps within the package for the right channel. Crossover networks using op-amp ICs are considerably less expensive and much less bulky than older types of circuits that use heavy inductors and large capacitors.

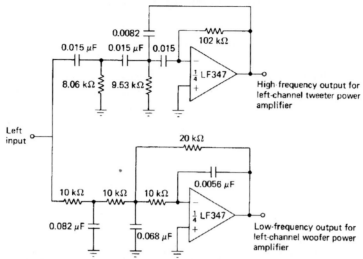

FIGURE 5-25 Active crossover network. (Courtesy National Semiconductor Corp.)

5-1-7-6 Two-Channel Panning Circuit

The circuit shown in Figure 5-26 has the ability of taking a single input signal and moving it to either output via the potentiometer. It can be set to divide the input signal evenly or by any amount between the two output channels. Because of this panoramic control, the circuit is called a "panning" or "pan-pot" circuit. Panning is how an audio engineer can manage to pick up a musical instrument and float the sound over to the other side of the stage and back again. The output of this circuit is required to have unity gain at each extreme of potentiometer travel; that is, one output will have all of the input signal while the other output will be zero. When the potentiometer is centered, each output will be -3 dB down from the input signal

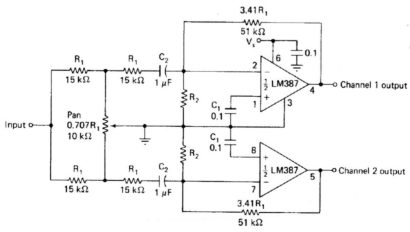

FIGURE 5-26 Two channel panning circuit. (Courtesy National Semiconductor Corp.)

5-1-8 SIMPLE MEDIUM-POWER AMPLIFIERS

Audio power-amplifier ICs are used for low- and medium-power applications, such as mono, stereo, or multichannel audio output for phono, tape, or radio. They utilize a power-supply range of 6 to 50 V.

These audio power-amplifier ICs do not differ significantly in circuit design from traditional op amps. Major design differences appear in the class AB high current output stages and special IC layout techniques to guarantee thermal stability throughout the chip. These IC packages resemble the standard 14-pin DIP, except that several pins on each side are replaced with a fin, which is used for connecting the IC to heat sinks. Normally, the circuits use a single power supply, but dual power supplies may be used without difficulty or degradation in output performance.

Unfortunately, circuits using these ICs are susceptible to picking up noise and self-oscillation at high frequencies. Component layout is extremely critical and extra circuitry may be needed to filter out noise and/or prevent oscillation.

Two circuit configurations using audio power-amplifier ICs are shown in Figure 5-27. The circuits are used for stereo output. The inverting amplifier requires the least amount of components, but must be driven by a relatively low-impedance circuit. Also given is the power output for each channel when using the rated supply voltage. The input signal voltage e_i should not be exceeded for each circuit to prevent output distortion. For applications requiring a high input impedance, the noninverting amplifier would normally be used, although it has a higher component count.

A typical mono amplifier capable of delivering 5 W of output power is shown in Figure 5-28. For applications where output ripple and high-frequency oscillations are not a problem, the 2.7-Ω resistor and all capacitors, except the 500-μF output capacitor, may be eliminated. For maximum efficiency the circuit must be driven by a low-impedance source.

When output power requirements exceed the limits of available audio power-amplifier ICs, the output may be boosted using two external power transistors, as shown in Figure 5-29. This simple circuit uses a complementary emitter-follower stage with a feedback circuit (components R_F, C_3, and the 27-kΩ resistor). Capacitors C_4 and C_5 are used for power-supply decoupling. At signal levels below 20 mW the IC supplies the speaker directly through the 5-Ω resistor. Above this level, the booster transistors are biased "on" by the same current through the 5-Ω resistor.

Figure 5-30 shows an improved 35-W boosted power amplifier using a specially designed power-driver IC. This circuit utilizes current and power limiting, which minimizes distortion and protects the output transistors from possible destruction. Resistors R_1 and R_6 are the actual current-limiting devices, while R_2–R_3 and R_4–R_5 form reference voltages about the transistors, which keep them properly biased under high load conditions. The 1-kΩ potentiometer is used to adjust the bias on the transistors so that 0 V appears between the transistors (at the load point R_L during the quiescent state.

SECTION 5-2 TERMINOLOGY EXERCISE

Write a brief definition for each of the following terms:
1. Audio frequency range
2. External noise
3. Internal noise
4. Single power-supply operation

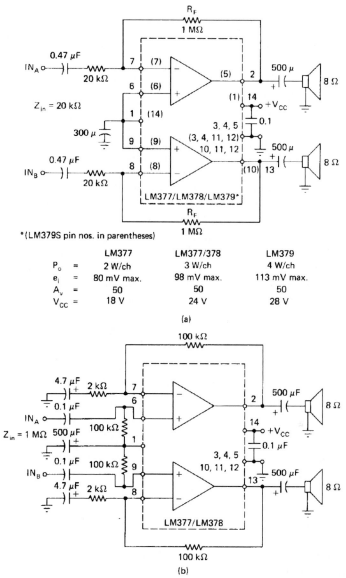

	LM377	LM377/378	LM379
P_o =	2 W/ch	3 W/ch	4 W/ch
e_i =	80 mV max.	98 mV max.	113 mV max.
A_v =	50	50	50
V_{CC} =	18 V	24 V	28 V

(a)

(b)

FIGURE 5-27 Stereo amplifiers: (a) inverting amplifier; (b) noninverting amplifier. (Courtesy National Semiconductor Corp.)

  5. RIAA equalization
  6. RIAA equalization amplifier
  7. NAB equalization
  8. NAB equalization amplifier
  9. Passive tone controls
 10. Active tone controls
 11. Audio mixers
 12. Scratch filter

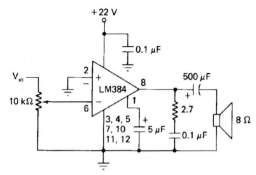

FIGURE 5-28 Typical 5 W amplifier. (Courtesy National Semiconductor Corp.)

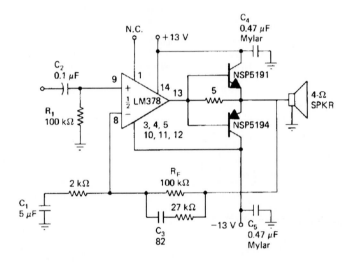

FIGURE 5-29 12-watt low-distortion power amplifier. (Courtesy National Semiconductor Corp.)

13. Rumble filter
14. Speech filter
15. Octave equalizer
16. Crossover networks
17. Panning circuit
18. Power amplifier

SECTION 5-3 PROBLEMS AND EXERCISES

1. Referring to Figure 5-2, what is the low-frequency cutoff when $C_i = 4.7$ μF and $R_i = 2.2$ kΩ ?
2. Draw an inverting amplifier and a noninverting amplifier using a single power supply.
3. Draw a noninverting preamplifier with a gain of 250, followed by an inverting amplifier with a gain of 50, which is driving an 8-Ω speaker.

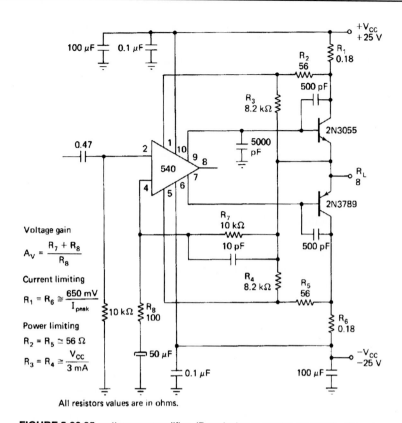

FIGURE 5-30 35-watt power amplifier. (Permission to reprint granted by Signetics Corporation, a subsidiary of U.S. Philips Corp., 811 E. Arques Avenue, Sunnyvale, CA 94086.)

4. Explain the function of the components that make up the RIAA preamplifier shown in Figure 5-11.
5. Explain the function of the components that comprise the NAB preamplifier shown in Figure 5-13.
6. Draw an active-tone-control (bass and treble) circuit.
7. List and explain three types of filters used in audio applications.
8. Explain the operation of an octave equalizer. How does it perform compared to normal tone-control circuits?
9. Explain the difference between an active crossover network and a panning circuit.
10. Draw a simple boosted-power-output amplifier and define the function of each component used. (*Hint*: See Figures 5-29 and 5-30.)

SECTION 5-4 EXPERIMENTS

EXPERIMENT 5-1 GENERAL AUDIO CIRCUITS

Objective:

For the reader to gain experience in working with op-amp applications to audio circuits.

Introduction:

This section does not contain any basic organized experiments to perform. The selection of circuits to construct is left to the discretion of the reader. However, you or your instructor may select one or more circuits from this unit to construct and perform some tests.

The standard 741 op amp can be used successfully with the circuits in the following figures: 5-2, 5-3, 5-4, 5-5, 5-6, 5-7, 5-8, 5-9, 5-17, 5-18, and 5-19. The other various op amps indicated in the remaining figures will give the best performance.

Test Procedure:

1. Decide which circuit you want to construct.
2. Obtain all of the components and test equipment before beginning construction of the circuit.
3. Follow the same precautions and procedures you did with the other experiments in this book.
4. Below is an outline which you might use to keep a record of your experiments. It will provide evidence to your instructor that you actually performed the experiment. You will have to fill in the title and state your objective, introduction (description of what equipment was used and how you performed the experiment), and a conclusion as to what you have gained from the experiment.

Experiment Title: _____

_____

Objective: _____

_____

_____

_____

_____

Introduction: _____

_____

_____

Test Procedure: Make a drawing of the circuit in the space above:

Conclusion:

_____

_____

_____

SECTION 5-5 SUMMARY POINTS

1. Inverting audio op amps are usually used with low-impedance sources.
2. Noninverting audio op amps are used with high-impedance sources.
3. Often, op-amp audio applications use a single power supply by biasing the noninverting input at $\frac{1}{2} V_{cc}$ (+ or −).
4. Special audio op amps are designed to operate from a single or a dual power supply.
5. RIAA equalization preamplifiers are designed to amplify frequencies below 500 Hz and to attenuate frequencies above 2 kHz.
6. NAB equalization preamplifiers are designed to have a rather linear attenuation for frequencies above 50 Hz.
7. Active-tone-control circuits maintain the input signal amplitude and may even have some gain.
8. Audio mixers are basically summing amplifiers.
9. A scratch filter is a low-pass filter.
10. A rumble filter is a high-pass filter.
11. A speech filter is a bandpass filter of 300 Hz to 3 kHz.
12. Octave equalizers are basically tone controls that provide greater flexibility over the entire audio range compared to simple bass and treble controls.
13. A crossover network directs low frequencies to the larger "woofer" speaker and directs the higher frequencies to the smaller "tweeter" speaker.
14. A panning circuit enables the operator to move a single audio source completely or proportionately from one audio channel to another.
15. Specially designed audio op amps are capable of delivering up to several watts of power directly to a speaker.
16. When more audio power is required, an audio op amp may drive booster-output transistors.

SECTION 5-6 SELF-CHECKING QUIZ

Referring to Figure 5-31, identify the op-amp component or circuit nomenclature for questions 1 through 6.
1. Audio mixer _____
2. Output driver_____
3. Bass-tone-control section_____
4. Volume control_____
5. Preamplifier_____
6. Treble-tone-control section_____

Multiple-Choice Questions

7. A circuit capable of selecting sound from one of two speakers or from both is known as:

    a.   A crossover network

    b.   A panning circuit

    c.   A tone control

    d.   An octave equalizer

8. The best circuit used to eliminate 60-Hz hum is:

    a.   A scratch filter

    b.   A speech filter

    c.   A rumble filter

    d.   An octave equalizer

9. An audio system requires a preamplifier with a gain of 200 to match a 50-kΩ impedance microphone. The best amplifier configuration to use is:

    a.   Noninverting

    b.   Inverting

    c.   Single follower

    d.   None of the above

10. A 10-section octave equalizer can adjust the frequency response of:

    a.   Low frequencies

    b.   High frequencies

    c.   Middle frequencies

    d.   All of the above

(Answers at back of book)

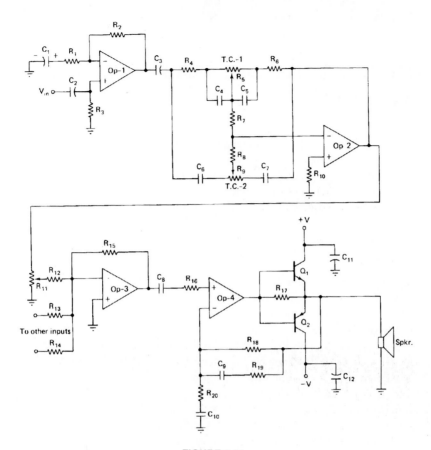

FIGURE 5-31

C H A P T E R 6

OP-AMP PROTECTION, STABILITY, AND TESTING

It is inevitable with any device that breakdown will occur sooner or later. Reliable manufacturers or persons constructing their own circuits will desire dependable trouble-free operation for their efforts. Certain precautions can be taken during the design and construction stages of op-amp circuits that will ensure proper operation even before the circuits are powered up. This chapter will present practical applications for overvoltage protection, circuit stability, and testing of op amps.

6-1-1 INPUT PROTECTION

As with any solid-state device, exceeding the manufacturer's voltage rating will probably destroy the op amp or alter its characteristics. Failure at the input can result from exceeding the differential input rating or the common-mode rating. The differential input transistors of an op amp form an equivalent circuit that resembles two zener diodes back to back. If a voltage across the input exceeds the zener breakdown point, sufficient reverse current could flow to damage the input transistors (usually a short). Current-limiting resistors and diodes may be used at the inputs of op amps to provide input protection, as shown in Figure 6-1.

Resistors R_1 and R_2 should be equal and may range up to 10 kΩ without any effect on circuit performance. The internal emitter-to-base zener breakdown point of the transistors within the op amp is about 7 V. Zener diodes with a lower breakdown voltage can be used to protect the op-amp input (Figure 6-1a). Very often, because it is less expensive, regular diodes are used in a reverse-connected parallel arrangement (Figure 6-1b). Where some op amps have internal input protection, only the resistors may need to be added (Figure 6-1c). In a practical working circuit, the input ends of the resistors may be considered the actual inputs of the op amp.

6-1-2 OUTPUT PROTECTION AND LATCH-UP

Most op amps currently manufactured have output short-circuit protection incorporated within the IC. You may encounter older types of op amps that require output short-circuit protection as shown in Figure 6-2. The output current is limited during a short circuit by a low-value resistor in series with the output. During normal operation the drop in voltage at the output is insignificant and performance is otherwise not impaired. Moreover, the circuit stability is improved, especially with capacitive loads.

A problem sometimes occurring in voltage-follower stages using op amps is called latch-up. If the input signal peak-to-peak voltage swing is greater than the input bias levels, the op amp can saturate. In the saturated condition, the op amp no longer has negative feedback, but goes into positive feedback. Positive feedback, of course, keeps the op amp in saturation, and the output will be latched up to a high voltage level (near $+V$ or $-V$ supply voltages).

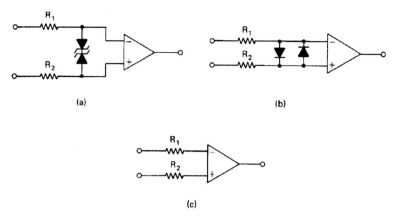

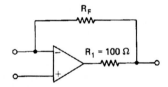

FIGURE 6-1 Input overvoltage/overcurrent protection methods: (a) zener diodes; (b) regular diodes; (c) internally protected.

The use of a high-value feedback resistor can reduce or eliminate the possibility of latch-up but may impair the input characteristics of an op amp. One commonly used method of preventing latch-up is shown in Figure 6-3a. A diode is placed from the output to one of the frequency-compensation terminals. This prevents the output voltage from rising above the potential on the terminal due to diode clamping action.

Since latch-up usually occurs from extreme limits of input voltage swing, a circuit that clamps the input voltage to a specific level will also prevent latch-up, as shown in Figure 6-3b. The input signal will not be able to swing greater than supply voltages $+V$ or $-V$.

FIGURE 6-2 Output short circuit protection.

6-1-3 POWER SUPPLY PROTECTION

Op-amp ICs are constructed in such a manner that they must always be operated with the correct power supply polarity, and the maximum power-supply voltage rating must not be exceeded. If the power-supply voltage ever becomes reversed, even for a moment, destructive currents will flow and the IC will be useless. A single amplifier can be reverse-polarity-protected by placing a diode in series with the $-V$ power supply, as shown in Figure 6-4a. Reverse-polarity protection for a group of amplifiers may be provided by connecting a pair of power diodes in reverse across the power supply, as shown in Figure 6-4b. The diodes should be capable of handling more current than the fuse or short-circuit current limit of the power supplies. If a polarity reversal occurs, D_1 and D_2 will clamp the power supplies to the limit or draw enough current to blow the fuse, thereby protecting the amplifiers.

General-type IC op amps usually have a maximum power-supply operating voltage of ± 18 V (36 V total) given by the manufacturer. If this limit is exceeded, even momentarily, the IC could be destroyed. Two power-supply overvoltage protection circuits are shown in Figure

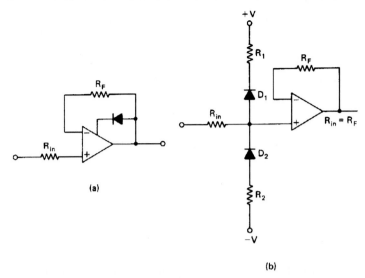

FIGURE 6-3 Preventing latch-up: (a) diode clamping; (b) input limiting.

6-5. A single zener diode with a V_Z of 36 V can be placed across the power-supply terminals. If this is not available, two 18-V zener diodes in series can be used.

Normally, the actual operating voltages will be lower than the rated maximum supply voltages and the zener diodes will not interfere with circuit operation. Just remember that the V_Z of the zener diodes for any power-supply overvoltage protection must be equal to or a little less than the rated maximum operating voltage of the op amp.

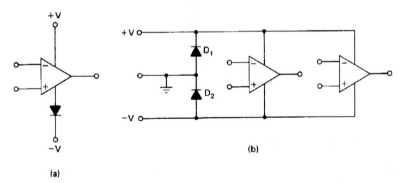

FIGURE 6-4 Power supply reverse polarity protection: (a) single amplifier; (b) group of amplifiers.

6-1-4 BASIC CIRCUIT STABILITY APPLICATIONS

Stabilizing a feedback amplifier means keeping it from oscillating, maintaining the constant gain for which it was designed, and reducing noise to a minimum. Proper circuit layout enhances the stability of a circuit. Component lead length should be kept to a minimum and, ideally, circuits be connected as directly as possible with short conductor lengths. Ground paths should have low resistance and low inductance.

It is important to keep the power-supply voltages constant for good stability. Power-supply decoupling as shown in Figure 6-6 can help accomplish this. The capacitors bypass

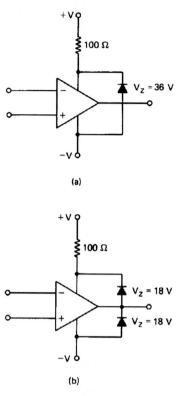

(a)

(b)

FIGURE 6-5 Power supply overvoltage protection methods: (a) using a single zener diode; (b) using two zener diodes.

power-supply variations to ground. These capacitors are usually 0.1-µF disk ceramic or 1.0-µF tantalum types. It is good practice to bypass each printed circuit board or at least every five op-amp circuits.

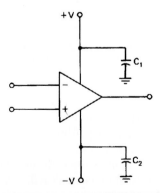

FIGURE 6-6 Power supply decoupling.

Stray input capacitance due to amplifier input capacitance and wiring capacitance can affect the stability of a circuit. Signal phase shifts can occur, which may even cause oscillation. A small feedback capacitor in the order of 3 to 10 pF placed in parallel with the feedback resistor can reduce or eliminate the problems caused by stray input capacitance. Examine Figure 6-7a.

Stray output capacitance can also cause stability problems. By adding a small output resistor in series with the output, the capacitance is isolated from the amplifier, as shown in Figure 6-7b.

High-frequency gain (and noise) is reduced by the feedback capacitor C_F. The reactance of C_F should be $\dfrac{1}{10}$ (or less) that of R_F at the unity-gain frequency.

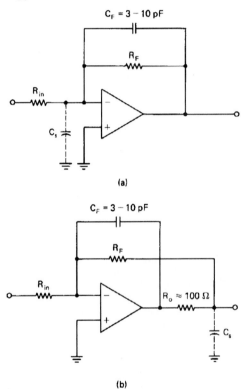

(a)

(b)

FIGURE 6-7 Stabilizing circuits with stray capacitance: (a) input capacitance; (b) stray output capacitance.

6-1-5 TESTING THE OP AMP

There are numerous tests that can be performed on op amps to determine their operating abilities. These exacting tests are comprised of bias current, offset voltage, offset current, slew-rate limiting, transient response, frequency response, voltage gain, CMRR, and other more specialized testing. These tests are normally performed by the manufacturer. But what about testing op amps from the functional standpoint? Will it work or not work in a circuit? Unlike other solid-state devices, ICs, particularly op amps, are too complex to perform simple ohmmeter tests for determining their "go–no go" ability.

This section gives four simple op-amp test circuits that determine if the output of the op amp can swing positive and negative and indicate some relative gain. Battery power supplies can be used for these circuits or you may want to construct an AC line-operated power supply as presented in Section 1-5.

These circuits can be constructed on a perforated board and are easily stored in a small space. Figure 6-8 illustrates a general layout for the op-amp testers. Connecting terminals are required for attaching the power supplies and having the flexibility of wiring op amps with various lead identification. Some of the terminal-lead methods that you might use are:

• mini-pin plug and jack
• mini-banana plug and jack
• spring connector and tinned wires
• mini-alligator clip lead

Two IC test sockets can be used: 14-pin DIP and 8-pin TO-99. All components are mounted on the board. Five terminals, labeled + *V*, – IN, + IN, OUT, and – *V*, have wires soldered to them which are used to wire the appropriate terminals of the IC socket.

Special care should be used when installing and removing the ICs from the socket. All power must be removed from the circuit. Make sure that the IC is properly aligned to the socket terminals. With the DIP socket, insert the pins on one side of the IC first and then with gentle pressure insert the other side. With the TO-99 socket, insert pin 1 first and then with a pointed object, such as a pencil or screwdriver, align each pin with a socket hole as you gently press down on the IC.

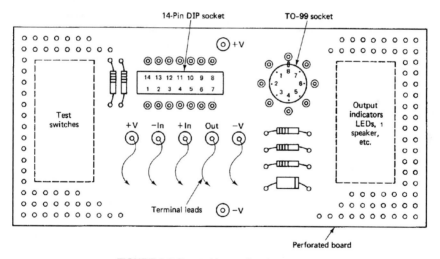

FIGURE 6-8 General layout for op-amp testers.

You may want to buy an IC puller or make one of your own from a pair of long tweezers by bending the tips $\frac{1}{8}$ in. inward 90 degrees, facing each other.

A very small screwdriver can be used to pry an IC out of a socket. Just remember to raise the IC evenly so that any pins are not overly bent as the IC comes free of the socket.

The circuit shown in Figure 6-9 uses LEDs (light-emitting diodes) to indicate the output swing. When the input polarity switch is in the positive position and the test switch is closed, the output of the "device under test" (D.U.T.) will go negative and LED-1 will light. Conversely, when the input polarity switch is set to negative and the test switch is closed, the output will swing positive, causing LED-2 to light.

If one or both of the LEDs fail to light, the op amp has an internal problem, which may be an open circuit. If the LEDs are on simultaneously anytime during the test, there could possibly be a short circuit within the op amp.

An automatic LED go–no go op-amp checker is shown in Figure 6-10. This circuit is a square-wave generator such as that discussed in Section 4-1. It proves the same test as the circuit in Figure 6-9. The output of the D.U.T. swings negative and positive, causing LED-1 and LED-2 to light, respectively.

By changing the values of the capacitor and resistor in the inverting input circuit of the square-wave generator you can produce an audible op-amp checker, as shown in Figure 6-11. The 1-kΩ load and AC voltmeter can test the op-amp output by giving a relative output reading. The output should be swinging nearly +V and −V; therefore, the output reading should be 50 percent or greater of the ±V supply. When SI is closed, there should be a 1-kHz audible sound in the loudspeaker. The meter reading should decrease drastically due to the speaker loading down the output. No sound, of course, would indicate a defective op amp.

A basic op-amp DC gain tester is shown in Figure 6-12. This tester uses a ±15-V supply but may be increased to ±18 V if it is decided to use batteries. The input resistors and diodes drop the voltage down for the input to the op amp. The diodes help to regulate the voltage at the input. Their forward voltage drop is about 0.7 V. The 470-Ω and 100-Ω resistors form a divider which provides approximately 0.1 V at the inverting input. The gain select switch, S_2, controls the gain of the circuit for $\times 1$, $\times 10$, and $\times 100$. The output voltages should be 0.1, 1.0, and 10 V, respectively for each setting of the gain select switch. When the input polarity switch, S_1, is in the positive position, the output voltages will be negative, and vice versa, since the circuit is a basic inverting amplifier. Any op amp that cannot produce the required gain for this tester should be discarded.

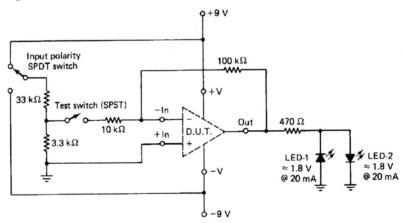

FIGURE 6-9 LED indicator GO-NO GO op-amp checker.

6-1-6 IN-CIRCUIT TESTING WITH A VOLTMETER

The voltmeter is basically used to test and measure the DC voltages in an electric circuit. As with any electronic servicing, it is always good practice to check power-supply voltages for proper values. With op amps, this voltage should be checked right at the supply-voltage pins of the IC. Improper readings may indicate that the IC is bad; however, the power supply could have a problem or another defective circuit could be upsetting the power to all circuits.

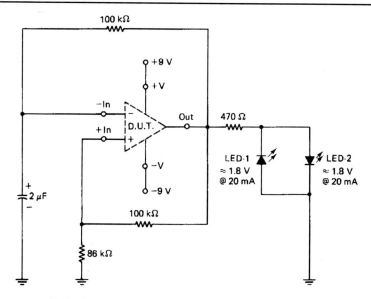

FIGURE 6-10 Automatic LED GO-NO GO op-amp checker.

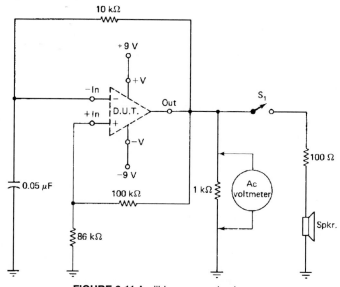

FIGURE 6-11 Audible op-amp checker.

Do not overlook faulty overvoltage protection or decoupling circuits, which may affect the power-supply voltages. Leaky diodes and capacitors can lower the supply voltages. Once it is determined that the power-supply voltages are correct, other DC voltage measurements can be made to ascertain where a problem is occurring.

Component aging can cause DC voltages to change and upset circuit stability. A check should be made of DC balance controls or null adjustments. These controls may be adjusted to restore circuits to their proper working condition, thereby eliminating the need for further troubleshooting.

When changes in DC levels occur, the problem is to tell whether these changes are

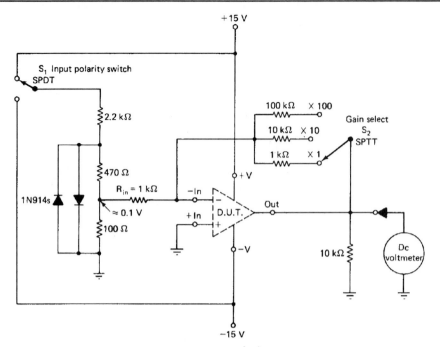

FIGURE 6-12 Basic op-amp DC gain tester.

caused by defects in the op amp or in the external circuit. One method of determining this is by removing the op amp and rechecking the voltage readings. If the voltage readings become normal, the IC (op amp) is probably defective. If the readings are still incorrect, the problem is most likely in the external circuitry. As an example, refer to Figure 6-13. The voltage at the noninverting input should read +4.8 V; however, our meter indicates about +2.0 V. If upon removing the op amp this voltage becomes normal, then the op amp seems to be defective. If the voltage remains at +2.0 V, R_1 has probably increased in value and R_2 is dropping less voltage.

Another troubleshooting technique is to short together the two inputs of the op amp, as shown in Figure 6-14. The differential input voltage becomes zero; therefore, the output voltage should also drop to zero. If this does not occur, the op amp is defective.

There are a few precautions to be observed with this technique. First, make sure that the IC is an op amp. Many other ICs cannot tolerate a short circuit across the inputs. Second, make sure that the pins being shorted are the inputs, because shorting other pins will destroy the IC. Third, do not use this method or at least open the output circuit if there is direct coupled circuitry following the op amp. Fourth, this test should be used only on circuits using dual polarity power supplies.

If the loss of gain is a problem within a system, individual amplifiers may be tested as shown in Figure 6-15. This is a DC gain test and it may be necessary to isolate the amplifier from other circuits by opening the input and output leads. A small 1.5-V battery and 10-kΩ potentiometer can be adjusted to provide the input voltage. Resistors R_{in} and R_F should be measured for accuracy and their values applied to the gain formula for determining the output voltage expected. Also, remember to observe the input/ output voltage polarity relationship of an inverting amplifier and noninverting amplifier.

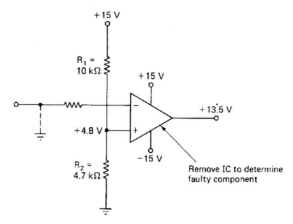

FIGURE 6-13 Testing DC input voltage.

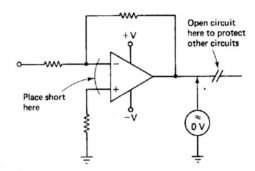

FIGURE 6-14 Testing for 0-volts output when inputs are shorted.

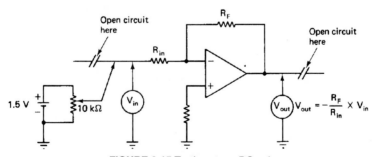

FIGURE 6-15 Testing stage DC gain.

6-1-7 IN-CIRCUIT TESTING WITH AN OSCILLOSCOPE

The oscilloscope is probably the best test instrument to use on any electronic circuit, since it can measure DC, signal, transient, and noise voltages. Its greatest advantage is in signal-tracing a system, as shown in Figure 6-16. Generally, a signal is placed or "injected" at the input to the system. An oscilloscope is used to check for the signal or any distortion from stage to stage. When a defective stage is located, the troubleshooting is concentrated in finding the faulty component or components. A blocking capacitor in series with the signal generator and the input to the first stage prevents any DC component from the generator getting to the unit under test. This extraneous DC component could upset the voltage measurements and cause distortion.

Testing a single stage with an oscilloscope is done in a similar manner, as shown in Figure 6-17. The signal generator is placed at the input and the oscilloscope detects the signal at the output. The gain of an amplifier can be determined and tested by using peak-to-peak voltage measurements.

6-1-7-1 Noise Problems

Since op amps are used in critical measuring or detecting circuits, noise presents a particularly bothersome condition. The oscilloscope is invaluable in locating noise in op-amp circuits as well as in any electronic circuit.

Hum and ripple is low-frequency noise that usually comes from the power-supply voltages feeding an amplifier. One method of localizing a hum or ripple problem is to short the input pins of an op amp as was done in Figure 6-14. The oscilloscope monitors the output. If the hum or ripple disappears, it is probably being picked up by the leads or at the terminals of the op amp. Look for cold-solder joints on lead shielding, loose shields, and loose ground terminals.

If the hum or ripple does not disappear with the op-amp input terminals shorted, the problem is probably in the power supply. Cheek the power-supply terminals of the op amp for an excessive amount of ripple. Remember that the amplifier may have considerable gain, and the ripple monitored at the output of the amplifier may be much greater than at the power-supply terminals.

Higher-frequency noise can be generated by aging components, such as leaky diodes and capacitors and resistors that have increased in value. These components are usually in the protection and stabilizing circuits associated with op amps. Leakage in these components is extremely difficult or impossible to detect with in-circuit testing. Replacement with a component known to be good and then observing the oscilloscope for noise seems to be the best possible remedy.

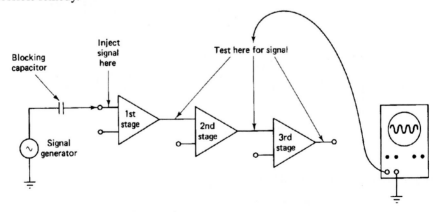

FIGURE 6-16 Signal tracing with an oscilloscope.

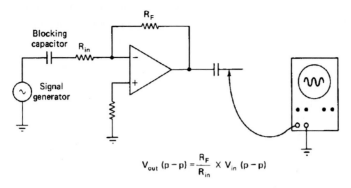

$$V_{out} \, (p-p) = \frac{R_F}{R_{in}} \times V_{in} \, (p-p)$$

FIGURE 6-17 Testing a single stage with an oscilloscope.

SECTION 6-2 TERMINOLOGY EXERCISE

Write a brief definition for each of the following terms:
1. Input protection
2. Output protection
3. Latch-up
4. Power supply protection
5. Stability
6. Go–no go test

SECTION 6-3 PROBLEMS AND EXERCISES

1. List and explain three types of op-amp input protection.
2. Explain one way to have output short-circuit protection for an op amp.
3. Explain what is meant by latch-up and what causes it.
4. List and explain two methods of preventing latch-up.
5. List two reasons power-supply protection is needed.
6. What is meant by power-supply decoupling, and why is it needed?
7. Draw and explain a stabilizing circuit to reduce input stray capacitance.
8. Draw and explain a stabilizing circuit to reduce output stray capacitance.
9. Explain three methods of DC voltage testing for an op-amp circuit.
10. List the uses that an oscilloscope can have when testing op-amp circuits.

SECTION 6-4 EXPERIMENTS

EXPERIMENT 6-1 OP AMP BASIC TROUBLESHOOTING

Objective:
To gain experience in troubleshooting op amp circuits by recognizing some common trouble symptoms.

Introduction:
In this experiment you will construct the circuit shown in Figure 6-18 and introduce specific circuit troubles by opening or shorting various circuit components. When you simulate an open component, simply pull the component lead out of the breadboard. When you simulate a short, place a wire across the component. With each trouble situation introduced in the circuit

you will make voltage measurements and record them in the data table. Compare the voltage readings of the trouble situation to the normal circuit voltage readings and note the comments.

Required Components:

1 4.7-kΩ resistor at 0.5 W
2 10-kΩ resistors at 0.5 W
1 100-kΩ resistor at 0.5 W
2 1-µF capacitors at 25 WVDC
1 741 op-amp or equivalent IC

Test Procedure:

1. Construct the circuit shown in Figure 6-18.
2. Using an oscilloscope, measure V_{in} and V_{out} and record their value in the data table. This is the signal voltage reading for a normal circuit.
3. For the remaining condition column, perform the indicated troubles and record the voltage readings in the data table.

QUESTIONS FOR FIGURE 6-18

1. When R_{in} opens, _____ signal is applied to the op amp.
2. When R_F opens, C_{in} charges up to a DC voltage level and the op amp _____ .
3. If C_{out} opens, you are unable to read _____ .
4. If one of the voltage sources becomes open, the output of the op amp will _____ toward the other power source voltage.

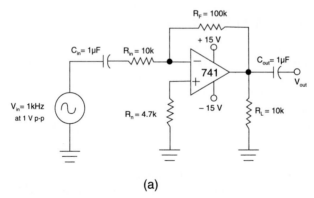

(a)

FIGURE 6-18 Op-amp ac inverting amplifier: (a) circuit; (b) data table.

SECTION 6-5 SUMMARY POINTS

1. Op amps may need input protection in the form of limiting resistors, zener diodes, and regular diodes.
2. Output protection and preventing latch-up also utilizes resistors and diodes.
3. Op amps should have power-supply protection from overvoltage and polarity reversal.
4. Stabilizing op-amp circuits involves counteracting stray capacitance with small feedback capacitors and decoupling power-supply terminals with capacitors.
5. Functional testing an op amp shows that its output can swing positive and negative and that it is capable of gain.

Condition	v_{out}	V_{out}	Comments
Normal			All voltages are proper
+15-V supply open			$-V_{sat}$ at output of op amp
−15-V supply open			$+V_{sat}$ at output of op amp
R_{in} open			No signal applied to op amp
R_F open			C_{in} charges up and op amp saturates
R_n open			$-V_{sat}$ at output of op amp
R_L open			No apparent trouble
C_{in} open			No signal applied to op amp
C_{in} shorted			V_{out} changes, maybe signal distorts
C_{out} open			No v_{out}
C_{out} shorted			Perhaps no problem, but maybe signal loading

(b)

FIGURE 6-18 Continued.

6. Check DC adjustments and null controls when testing op-amp circuits to see if the circuit can be restored to normal operation.
7. Check for leaky diodes and capacitors and resistors that are out of tolerance when testing op-amp circuits.
8. A circuit may be tested by removing the op amp and making voltage measurements.
9. An op amp may be tested by shorting the inputs and measuring the output for zero volts.
10. An in-circuit gain test can be performed by applying the formula $V_{out} = R_F/R_{in} \times V_{in}$.
11. The voltmeter is used to check DC power-supply voltages and DC voltages at the terminals of op amps.
12. The oscilloscope is used for signal tracing and can detect transient voltages and noise.

SECTION 6-6 SELF-CHECKING QUIZ

Match each circuit in Figure 6-19 with its proper description in column A.

Column A
1. Input protection
2. Output short-circuit protection
3. Latch-up protection
4. Reverse-polarity protection
5. Overvoltage protection
6. Power-supply decoupling
7. Stray capacitance stabilization

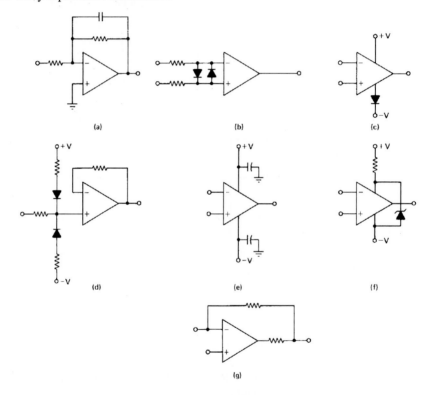

FIGURE 6-19

MULTIPLE-CHOICE QUESTIONS

8. If both inputs of an op amp are at the same voltage potential, the output should be at:
   a. $+V$
   b. $-V$
   c. Depends on A_v factor
   d. Zero volts
9. Low voltage at a power-supply terminal of an op amp could be caused by:
   a. An open decoupling capacitor

b. A leaky protection diode
c. An open feedback resistor
d. A shorted stabilizing feedback capacitor
10. The gain of an op-amp inverting amplifier with an input of 0.25 V and an output of 17.5 V is:
a. 4.375
b. 17.75
c. 17.25
d. 70
(Answers at back of book)

CHAPTER 7

SPECIAL TYPE OP AMPS

There are countless numbers of op-amp ICs produced by various manufacturers for special circuits. The main differences among these op amps are the slew rate, frequency response, input bias current, output-offset voltage, input impedance, CMRR, and gain and electrical characteristics. Most manufacturers' component manuals have a good selection of op amps to choose from for designing special circuits. There are also other types of op amps with added components or features that make it important for the engineer and technician to have some familiarity.

7-1-1 JFET-INPUT OP AMP

A bipolar transistor operates in the forward biased condition and a current must flow through the emitter/base junction, resulting in a low input resistance. Leakage currents are also more pronounced. The JFET operates in reverse bias with an extremely high resistance, resulting in little or no current flow between the source and gate. Leakage currents with the JFET are much less.

An op amp using a JFET input stage as shown in Figure 7-1 will have many improved features over an all-bipolar transistor device.

Transistors Q_1 and Q_2 are the two JFET differential inputs. Transistor Q_3 acts as a constant current source for the input transistors. The differential output taken from the drains of Q_1 and Q_2 is applied to other bipolar transistor circuits in the op amp. The main advantages of a JFET-input op amp are:

1. Extremely high input impedance (10^{12} Ω or more)
2. Low input bias currents (50 pa or less)
3. Low input offset current (10 pa or less)
4. Low input offset voltage (0.5 mV or less)
5. Low input offset voltage temperature drift (5 μV/$^\circ$ C or less)
6. Low input noise current
7. Low input noise voltage
8. High common-mode rejection ratio (90 dB or more)

Some op amps use MOSFET input transistors, which extend these advantages but must be physically handled more carefully and require other precautions to prevent rupturing the insulated gate region from high static charges.

7-1-2 OPERATIONAL TRANSCONDUCTANCE AMPLIFIER

Conventional op amps are essentially voltage-amplifying devices with a high impedance differential input, low impedance output, and a fixed open loop voltage gain (A_o), typically of 100,000. The output voltage is the gain times the differential input voltage, i.e., the voltage difference between the inverting input V_1 and the noninverting input V_2, expressed as $V_{out} = A_o \times (V_2 - V_1)$.

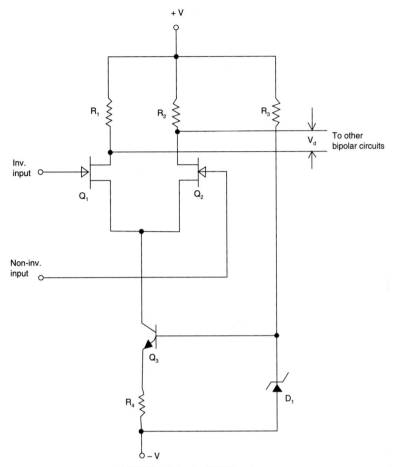

FIGURE 7-1 Basic JFET input op amp

An *operational transconductance amplifier* (OTA) is a variable-gain voltage-to-current amplifier. The OTA has similar connections as a conventional op amp, except for an extra connection to externally set the bias current as shown in Figure 7-2b. The constant current symbol may be shown, indicating the output is related to current gain.

The input voltages produce an output in the form of a high-impedance current. The current gain or transconductance (gm) of the OTA can be controlled by the amount of external bias current applied to the I_{bias} terminal. The current can usually be varied from 0.1 μA to 1 mA, providing a 10,000:1 gain-control range. The output current is proportional to the differential input voltage times the gm (in mhos), expressed as $I_o = gm \times (V_2 - V_1)$.

A well known OTA is the CA3080 or LM3080, of which the internal circuitry is shown in Figure 7-2a. The pin connections are shown in Figures 7-2c and d. This circuit consists of one differential amplifier and four current mirror (CM) circuits. A *current mirror circuit* is a three-terminal circuit that will produce an in-phase output current of similar value as the input current applied to it. Figure 7-3a shows a basic current mirror circuit. The characteristics of the two transistors must be closely matched for proper operation. Let's assume the beta of the transistors is 200. If the base current of each transistor is 5 μA, then the collector cur-

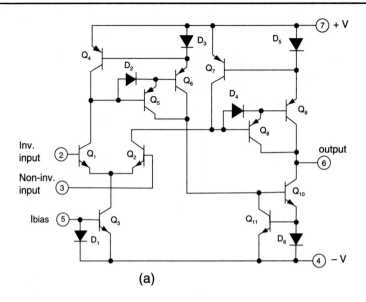

(a)

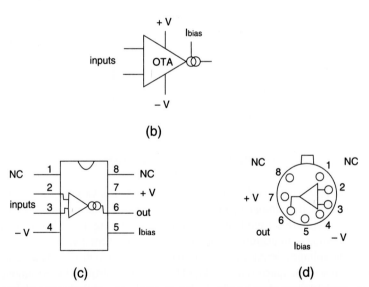

(b)

(c)   (d)

FIGURE 7-2 Operational transconductance amplifier (OTA): (a) schematic diagram; (b) symbol; (c) mini-DIP package; (d) plug-in package T0-99, T0-100 or T0-5.

rent would be 1000 μA or 1 mA. Notice how the collector and base are connected together for Q_1. In effect, it becomes a diode, as shown in Figure 7-3b. The input current, I_{in}, is equal to $i_{C1} + i_{B1} + i_{B2}$ for a total of 1010 μA or 1.01 mA. The output current through Q_2 is equal to 1000 μA or 1 mA, which is very close to the input current and is, therefore, said to be a mirror of the input current. The current mirror circuit symbol is shown in Figure 7-3c.

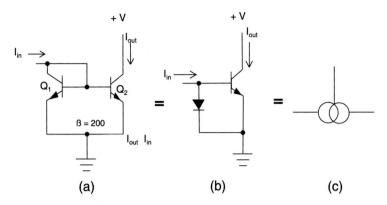

FIGURE 7-3 Basic current mirror circuit: (a) Q_1 and Q_2 must be matched transistors; (b) equivalent circuit; (c) circuit symbol.

When two current mirror circuits are connected together as shown in Figure 7-4, they generate a differential output current through an external load. The *source circuit* is connected between a positive voltage supply and the output.

The *sink circuit* is connected between a negative voltage supply or ground and the output. The current through the load resistor is the difference between the source current and the sink current, $I_{out} = I_{source} - I_{sink}$.

An OTA can be made to operate like a conventional voltage-amplifying op amp by

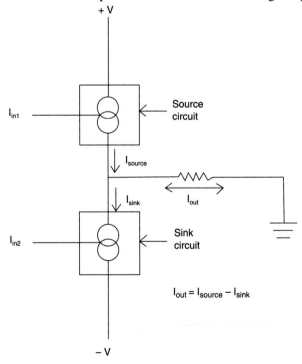

FIGURE 7-4 Two current mirrors connected together.

connecting a suitable load resistor to its output terminal so that the output current is converted into a proportional voltage.

All of the major operating parameters of the OTA are adjustable and depend on the value of the input bias current (I_{bias}). The I_{bias} range is from 0.1 µA to 1000 µA or 1 ma with a corresponding gm range from 0.2 µmho to 20000 µmhos. Therefore, an I_{bias} of 500 µA would produce a gm of about 10000 µmhos. The maximum output current is equal to I_{bias} and the total operating current of the op amp is twice the I_{bias} value. Since the I_{bias} can be as low as 0.1 µA, the total current would be 0.2 µA making the device ideal for micropower applications.

7-1-2-1 Calculating R_{bias}

Setting I_{bias} is determined by an external resistor, R_{bias}, connected to pin 5 as shown in Figure 7-5. Once the value I_{bias}, (500 µa), has been decided upon, R_{bias} can be calculated, applying Ohm's law, using the formula:

$$R_{bias} = \frac{(+V) - (-V) - (0.7V)}{I_{bias}}$$

The total voltage in this case is the difference between +12 V and –12 V less 0.7 V (the forward voltage drop across D_1 as shown in Figure 7-2a).

$$R_{bias} = \frac{(+V) - (-V) - 0.7V}{I_{bias}}$$

$$= \frac{(+12) - (-12) - 0.7}{500 \times 10^{-6}}$$

$$= \frac{24 - 0.7}{500 \times 10^{-6}}$$

$$= \frac{23.3}{500 \times 10^{-6}}$$

$$= 46600\Omega \quad \text{or} \quad 47k\Omega$$

Since $I_{out} = I_{bias}$, the output voltage can now be calculated, which is determined by R_L and can be found by the formula

$$V_{out} = I_{out} \times R_L$$

$$= 500\mu a \times 10k\Omega$$

$$= 500 \times 10^{-6} \times 10 \times 10^3$$

$$= 5000 \times 10^{-3}V \quad \text{or} \quad 5V$$

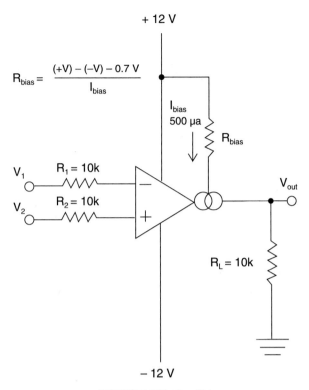

$$R_{bias} = \frac{(+V) - (-V) - 0.7\,V}{I_{bias}}$$

FIGURE 7-5 Finding Rbias.

7-1-2-2 OTA Schmitt Trigger Circuit

Since the I_{bias} of the OTA can be controlled, it is often called a *programmable op amp*. The advantage of programming or controlling the parameters of the OTA become apparent when applied to practical circuits. Figure 7-6 shows how the OTA 3080 can be constructed to produce a Schmitt trigger circuit.

When V_{out} is high, a positive reference voltage (V_{ref}), is present at the noninverting input, $V_{ref} = I_{bias} \times R_L$. The voltage drop across R_L is the V_{ref}. When V_{in} exceeds the value of V_{ref}, the op amp switches the output low. Now the V_{ref} is the same value, but of the opposite or negative polarity. When V_{in} falls below this value, the op amp will switch the output back to the positive polarity.

To set the desired V_{ref}, you must first decide on the value of I_{bias}. In this case $I_{bias} = 106$ μA with the use of R_{bias} at 220 kΩ. Let's choose V_{ref} to be 5 V. The value of R_L can be found from the formula:

$$R_L = \frac{V_{ref}}{I_{bias}}$$

$$= \frac{5\,V}{106\mu A}$$

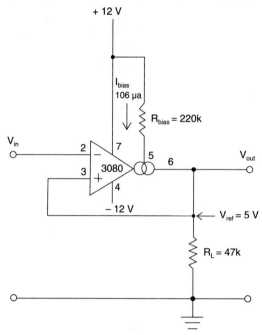

FIGURE 7-6 OTA Schmitt trigger circuit.

$$= \frac{5}{106 \times 10^{-6}}$$

$$= 47,169\Omega \quad \text{or} \quad \approx 47\text{k}\Omega$$

7-1-2-3 OTA Micropower Amplifier

The 3080 OTA can be used successfully as a micropower amplifier, as shown in Figure 7-7. The object of this circuit is to achieve the largest V_{out} with the least amount of power expended. If I_{bias} is set as 50 µA, then the entire circuit will consume about 150 µA. The voltage gain A_v, is determined by the ratio of R_1/R_2, as with a conventional op amp. However, the gain equation is only valid when the value of R_L is infinite. Any external load less than infinite appears in parallel with R_2 and lessens the output impedance of the op amp which in turn reduces V_{out}.

An OTA can be used as a voltage-controlled oscillator (IVCO), voltage-controlled amplifier (VCA), or voltage-controlled filter (VCF).

Other OTA 3080 IC characteristics are given below.

Characteristic	Parameters
Supply voltage range	+2 to +15 V or +4 to +30 VDC
MAX power dissipation	125 mW
MAX differential input voltage	+15 V

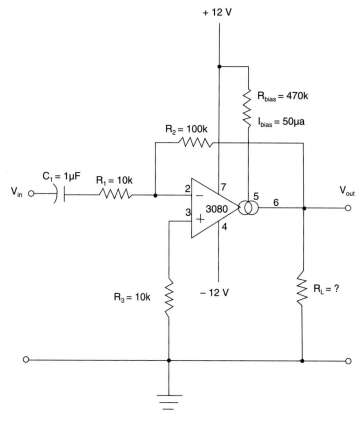

FIGURE 7-7 Micropower inverting AC amplifier.

Characteristic	Parameters
MAX input signal current	1 mA
MAX amplifier bias current	2 mA
Forward transconductance, gm	10 to 100,000 μmho
Open loop bandwidth	2 MHz
Unity-gain slew rate	50 V/μs
Common-mode rejection ratio	110 dB typical
Output short-circuit duration	Indefinite

7-1-3 CURRENT-DIFFERENCING AMPLIFIER

Another type of op amp that utilizes current mirror circuits is the current-differencing amplifier, also called the *Norton op amp*. A *current-differencing amplifier (CDA)* is an amplifier that has a voltage output proportional to the difference between the currents applied to the two input terminals. The ability of an op amp to provide an output that swings both positive and negative is not always desirable or necessary, and the required bipolar power supply increases the complexity and cost of equipment. External resistors can be used to bias conventional op amps using a single-ended power supply, as we saw in Chapter 5. However, op amps designed to operate from a single-ended power supply with the minimum of external components are most desirable. One of the most popular CDAs that were designed to operate from a single-ended power supply is the LM3900, shown in Figure 7-8.

The LM3900 contains four identical op amps, each having the circuit shown in Figure

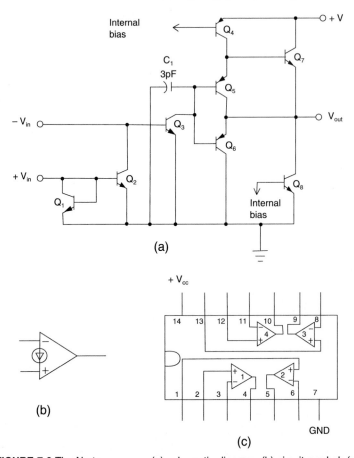

FIGURE 7-8 The Norton op amp: (a) schematic diagram; (b) circuit symbol; (c) LM 3900 14-pin DIP-IC.

7-8a. The term *quad* is applied to ICs that contain four separate circuits, although there is one + Vcc connection and one ground connection that supply all of the op amps.

Transistors Q_1 and Q_2 form the current mirror circuit, which is driven by the non-inverting input, and the mirror current is drawn from the inverting input. The base current of Q_1 is equal to the input current at the inverting input minus the input current at the non-inverting input. Transistors $Q_3 - Q_6$ are the high voltage gain stage with Q_4 being a high impedance active load. The output is taken from the emitter circuit of Q_7 and Q_8 is the high impedance active load. This arrangement forms an emitter-follower circuit at the output. The internal bias for the active loads of all op amps is developed from components built into the IC.

The symbol for the Norton amplifier is shown in Figure 7-8b. The current source symbol between the inputs implies the current-mode of operation.

The pin identification for the LM3900 is shown in Figure 7-8c. Notice the direction of the op amps and how their inputs and outputs are connected to the respective pins.

The main 3900 IC characteristics are given below.

Characteristic	Parameters
Supply voltage range	4 – 36 VDC
MAX power dissipation	570 mW
MAX input currents, I_{in+} or I_{in-}	20 mA
Input bias current	30 nA typical
Open loop voltage gain	2800 typical
Slew rate, Positive output swing	0.5V/μs
Slew rate, Negative output swing	20V/μs
Unity gain bandwidth	2.5 MHz
MAX output voltage swing	+V – 0.7 V
Output short-circuit duration	Continuous

7-1-3-1 Biasing the Norton Op Amp

Unlike a conventional op amp, which does not require any special biasing to be useful, the CDA must take biasing into consideration. There are several methods in which the CDA can be biased: single-supply biasing, fixed-voltage biasing (positive or negative), and a resistive divider from the output to one of the inputs of the op amp. As an example, let's consider the simplest method, single-supply biasing.

Assume we want an inverting amplifier with a maximum output swing. In a conventional op-amp circuit the output voltage swings plus and minus about a zero reference point called the quiescent voltage (V_Q). To obtain a maximum output voltage swing with a single-supply voltage, the circuit must be biased so that the V_Q is one half of V_{CC}, $V_Q = +V_{CC}/2$.

With single-supply biasing, a single resistor (R_2), is used between +Vcc and the non-inverting input, as shown in Figure 7-9. The input transistors are shown to help explain how the biasing is accomplished. In order to obtain the current mirror effect at the inputs, the feedback current, I_F, which flows into the inverting input, will attempt to be equal to the non-inverting input current, I_{in+}. In this situation the current flowing through R_F and R_2 is the same value. However, the voltage drop across R_2 Will be $+V_{CC} - 0.6$ V (the voltage drop of the EB junction of Q_2), or 11.4 V, while the voltage drop across R_F is V_Q, or one half of $+V_{CC} - 0.6$ V(the voltage drop across the EB junction of Q_3) or 5.7 V.

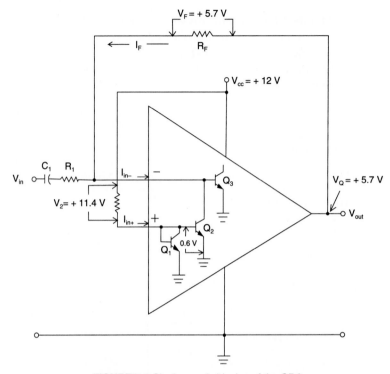

FIGURE 7-9 Single supply biasing of the CDA.

We now have objectives with which to work

$V_F = V_Q = V_{CC} - 0.6$ V/2 $= 12$ V $- 0.6$ V/2 $= 5.7$ V
$V_2 = V_{CC} = 0.6$ V $= 12$ V $- 0.6$ V $= 11.4$ V
Also, $V_F = V_2/2$

The input current to the noninverting input is usually held at about 10 μA in order to obtain a good match for the mirror current, therefore, $I_{in+} = 10$ μA. The value of R_2 can now be calculated

$$R_2 = \frac{V_{CC} - 0.6\text{V}}{I_{in+}} = \frac{12 - 0.6\text{V}}{10 \times 10^{-6}\text{A}} = 1.14\text{M}\Omega$$

Since $I_{in+} = I_F$, we can solve for R_F

$$R_F = \frac{V_F}{I_F} = \frac{5.7\text{V}}{10 \times 10^{-6}\text{A}} = 570 \times 10^3 \Omega \qquad \text{or} \qquad 570\text{k}\,\Omega$$

The stage gain can be found as with conventional op amp circuits, $A_\upsilon = -R_F/\,R_1$, or R_1

$= R_F/A_v$. If we desire a gain of 10, then

$$R_1 = \frac{R_F}{A_v} = \frac{570 \times 10^3}{10} = 57 \times 10^3 \qquad \text{or} \qquad 57\,\text{k}\Omega$$

Since these values are difficult to find in common carbon-type resistors, we could approximate the values of the resistors and obtain the following, $R_F = 560$ kΩ, $R_1 = 56$ kΩ, and $R_2 = 1.2$ MΩ.

7-1-3-2 The CDA as a Comparator

The LM 3900 IC is particularly suited for comparators that require a single supply voltage. Instead of the output swinging positive and negative, as with a conventional op amp comparator, the CDA comparator can switch from ground to a selected supply voltage and back to ground again, or vice versa. The CDA comparator is quite simple, with only two input resistors, as shown in Figure 7-10.

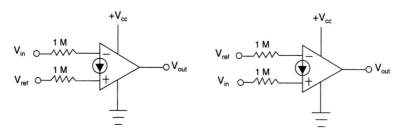

FIGURE 7-10 CDAs used as comparators: (a) negative going output; (b) positive going output.

The V_{ref} voltage sets the threshold at which the comparator switches its output. The V_{in} voltage is the active input voltage that is being sensed. If V_{in} is below V_{ref}, the output of the CDA will be in a specified state. When V_{in} rises above V_{ref}, the output will switch to the opposite state. Either input can be used for V_{ref}, with the other input being used for V_{in}. A positive-voltage or negative-voltage supply can be used and connected as shown.

In Figure 7-10a, the noninverting input is used for V_{ref} and the inverting input for V_{in}. When V_{in} is less than V_{ref}, V_{out} equals approximately $+V_{CC}$. When V_{in} rises above V_{ref}, V_{out} switches to about 0 V or ground.

In Figure 7-10b, V_{ref} is at the inverting input and V_{in} is at the noninverting input. When V_{in} is less than V_{ref}, V_{out} equals about 0 V. When V_{in} is above V_{ref}, V_{out} switches to about $+V_{CC}$.

CDA comparators can be wired to use a negative voltage power supply and operate in a similar manner. Comparators are very useful in digital-to-analog converters and in analog-to-digital converters. Their output must change very rapidly when the input voltage V_{in} changes through a reference voltage.

SECTION 7-2 TERMINOLOGY EXERCISE

Write a brief definition for the following terms:
1. OTA

2. Current mirror circuit
3. Source circuit
4. Sink circuit
5. I_{bias}
6. R_{bias}
7. Programmable op amp
8. CDA
9. Norton op amp
10. Quad

SECTION 7-3 PROBLEMS AND EXERCISES

1. Give the major advantage of a JFET-input-type op amp.
2. Name the type of op amp that converts a voltage change at the inputs to a voltage change at the output.
3. Name the type of op amp that converts a voltage change at the inputs to a current change at the output.
4. Name the type of op amp that converts a current change at the inputs to a voltage change at the output.
5. Referring to Figure 7-5, if the dual power supply is +15 V, and I_{bias} is chosen as 500 µA, find R_{bias}.
6. Referring to Figure 7-6, if the reference chosen is at 3.5 V, find the value of R_L.
7. What happens to the output voltage in the circuit shown in Figure 7-7 when the value of R_L decreases?
8. Referring to Figure 7-9, if +V_{CC} = +9 V and I_{in+} = 10 µA find the value of R_F and R_2 with V_Q set for +V_{CC}/2.
9. Referring to problem 8, find the value of R_1 for a gain of 50.
10. Explain in your own words the operation of the comparators shown in Figure 7-10.

SECTION 7-4 EXPERIMENTS

EXPERIMENT 7.1 CDA AC INVERTING AMPLIFIER

Objective:
To demonstrate how a CDA op amp can be used as an inverting amplifier.
Introduction:
The CDA must be externally biased with resistor R_2. The two input currents will equal each other. If one input current changes, the output of the op amp will change in an attempt to keep the two input currents equal. It is desirable to have the output quiescent voltage, V_Q, set at one half of +V_{CC} in order to achieve the maximum undistorted output voltage waveform. For this reason, R_F is chosen to be one half the value of R_2. The gain of the stage is determined by the ratio of R_F/R_1. Capacitor C_1 blocks any DC voltage component from the audio generator circuit, which could upset the biasing of the circuit.
Required Components:
1 39-kΩ resistor at 0.5 W (R_1)
1 750-kΩ resistor at 0.5 W (R_F)
1 1.2-MΩ resistor at 0.5 W (R_2)
1 0.1-µF capacitor at 15 WVDC (C_1)

1 LM-3900 CDA op-amp IC
1 breadboard for constructing circuit
   miscellaneous wires

Test Procedure:

1. Construct the circuit shown in Figure 7-11.
2. Apply power to the circuit.
3. Using a voltmeter, measure the voltage drop across R_2 and record here. _____
4. Calculate V_Q and record here. _____
5. Using a voltmeter, measure V_Q and record here. _____
6. Calculate A_v and record here. _____
7. Using an audio signal generator and oscilloscope, apply a sine wave signal to V_{in} that is 1 kHz at 0.5 V p-p.
8. Measure the output signal with an oscilloscope and record here. _____ V p-p
9. Divide the input signal into the output signal to establish the actual circuit gain.
10. Compare the calculated gain of the circuit to the actual gain measured.

QUESTIONS FOR FIGURE 7-11

1. Resistor _____ establishes the bias on the CDA amplifier.
2. Resistors _____ and _____ determine the stage gain of the amplifier.
3. The actual gain of the circuit was _____ .

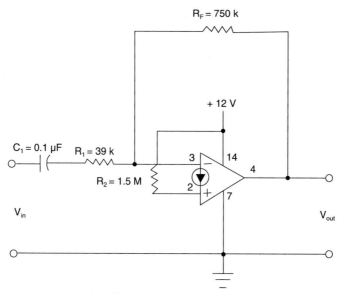

FIGURE 7-11 CDA AC inverting amplifier.

EXPERIMENT 7-2 CDAS USED AS COMPARATORS

Objective:

To show how CDA comparators operate from a single supply voltage source.

Introduction:

The LM3900 IC can operate over a power supply range of 4 to 36 VDC. It can be matched to several types of circuits and standard electronic systems. In this experiment, you will see how simple comparators perform from a +5 V power supply that might be used with 7400-series digital circuits.

Required Components:

1 220-Ω resistor at 0.5 W (R_6)

1 2.2-kΩ resistor at 0.5 W (R_2)

1 3.3-kΩ resistor at 0.5 W (R_1)

1 10-kΩ linear potentiometer (R_3)

2 1-MΩ resistor at 0.5 W (R_4, R_5)

1 LM-3900 IC

1 breadboard for constructing circuit

miscellaneous wires

Test Procedure:

1. Construct the circuit shown in Figure 7-12.
2. Place the wiper of R_3 at ground potential.
3. Record the condition of LED$_1$ here. _____
   What is the condition of V_{out}, high or low?
4. Using a voltmeter, measure V_{out} and record here. _____
5. Adjust R_3 until the LED changes states.
   Record the condition of the LED here. _____
6. Using a voltmeter measure V_{out} and record here. _____
7. Exchange the left-hand side of resistors R_4 and R_5, so that the inverting input has V_{ref} and the wiper of R_3 (V_{in}) is applied to the noninverting input.
8. Place the wiper of R_3 at ground potential.
9. Record the condition of LED$_1$ here. _____
   What is the condition of V_{out}, high or low?
10. Using a voltmeter measure V_{out} and record here. _____
11. Adjust R_3 until the LED changes states. Record the condition of the LED here.
   _____
12. Using a voltmeter measure V_{out} and record here. _____

QUESTIONS FOR FIGURE 7-12

1. When V_{in} is at the inverting input, and this voltage increases above V_{ref}, the output will go _____ .
2. When V_{in} is at the noninverting input, and increases above V_{ref}, the LED will turn _____ .

SECTION 7-5 SUMMARY POINTS

1. The main advantage of a JFET-input op amp is the extremely high input impedance.
2. A JFET op amp also has low bias currents, low offset currents, and low noise currents.
3. An operational transconductance amplifier is a variable-gain voltage-to-current amplifier.
4. The OTA is also referred to as a programmable op amp.
5. A current mirror circuit is a circuit that will produce an in-phase current of similar value as the input current applied to it.
6. The I_{bias} current of the OTA must be set externally by a bias resistor.
7. A source circuit connects an output or other part of a circuit to the voltage supply.
8. A sink circuit connects an output or other part of a circuit to the ground potential.

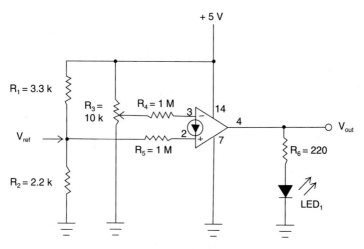

FIGURE 7-12 CDA as a comparator to match 7400 series digital circuits.

9. A current-differencing amplifier has current mirror circuits.
10. The CDA will produce an output voltage proportional to the difference between the currents applied at the inputs.
11. The CDA amplifier also has its bias current set by an external resistor.
12. The CDA amplifier is often referred to as a Norton op amp.
13. Quad means four and refers to four op amps in a single package.

SECTION 7-6 SELF-CHECKING QUIZ

Circle the correct answer for each of the following questions.
1. If a specific gain of an op amp was needed, you could use:
   a. A CDA
   b. An OTA
   c. A JFET-input op amp
   d. None of the above
2. When the output of an op amp is pulled toward ground, the conducting circuit is referred to as the:
   a. Mirror circuit
   b. Source circuit
   c. Sink circuit
   d. Bias circuit
3. An op amp that is excellent for use in micropower applications is the:
   a. OTA
   b. CDA
   c. JFET-input op amp
   d. All of the above
4. The op amp that produces an output voltage proportional to the difference of the currents at its inputs is the:
   a. OTA
   b. JFET-input op amp

c. CDA

d. None of the above

5. An op amp which is normally used with a single-ended power supply is the:

a. OTA

b. JFET-input op amp

c. CDA

d. None of the above

6. The op amp which produces a proportional output current with respect to a voltage difference at its inputs is the:

a. OTA

b. JFET-input op amp

c. CDA

d. None of the above

7. A current mirror circuit:

a. produces an output current twice as large as the input current

b. produces an out-of-phase output current of the same value as the input current applied to it

c. is seldom used in op amps

d. produces an in-phase output current very close to the value of input current applied to it

8. If it is desired to have the maximum output swing from a Norton op amp, you bias the quiescent output, V_Q, so that it would be:

a. $2 + V_{CC}$

b. $2/+V_{CC}$

c. $+V_{CC}/2$

d. None of the above

9. If the output of an op amp is pulled up toward $+V_{CC}$, the conducting circuit is referred to as the:

a. Mirror circuit

b. Source circuit

c. Sink circuit

d. Bias circuit

10. An op amp that produces an output voltage proportional to the difference of the voltage at its inputs is the:

a. OTA

b. JFET-input op amp

c. CDA

d. None of the above

(Answers at back of book)

CHAPTER 8

BASIC OP-AMP CIRCUIT DESIGN

Many op-amp circuits evolve from simple basic design procedures. Most of the formulas needed for basic design have been covered in the preceding chapters. This chapter will provide practical, easy-to-follow, step-by-step design procedures for some basic op-amp circuits. The results of the design techniques can be proven with the test procedures given in Section 1-4 and other sections of the book.

A standard glossary of definitions, which will be used throughout each circuit design procedure, is given below.

V_{in}—DC input voltage
V_{out}—DC output voltage
I_{in}—DC input current (current through source)
I_{out}—DC output current (current through load)
v_{in}—AC peak-to-peak input signal voltage
v_{out}—AC peak-to-peak output signal voltage
i_{in}—AC peak-to-peak input signal current (current through source)
i_{out}—AC peak-to-peak output signal current (current through load)
A_V—DC voltage gain
A_I—DC current gain
A_v—AC peak-to-peak voltage gain
A_i—AC peak-to-peak current gain
R_S—source resistance
R_L—load resistance
R_{in}—input resistance
R_F—feedback resistance
All other R's numbered as needed by circuit
C_{in}—input capacitance
C_{out}—output capacitance
Z_{in}—input impedance
Z_{out}—output impedance
$+V$—positive power-supply voltage
$-V$—negative power-supply voltage

Certain design procedures are common to all design problems and do not have to be repeated for each circuit. These procedures include:

1. *Selecting a ± power supply.* Make sure that the required V_{out} is about 2 V less than the ±V used. Choose the proper ± power supply required or desired for each application. (Example: $+V = +15$ V, $v_{out} = +13$ V; $-V = -15$ V, $v_{out} = -13$ V.)
2. *Using test equipment for design verification.* The design circuit problems in this chapter can be accurately tested with the same type of equipment listed in Chapter 1.

3. *Offset null adjusting.* With circuits requiring a high degree of accuracy, offset null adjustments should be made according to Experiment 1-9 or 1-11.

4. *Selecting the proper op amp.* Choose an op amp that has the required open-loop gain, slew rate, and frequency response for the designed circuit.

DESIGN 8-1 COMPARATOR CIRCUITS

Op-amp comparator circuits are used to clamp large-output DC voltage levels with the use of smaller DC control voltages. The input control voltages may be positive or negative, which clamp the output voltage at zero or some specific positive or negative level. Section 2-1-1 shows one method of utilizing comparators. These design examples will show another method using clamping diodes.

8-1-1 Basic Positive-Clamped Comparator

Referring to Figure 8-1, the diode in the feedback loop causes the circuit to respond in the open-loop mode for positive input levels and in the closed-loop mode for negative input levels. A reference voltage ($-V_{ref}$) is compared through R_1 with the variable V_{in}, through R_2. The voltage waveforms show the results for a desired clamping level of +2 V. When V_{in} is below +2 V, V_{out} is approximately +0.5 V (the forward voltage drop of the diode). When V_{in} reaches the desired clamping level, V_{out} changes states and swings to approximately –13 V ($-V_{sat}$). V_{ref} can be any voltage greater than V_{in} up to the $-V$ supply.

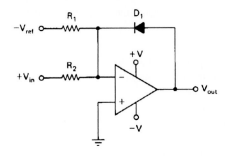

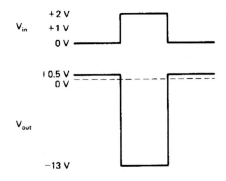

FIGURE 8-1 Positive-clamping level comparator (negative output).

DESIGN PROCEDURES

1. Choose R_1 (typically 100 kΩ).
2. Select V_{in} (desired input clamping level).
3. Calculate

$$R_2 = \frac{R_1 V_{in}}{-V_{ref}}$$

4. Construct the circuit and verify the design results.

If the diode in the feedback loop is reversed as shown in Figure 8-2, V_{out} will be positive when V_{in} is less than the clamped input level, and about – 0.5 V when V_{in} is greater than the clamped level.

8-1-2 Basic Negative-Clamped Comparator

The circuit shown in Figure 8-3 will respond to a negative input level. A reference voltage (+ V_{ref}) is compared through R_1 with the variable V_{in}, through R_2. The voltage waveforms show the results for a desired clamping level of – 2 V. When V_{in} is above – 2 V, V_{out} is about – 13 V (– V_{sat}). When V_{in} reaches the desired clamping level, V_{out} changes states and swings to about + 0.5 V (the forward voltage drop of the diode). + V_{ref} can be any voltage greater than V_{in} up to the + V supply.

DESIGN PROCEDURES

1. Choose R_1 (typically 100 kΩ).
2. Select V_{in} (desired input clamping level).
3. Calculate

$$R_2 = \frac{R_1 V_{in}}{+V_{ref}}$$

4. Construct the circuit and verify the design results.

If the diode in the feedback loop is reversed as shown in Figure 8-4, V_{out} will be about – 0.5 V when V_{in} is less than the clamped input level, and will be positive when V_{in} is greater than the clamped level.

8-1-3 Output Clamping to a Specific Level

The output of a comparator can be clamped to two specific levels with the use of a zener diode in the feedback loop, as shown in Figure 8-5. When V_{in} is below the input clamping level, zener diode is conducting in the zener region and V_{out} will equal + V_Z (the zener breakdown voltage). When V_{in} goes above the input clamping level, the zener diode is forward-biased like a normal diode and the output will be clamped to – 0.6 V.

If the zener diode in the feedback loop is reversed, V_{out} will be about +0.6 V when V_{in} is below the input clamping level. When V_{in} goes above the input clamping level, V_{out} will go

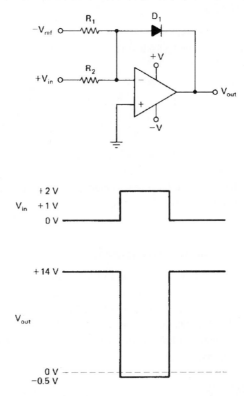

FIGURE 8-2 Positive-clamping level comparator (positive output).

to $- V_Z$.

DESIGN PROCEDURES

1. Choose R_1 (typically 100 kΩ).
2. Select V_{in} (desired input clamping level).
3. Calculate

$$R_2 = \frac{R_1 V_{in}}{-V_{ref}}$$

4. Choose a zener diode with the proper V_Z for the desired output clamping level.
5. Construct the circuit and verify the design results.

DESIGN 8-2 INVERTING AMPLIFIER CIRCUITS

Op-amp inverting amplifiers provide high voltage gain and high current gain. Basic inverting amplifiers are relatively easy to design and construct. These design examples will show how to determine voltage gain, current gain, and the values of related external components.

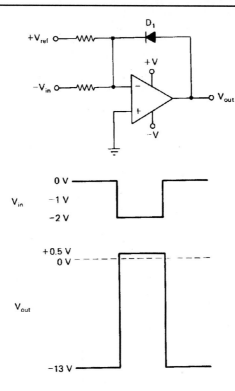

FIGURE 8-3 Negative-clamping level comparator (negative output).

8-2-1 Inverting DC Amplifier

The input impedance (in this case R_{in} of an inverting DC amplifier is usually chosen to be about 50 times greater than the source impedance, as shown in Figure 8-6. The output impedance is very low, typically 25 to 50 Ω, and is usually ignored in design.

DESIGN PROCEDURES

1. Determine or select V_{in}.
2. Determine source resistance R_s, either by direct ohmic measurement or using Ohm's Law $(R_s = V_{in}/I_{in})$.
3. Choose R_{in}. to be about 50 times greater than R_s.
4. Calculate the desired voltage gain by the formula $A_v = V_{out}/V_{in}$.(Remember that maximum V_{out} should be about 2 V less than the $\pm V$ supply.)
5. Calculate R_F from the formula $R_F = -A_v R_{in}$. (Disregard the minus sign in the calculations.)
6. Determine R_L by the following circuit to be driven, or arbitrarily select R_L for 2.2 kΩ.
7. Calculate V_{out} from the formula $V_{out} = (-R_F/R_{in})V_{in}$.
8. Calculate I_{in} from the formula $I_{in} = V_{in}/(R_S + R_{in})$.
9. Calculate I_{out} from the formula $I_{out} = V_{out}/R_L$.
10. Calculate A_I from the formula $A_I = I_{out}/I_{in}$.
11. Construct the circuit and verify the design results.

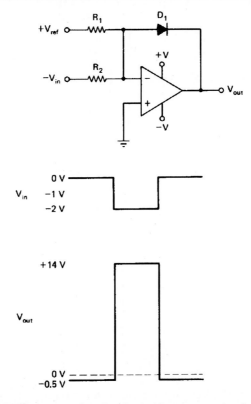

FIGURE 8-4 Negative-clamping level comparator (positive output).

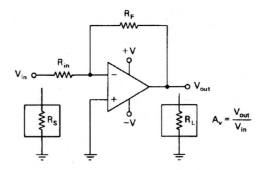

FIGURE 8-6 Inverting DC amplifier.

8-2-2 Inverting AC Amplifier

A capacitor is used at the input of an inverting amplifier when amplifying AC signals, as shown in Figure 8-7. This capacitor C_1 blocks any DC component from the source, thus minimizing any distortion of the AC signal at the output. Design procedures for an AC inverting amplifier are similar for those of the DC inverting amplifier, except that C_1 must be calcu-

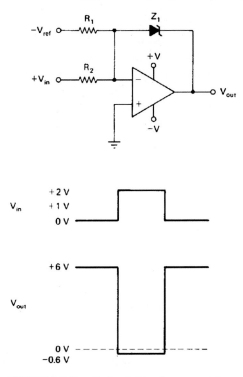

FIGURE 8-5 Specific lavel-clamping comparator.

lated for a specific break frequency.

Noise may be a problem, so remember that the larger R_F is made, the more susceptible the circuit is to noise.

Depending on the op amp chosen and the circuit gain selected, the output signal voltage will roll off rapidly beyond the bandwidth for a given circuit. (Refer to Section 1-4-11.)

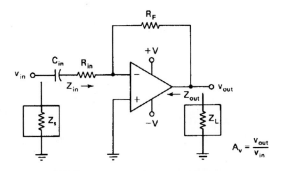

FIGURE 8-7 Inverting AC amplifier.

DESIGN PROCEDURES

1. Determine or select v_{in}.

2. Determine source impedance Z_s.
3. Choose R_{in} to be about 50 times greater than Z_s.
4. Calculate desired voltage gain by the formula $A_v = v_{out}/v_{in}$.
   (Remember that maximum v_{out} should be about 2 V less than the $\pm V$ supply.)
5. Calculate R_F from the formula $R_F = -A_v R_{in}$. (Disregard the minus sign in the calculations.)
6. Determine Z_L by the following circuit to be driven, or arbitrarily select Z_L for 2.2 kΩ.
7. Calculate vout from the formula $v_{out} = -(R_F/R_{in})v_{in}$.
8. Calculate i_{in} from the formula $i_{in} = v_{in}/(Z_s + R_{in})$.
9. Calculate i_{out} from the formula $i_{out} = v_{out}/R_L$
10. Calculate A_i from the formula $A_i = i_{out}/i_{in}$.
11. Calculate C_1 for a break frequency of 10 Hz from the formula

$$C_1 = \frac{1}{2\pi (Z_s + R_{in})f_c}$$

12. Construct the circuit and verify the design results.

8-2-3 Basic Two-Stage Cascaded Amplifier

Designing a basic two-stage cascaded inverting amplifier, as shown in Figure 8-8, is simply a matter of designing the gain of each stage. The important aspect to remember is not to have too much gain for each stage, since the total gain (A_{vT}) is equal to the first-stage gain (A_{v1}) times the second-stage gain (A_{v2}), or $A_{vT} = A_{v1} \times A_{v2}$.

Depending on the specific application, the first stage may be required to have more gain than the second stage. However, in this design problem the first stage could have the lower gain to reduce the input noise level. As an example, if $v_{in} = 10$ mV and $A_{v1} = 10$, v_{out} of OP-1 would be 100 mV. If $A_{v2} = 100$, then v_{out} of OP-2 would be 10 V. Total circuit gain is $A_v = v_{out}/v_{in} = 10$ V/0.01 V = 1000.

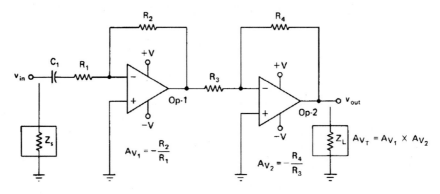

FIGURE 8-8 Two-stage inverting amplifier.

DESIGN PROCEDURES

1. Determine or select v_{in}.
2. Determine source impedance Z_s.

3. Choose R_1 to be about 50 times greater than Z_s.
4. Calculate C_1 for a break frequency of 10 Hz from the formula

$$C_1 = \frac{1}{2\pi \, (Z_s + R_1) f_c}$$

5. Choose the desired voltage gain for the first stage, A_{v1}.
6. Calculate R_2 from the formula $R_2 = -A_{v1}R_1$. (Disregard the minus sign in the calculations.)
7. Choose R_3 to be about 10 times greater than the output impedance of OP-1. (This impedance is about 25 to 50 Ω.)
8. Select the desired voltage gain for the second stage, A_{v2}. (Make sure that A_{vT} will not cause distortions of v_{out} for the v_{in} of step 1.)
9. Calculate R_4 from the formula $R_4 = -A_{v2}R_3$. (Disregard the minus sign in the calculations.)
10. Determine Z_L by the following circuit to be driven, or arbitrarily select Z_L for 2.2 kΩ.
11. Calculate the total circuit gain from the formula $A_{vT} = A_{v1} \times A_{v2}$.
12. Calculate v_{out} from the formula $v_{out} = A_{vT}v_{in}$. (Remember that v_{out} should be about 2 V less than the $\pm V$ supply.)
13. Calculate i_{in} from the formula $i_{in} = v_{in} /(Z_s + R_1)$.
14. Calculate i_{out} from the formula $i_{out} = v_{out}/Z_L$.
15. Calculate A_i from the formula $A_i = i_{out}/i_{in}$.
16. Construct the circuit and verify the design results.

DESIGN 8-3 NONINVERTING AMPLIFIER CIRCUITS

Op-amp noninverting amplifiers provide high voltage gain and high current gain together with high input impedance. Basic noninverting amplifiers are also relatively easy to design and construct. These design examples will show how to determine voltage gain, current gain, and the values of related external components.

8-3-1 Noninverting DC Amplifier

The input impedance of a noninverting DC amplifier is very large, usually a few megaohms. For this reason the circuit is capable of accommodating most source impedances without appreciable loading. The gain of the non-inverting amplifier, as shown in Figure 8-9, is dependent on the same resistance ratio as the inverting amplifier.

DESIGN PROCEDURES

1. Determine source resistance R_s.
2. Choose R_{in} to equal R_s.
3. Determine or select V_{in}.
4. Calculate desired voltage gain from the formula $A_v = V_{out}/V_{in}$.?(Remember that maximum V_{out} should be about 2 V less than the $\pm V$ supply.)
5. Calculate R_F from the formula $R_F = A_v R_{in} - R_{in}$.
6. Determine R_L by the following circuit to be driven, or arbitrarily select R_L for 2.2 kΩ.
7. Calculate V_{out} from the formula $V_{out} = (1 + R_F/R_{in})V_{in}$.

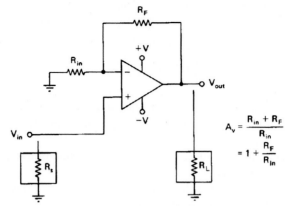

FIGURE 8-9 Non inverting DC amplifier.

8. Calculate I_{in} from the formula $I_{in} = V_{in}/(R_s + Z_{in})$. (Let $Z_{in} \approx 1\ M\Omega$.)
9. Calculate I_{out} from the formula $I_{out} = V_{out}/R_L$.
10. Calculate A_I from the formula $A_I = I_{out}/I_{in}$.
11. Construct the circuit and verify the design results.

8-3-2 Noninverting AC Amplifier

The input impedance of a noninverting amplifier is usually between 5 and 50 kΩ and is determined by R_1, as shown in Figure 8-10. Capacitor C_1 blocks any DC component from the source, thus minimizing any distortion of the AC signal at the output. Design procedures for an AC noninverting amplifier are similar for those of the DC noninverting amplifier, except that C_1 must be calculated for a specific break frequency.

Depending on the op amp chosen and the circuit gain selected, the output signal voltage will roll off rapidly beyond the bandwidth for a given circuit. (Refer to Section 1-4-11.)

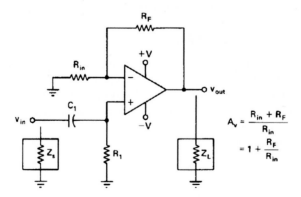

FIGURE 8-10 Noninverting AC amplifier.

DESIGN PROCEDURES

1. Choose R_1 between 5 and 50 kΩ.

2. Calculate C_1 from the formula

$$C_1 = \frac{1}{2\pi(Z_s + R_1)f_c}.$$

3. Choose R_{in} equal to R_1.
4. Determine or select v_{in}.
5. Calculate desired voltage gain by the formula $A_v = v_{out}/v_{in}$. (Remember that maximum v_{out} should be about 2 V less than the $\pm$V supply.)
6. Calculate R_F from the formula $R_F = A_v R_{in} - R_{in}$.
7. Determine Z_L by the following circuit to be driven, or arbitrarily select Z_L for 2.2 kΩ.
8. Calculate v_{out} from the formula $v_{out} = (1 + R_F/R_{in})v_{in}$.
9. Calculate i_{in} from the formula $i_{in} = v_{in}/(Z_s + R_1)$.
10. Calculate i_{out} from the formula $i_{out} = v_{out}/Z_L$.
11. Calculate A_i from the formula $A_i = i_{out}/i_{in}$.
12. Construct the circuit and verify the design results.

8-3-3 Basic Two-Stage Cascaded Noninverting Amplifier

Designing a basic two-stage cascaded noninverting amplifier, as shown in Figure 8-11 is accomplished by designing the gain of each stage. The total circuit gain is equal to the gain of the first stage times the gain of the second stage, $A_{vt} = A_{v1} \times A_{v2}$. As an example, if $A_{v1} = 11$ and $A_{v2} = 22$, $A_{vt} = 242$. If $v_{in} = 0.1$ V, the v_{out} of OP-1 would be 1.1 V and the v_{out} of OP-2 would be 24.2 V.

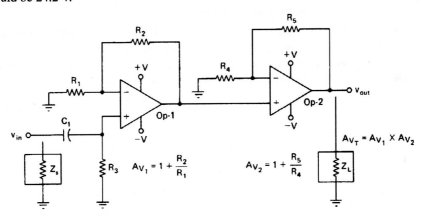

FIGURE 8-11 Two-stage noninverting amplifier.

DESIGN PROCEDURES

1. Determine or select v_{in}.
2. Choose R_3 between 5 and 50 kΩ.
3. Calculate C_1 from the formula

$$C_1 = \frac{1}{2\pi(Z_s + R_3)f_c}$$

4. Choose R_1 equal to R_3.
5. Choose the desired voltage gain for the first stage, A_{v1}.
6. Calculate R_2 from the formula $R_2 = A_{v1} R_1 - R_1$.
7. Choose R_4 equal to R_1.
8. Select the desired voltage gain for the second stage, A_{v2}. (Make sure that A_{vt} will not cause distortion of v_{out} for the v_{in} of step 1.)
9. Calculate R_5 from the formula $R_5 = A_{v2}R_4 - R_4$.
10. Determine Z_L by the following circuit to be driven, or arbitrarily select Z_L for 2.2 kΩ.
11. Calculate total circuit gain from the formula $A_{vt} = A_{v1} \times A_{v2}$
12. Calculate v_{out} from the formula $v_{out} = A_{vt}v_{in}$. (Remember that v_{out} should be about 2 V less than the ±V supply.)
13. Calculate i_{in} from the formula $i_{in} = v_{in}/(Z_s + R_3)$.
14. Calculate i_{out} from the formula $i_{out} = v_{out}/Z_L$.
15. Calculate A_i from the formula $A_i = i_{out}/i_{in}$.
16. Construct the circuit and verify the design results.

DESIGN 8-4 VOLTAGE-FOLLOWER CIRCUITS

Voltage followers are used to transfer signals from large impedances to small impedances while maintaining a gain of near unity. In other words, they are buffer or impedance-matching devices with controlled output voltage, but have the capability of current amplification.

8-4-1 Noninverting DC Voltage Follower

A basic noninverting DC voltage follower requiring no external components is shown in Figure 8-12. The input impedance is several megaohms, and the output impedance is about 25 to 50 Ω. Voltage gain will be approximately 1, with current gains usually less than 1000, depending on the source resistance and the load resistance.

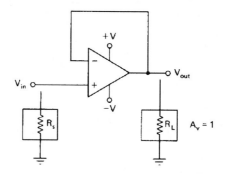

FIGURE 8-12 Noninverting DC voltage follower.

DESIGN PROCEDURES

1. Determine or select the required V_{in}.
2. Calculate A_v required from the formula $A_v = V_{out}/V_{in}$.
3. Calculate I_{in} from the formula $I_{in} = V_{in}/(R_1 + Z_{in})$. (Let $Z_{in} \approx 2$ MΩ.)

4. Calculate I_{out} from the formula $I_{out} = V_{out}/R_L$
5. Calculate A_I from the formula $A_I = I_{out}/I_{in}$.
6. Construct the circuit and verify the design results.

8-4-2 Noninverting AC Voltage Follower

The input impedance of a noninverting AC voltage follower, as shown in Figure 8-13, is determined by R_1. This resistor is typically selected to be 50 times greater than the source impedance (Z_s). Feedback resistor R_F is equal to R_1. Capacitor C_1 blocks any DC component from the source that may cause output distortion. The value of C_1 is determined by the desired frequency range.

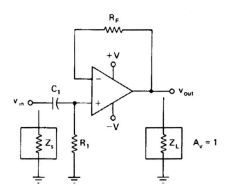

FIGURE 8-13 Noninverting AC voltage follower.

DESIGN PROCEDURES

1. Determine or select the required v_{in}.
2. Calculate the A_v required from the formula $A_v = v_{out}/v_{in}$.
3. Calculate C_1 from the formula

$$C_1 = \frac{1}{2\pi\sqrt{(Z_s + R_1)}f_c}.$$

(Choose for a break frequency of 10 Hz.)
4. Choose R_1 to be about 50 times greater than Z_s.
5. Choose R_F equal to R_1.
6. Calculate i_{in} from the formula $i_{in} = v_{in}/(Z_s + R_1)$.
7. Calculate i_{out} from the formula v_{out}/Z_L.
8. Calculate A_i from the formula $A_i = i_{out}/i_{in}$.
9. Construct the circuit and verify the design results.

8-4-3 Inverting DC Voltage Follower

An inverting DC voltage follower, as shown in Figure 8-14, is the same configuration as an inverting amplifier. Resistors R_{in} and R_F are equal, resulting in unity gain. The input impedance of this follower is much less than that of the noninverting follower and is dependent on R_{in}.

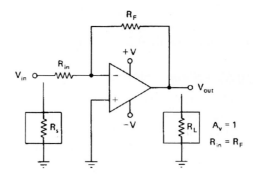

FIGURE 8-14 Inverting DC voltage follower.

DESIGN PROCEDURES

1. Determine or select V_{in}.
2. Calculate A_v from the formula $A_v = V_{out}/V_{in}$.
3. Choose R_{in} to be 50 times greater than R_s.
4. Choose R_F to equal R_{in}.
5. Calculate I_{in} from the formula $I_{in} = V_{in}/(R_s + R_{in})$.
6. Calculate I_{out} from the formula $I_{out} = V_{out}/R_i$.
7. Calculate A_I from the formula $A_I = I_{out}/I_{in}$.
8. Construct the circuit and verify the design results.

8-4-4 Inverting AC Voltage Follower

The inverting AC voltage follower shown in Fig. 8-15 is similar to the inverting DC voltage follower, except for C_1 which blocks the DC component from the source, thereby minimizing distortion at the output.

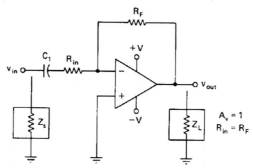

FIGURE 8-15 Inverting AC voltage follower.

DESIGN PROCEDURES

1. Determine or select v_{in}.
2. Calculate A_v from the formula $A_v = v_{out}/v_{in}$.
3. Calculate C_1 from the formula

$$C_1 = \frac{1}{2\pi\,(Z_s + R_{in})f_c}$$

(Choose for a break frequency of 10 Hz.)

4. Choose R_{in} to be 50 times greater than Z_s.
5. Choose R_F to equal R_{in}.
6. Calculate i_{in} from the formula $i_{in} = v_{in}\,/(Z_s + R_{in})$.
7. Calculate i_{out} from the formula $i_{out} = v_{out}/Z_L$.
8. Calculate A_i from the formula $A_i = i_{out}/i_{in}$.
9. Construct the circuit and verify the design results.

DESIGN 8-5 VOLTAGE-SUMMING-AMPLIFIER CIRCUITS

Op amp voltage-summing amplifiers are used for summing several input signals to provide a single output signal. The output signal may be a direct mathematical summation of the input signals or may include a determined amount of gain. With a direct mathematical summation, all of the input resistors and the feedback resistors are of the same value. Where gain is desired, the feedback resistor is made larger. The summing amplifier may be a scaling adder, where the input resistors are selected to provide different gains for each input. Summing amplifiers may be inverting or noninverting; however, the inverting type is less complex to design and easier to construct. If an in-phase signal is needed from an inverted summing amplifier, it is usually easier to add an inverting follower stage.

8-5-1 Inverting DC Summing Amplifier

The inverting DC summing amplifier shown in Figure 8-16 is a basic circuit that can be used for direct mathematical summation, with summation at a specific gain, or with scaling adder inputs. The design procedures for this circuit will cover all three aspects of its use.

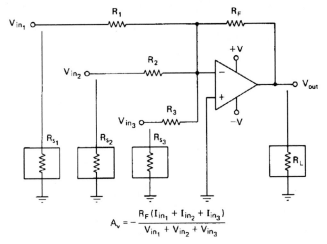

$$A_v = -\frac{R_F\,(I_{in_1} + I_{in_2} + I_{in_3})}{V_{in_1} + V_{in_2} + V_{in_3}}$$

FIGURE 8-16 Inverting DC summing amplifier.

DESIGN PROCEDURES

1. Determine or select V_{in_1}, V_{in_2}, and V_{in_3}.

2.   Calculate the A_v required from the formula

$$A_v = \frac{V_{out}}{V_{in_1} + V_{in_2} + V_{in_3}}$$

3.* A. *For direct mathematical summation, select*
     $R_1 = R_2 = R_3 = R_F$ (typically 10 to 25 kΩ)

   B. *For summation with gain, select*
      $R_1 = R_2 = R_3$ (typically 10 to 25 kΩ)

Select the proper step with respect to the type of summing amplifier you are designing. All other design steps apply to all three summing amplifiers.

   C. *For scaling adder input resistors, calculate*

$$R_1 = \frac{V_{in1}}{I_{in1}} - R_{s_1}$$

$$R_2 = \frac{V_{in_2}}{I_{in_2}} - R_{s_2}$$

$$R_3 = \frac{V_{in_3}}{I_{in_3}} - R_{s_3}$$

   Select $I_{in_1} = I_{in_2} = I_{in_3}$ (typically 0.1 mA).

4.* *Calculate I_{in} for direct mathematical summation or summation with gain from the formulas*

$$I_{in_1} = \frac{V_{in_1}}{R_{s_1} + R_1}$$

$$I_{in_2} = \frac{V_{in_2}}{R_{s_2} + R_2}$$

$$I_{in_3} = \frac{V_{in_3}}{R_{s_3} + R_3}$$

Select the proper step with respect to the type of summing amplifier you are designing. All other design steps apply to all three summing amplifiers.

5.   Calculate I_{out} from the formula $I_{out} = V_{out}/R_L$.
6.   Calculate A_I from the formula

$$A_I = \frac{I_{out}}{(I_{in_1} + I_{in_2} + I_{in_3})}$$

7.* *Calculate R_F for summation with gain and scaling adder inputs from the formula*

$$R_F = \frac{-A_\upsilon\,(V_{in_1} + V_{in_2} + V_{in_3})}{I_{in_1} + I_{in_2} + I_{in_3}}$$

(Disregard minus signs in making the calculations.)

*Select the proper step with respect to the type of summing amplifier you are designing. All other design steps apply to all three summing amplifiers.

8.   Construct the circuit and verify the design results.

8-5-2 Inverting AC Summing Amplifier

The inverting AC summing amplifier is similar to the inverting DC summing amplifier, except for the input capacitors, as shown in Figure 8-17. Follow the same design procedures given for the inverting DC summing amplifier and use the additional design procedures given below for the inverting AC summing amplifier.

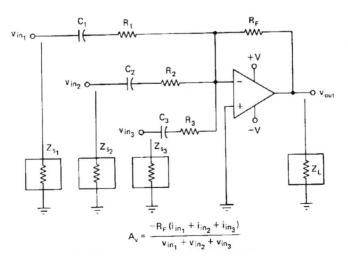

$$A_v = \frac{-R_F\,(i_{in_1} + i_{in_2} + i_{in_3})}{v_{in_1} + v_{in_2} + v_{in_3}}$$

FIGURE 8-17 Inverting AC summing amplifier.

ADDITIONAL DESIGN PROCEDURES

1. Use lowercase AC signal symbols, as shown in Figure 8-17.
2. The input resistors R_1, R_2, and R_3 for the direct mathematical summing and summing circuits with gain should be about 50 to 100 times greater than their source impedances.
3. Calculate C_1, C_2, and C_3 from the formulas

$$C_1 = \frac{1}{2\pi (R_{s_1} + R_1)f_c}$$

$$C_2 = \frac{1}{2\pi (R_{s_2} + R_2)f_c}$$

$$C_3 = \frac{1}{2\pi (R_{s_3} + R_3)f_c}$$

(f_c = 10 Hz, typically)

4. Construct the circuit and verify the design results.

DESIGN 8-6 DIFFERENTIAL AMPLIFIER CIRCUITS

Differential amplifiers are used where input voltage differences must be amplified. A differential amplifier has low voltage gain but high current gain. Both inputs are used and the circuit operation resembles that of a voltage comparator, except with controlled gain. The output will be inverted depending on the polarity of the inverting input with respect to the noninverting input.

8-6-1 Differential DC Amplifier

The differential DC amplifier shown in Figure 8-18 has input impedances of about 1 MΩ. The output impedance, as with most op amps, is between 25 and 50 Ω and is usually considered zero for design purposes. Input voltages are not critical and may be up to 70 to 80 percent of the ±V supply. The design procedures given are for symmetrical gain; however, other gains may be found from the formula

$$V_{out} = \left[\left(\frac{R_1 + R_3}{R_2 + R_3} \right) \left(\frac{R_3}{R_1} \right) \right] \times \left[\left(\frac{V_{in_2} - R_F}{R_1} \right) (V_{in_1}) \right]$$

DESIGN PROCEDURES

1. Determine or select V_{in_1} and V_{in_2}.
2. Select R_1 to be 50 times R_{s_1}.

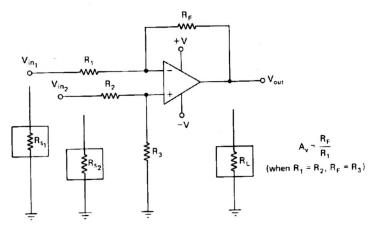

FIGURE 8-18 Differential DC amplifier.

3. Select R_2 to be equal to R_1.
4. Calculate A_v from the formula

$$A_v = \frac{V_{out}}{(V_{in_2} - V_{in_1})}$$

5. Calculate R_F from the formula $R_F = - A_v R_1$.
6. Select R_3 to equal R_F.
7. Calculate I_{in_1} from the formula

$$I_{in_1} = \frac{V_{in_1}}{R_{s_1} + R_1 + \dfrac{R_F Z_{in_1}}{R_F + Z_{in_1}}}$$

8. Calculate I_{in} from the formula

$$I_{in_2} = \frac{V_{in_2}}{R_{s_2} + R_2 + \dfrac{R_F Z_{in_2}}{R_F + Z_{in_2}}}$$

9. Calculate I_{out} from the formula $I_{out} = V_{out}/R_L$
10. Calculate A_I from the formula

$$A_I = \frac{I_{out}}{(I_{in_1} - I_{in_2})}$$

11. Construct the circuit and verify the design results.

8-6-2 Differential AC Amplifier

The differential AC amplifier is similar to the differential DC amplifier, except for the input capacitors, as shown in Figure 8-19. Follow the same design procedures given for the differential DC amplifier and use the additional design procedures given below for the differential AC amplifier.

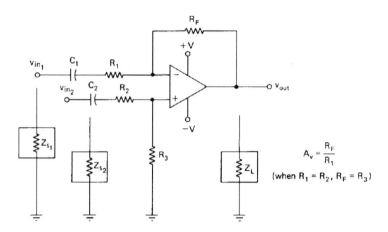

FIGURE 8-19 Differential AC amplifier.

ADDITIONAL DESIGN PROCEDURES

1. Calculate C_1 from the formula

$$C_1 = \frac{1}{2\pi\left[R_{s_1} + R_1 + \left(\dfrac{R_F Z_{in_1}}{R_F + Z_{in_1}}\right)\right]f_c}.$$

2. Calculate C_2 from the formula

$$C_2 = \frac{1}{2\pi\left[R_{s_2} + R_2 + \left(\dfrac{R_3 Z_{in_2}}{R_3 + Z_{in_2}}\right)\right]f_c}.$$

(f_c = 10 Hz, typically)

3. Construct the circuit and verify the design results.

DESIGN 8-7 SQUARE-WAVE-GENERATOR CIRCUIT

Using feedback capabilities, an op amp can produce a fairly stable oscillator circuit. The simplest oscillator circuit is the astable multivibrator, often referred to as a square-wave generator, as shown in Figure 8-20. Exact frequencies can be obtained by the proper selection of R_1 and C_1 , which provide an RC time constant that determines the desired frequency. Resistors R_2 and R_3 form a voltage divider whose ratio equals two time constants, which permits the frequency to be found by a simple formula.

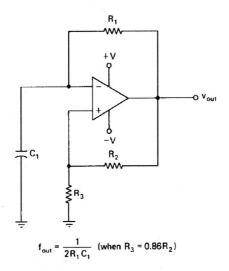

$$f_{out} = \frac{1}{2R_1C_1} \quad \text{(when } R_3 = 0.86R_2\text{)}$$

FIGURE 8-20 Square wave generator.

DESIGN PROCEDURES

1. Select R_1 (usually 100 kΩ).
2. Select R_2 equal to R_1.
3. Calculate R_3 from the formula $R_3 = 0.86\ R_2$.
4. Choose the desired frequency.
5. Calculate C_1 from the formula $C_1 = \frac{1}{2}\ fR_1$.
6. Construct the circuit and verify the design results.

CHAPTER 9

COLLECTION OF PRACTICAL OP-AMP CIRCUITS

This chapter presents a collection of practical op-amp circuits that will enable you to realize the versatility of the op amp. It is hoped that you may find some circuits in this chapter that will fit your particular application or that you will find satisfaction from the enjoyment of just constructing some of the circuits. Each circuit has a description of its use, theory of operation, and/or any related pertinent facts.

Special appreciation is given to Signetics Corporation, Fairchild Semiconductor Incorporated, and National Semiconductor Corporation for their contributions to this chapter.

SECTION 9-1 POWER-SUPPLY APPLICATIONS

9-1-1 Voltage Regulator

The op-amp voltage regulator shown in Figure 9-1 is a noninverting amplifier. This circuit is a positive voltage regulator with R_{in} and R_F determining the gain. The zener diode provides the reference voltage. The regulated output voltage for the values given is then $3 \times (+5)$ V = + 15 V. The output voltage to be regulated should be at least 2 V lower than the unregulated voltage from the power supply to keep the zener diode operating in its breakdown region.

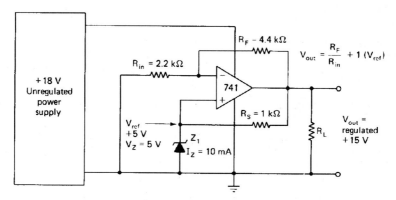

FIGURE 9-1 Op amp voltage regulator.

9-1-2 Dual-Tracking Op-Amp Power Supply

A dual-tracking op-amp power supply is shown in Figure 9-2. The positive voltage regulator is similar to the circuit in Figure 9-1. The positive output is fed to an inverting follower to produce the negative output voltage.

228

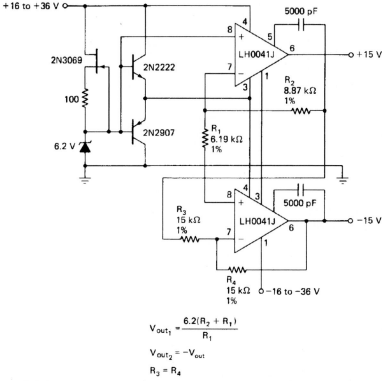

FIGURE 9-2 Dual tracking op-amp power supply. (Courtesy National Semiconductor Corp.)

9-1-3 Crowbar Overvoltage Protection

Some ICs cannot withstand overvoltage. The crowbar overvoltage protection circuit of Figure 9-3 is fast-acting to protect the load R_L against damaging effects of an overvoltage. The zener diode sets the inverting input at the reference +2.5 V. The trip adjust pot sets the noninverting input at +2.5 V. Differential input voltage is zero; therefore, the op-amp output is zero and the SCR is open. If the 5-V power supply increases, the voltage at the noninverting input increases. The output of the op amp increases, causing the SCR to fire. The SCR appears as a short around the load and activates the fuse, circuit breaker, or current limiter. When the trouble is cleared and the power supply is again at 5 V, the reset switch is used to disable the SCR, allowing full voltage to the load.

9-1-4 Crowbar Undervoltage Protection

In some applications it is desirable to shut down the power supply if the voltage level drops below a specific level. The circuit in Figure 9-4 is similar to the previous circuit except that the reference voltage is on the noninverting input. The trip adjust pot sets the inverting input at +2.5 V. Differential input voltage is zero, the op-amp output is zero, and the SCR is open.

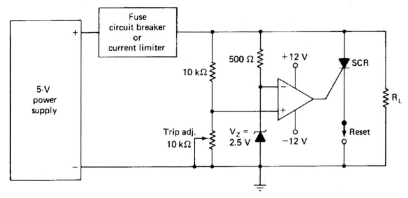

FIGURE 9-3 Crowbar overvoltage protection.

When the power-supply voltage drops below +5 V, the voltage at the inverting input decreases, the op-amp output voltage increases, and the SCR fires. Voltage across the load decreases and an alarm or indicator is activated. The capacitor across the zener diode temporarily holds the noninverting input at a lower voltage than the inverting input during initial turn-on. This allows the zener diode time to conduct and prevents false triggering the SCR.

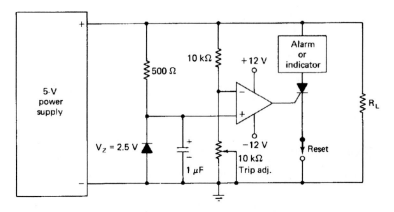

FIGURE 9-4 Crowbar undervoltage protection.

SECTION 9-2 AMPLIFIERS

9-2-1 Bridge Amplifier

A bridge amplifier is a balanced circuit where the input resistances are equal. The feedback resistor may be any value, depending on the desired output. All resistors in Figure 9-5 are considered equal, and with the bridge balanced, V_{out} is zero. A transducer is used as a sensing element and can be used in various parts of the circuit as shown. The transducer is a device that con-verts an environmental change to a resistive change and could be a thermistor, photodetector, or strain gauge. When the resistance of the transducer changes (ΔR_T), an output voltage will occur. The formulas give the V_{out} for each circuit.

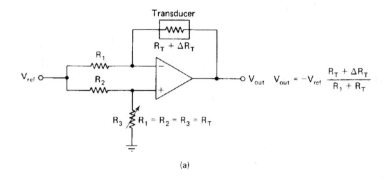

(a)

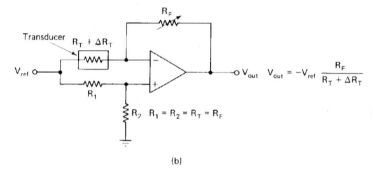

(b)

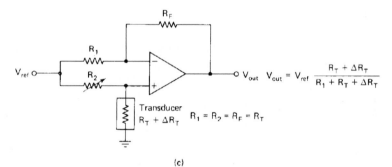

(c)

FIGURE 9-5 Bridge amplifier.

9-2-2 Buffer Amplifier

A practical buffer amplifier for isolating circuits is shown in Figure 9-6. If the 1 MΩ causes any noise problems, the resistors could be reduced, but should be at least 10 times the impedance of the circuit feeding the buffer.

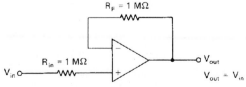

FIGURE 9-6 Buffer amplifier.

9-2-3 Current Amplifier

An op amp can detect a small current and amplify it up to its maximum output current, with the circuit shown in Figure 9-7. The amount of load current depends on the factor $F = R_2/R_1$ and the input current I_s. As an example, the small current from a solar cell can be amplified to cause the LED to give a visible indication. If $I_s = 0.1$ mA, then by the formula, $I_L = 10.1$ mA. The LED might be part of an optical coupler that could drive a higher-voltage circuit.

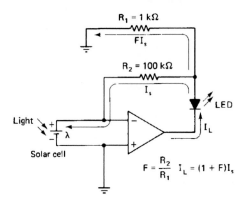

FIGURE 9-7 Current amplifier.

9-2-4 Lamp Driver

A simple op-amp lamp driver is shown in Figure 9-8. The output of the op amp has to be positive-going for an NPN transistor to turn on and be of sufficient amplitude to drive the transistor into saturation. Resistor R_1 should be selected to limit the base current below the recommended maximum rating. The transistor I_c must have a maximum higher rating than the current that the lamp will draw.

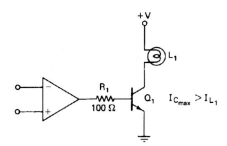

FIGURE 9-8 Lamp driver.

9-2-5 LED Driver

An op amp can drive an LED directly, provided that its maximum output current is not exceeded. A positive-going output will turn on the LED in Figure 9-9a, while a negative-going output will turn on the LED of Figure 9-9b. The value of R_1 is determined by the formulas given, where V_{FLED} is the forward voltage drop of the LED and I_{FLED} is the desired forward current through the LED.

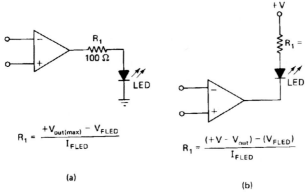

FIGURE 9-9 LED driver.

9-2-6 Photodiode/Phototransistor Amplifier

For normal operation the photodiode must be reversed-biased, as shown in Figure 9-10a. Light striking the diode will decrease its resistance, causing the output voltage to increase in a negative direction. The same action will occur for the phototransistor amplifier shown in Figure 9-10b. The output voltage depends on the current drawn through R_F. Considering the basic gain formula $A_\upsilon = -R_F/R_{in}$, when R_{in} decreases, A_υ increases.

9-2-7 Photoresistor Amplifier

Similar to the two previous circuits, a photoresistor amplifier is shown in Figure 9-11. Again, the varying input resistance will cause a varying output.

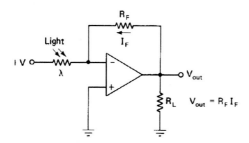

FIGURE 9-11 Photoresistor amplifier.

9-2-8 Solar-Cell Amplifier

The solar-cell amplifier shown in Figure 9-12 is similar to the previously mentioned circuits, although its operation is somewhat different. The solar cell sees essentially a short circuit, since the inverting input is at virtual ground. The current generated by the solar cell is proportional to the light striking its surface. The current is converted to voltage by R_F as given by the formula. (Also see Section 9-2-3.)

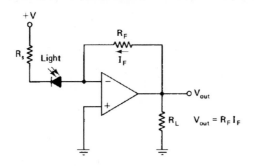

(a) Photodiode amplifier

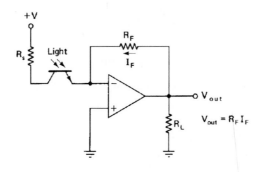

(b) Phototransistor amplifier

FIGURE 9-10 Photodiode/phototransistor amplifier: (a) photodiode amplifier; (b) phototransistor amplifier.

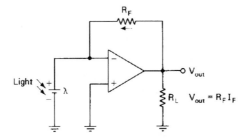

FIGURE 9-12 Solar cell amplifier.

9-2-9 Power-Booster Amplifier

Although the available power from op amps is usually sufficient, there are occasions when more power-handling capability is needed. The power-booster amplifier shown in Figure 9-13 is capable of driving moderate loads. The complementary transistor push-pull circuit will allow the output voltage to swing nearly to the maximum ± voltage supply and be able to handle more current. (See Figures 5-29 and 5-30.)

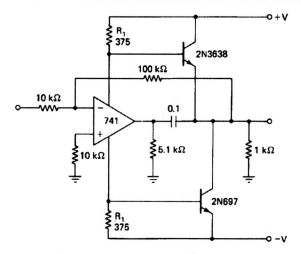

All resistor values are in ohms.

FIGURE 9-13 Power booster amplifier. (Permission to reprint granted by Signetics Corp., a subsidiary of U.S. Philips Corp., 811 E. Arques Ave., Sunnyvale CA 94086

9-2-10 Phono Amplifier

The basic phono amplifier shown in Figure 9-14 uses an LM 380 power audio amplifier IC that will produce at least 2.5 W (rms) of power. A large signal output cartridge is required. This circuit uses a voltage-divider volume control and a high-frequency rolloff tone control. If the circuit tends to oscillate, a 2.7-Ω resistor in series with a 0.1-μF capacitor can be connected from pin 8 to ground.

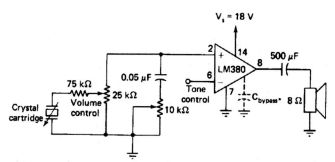

FIGURE 9-14 Phono amplifier. (Courtesy National Semiconductor Corp.)

9-2-11 Squaring Amplifier

A squaring amplifier, as shown in Figure 9-15, is often needed to amplify low-level signals provided by variable-reluctance transducers. The output incorporates symmetrical hysteresis above and below the zero level, which improves noise immunity. The large input resistors provide a low-pass filter due to the "Miller effect" input capacitance of the amplifier. With the values shown, the output is approximately 0.3 V p-p.

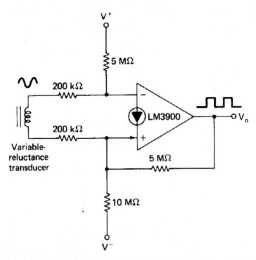

FIGURE 9-15 Squaring amplifier. (Courtesy National Semiconductor Corp.)

9-2-12 Instrumentation Amplifier

A very popular circuit used for precision measurement and control is the instrumentation amplifier shown in Figure 9-16. This commonly used configuration consists of two input voltage followers feeding a differential amplifier. The followers exhibit extremely high input impedance with low error and allow the source (driving) resistances to be unbalanced by over 10 kΩ. The differential amplifier provides gain and high common-mode rejection. The gain is determined by R_6 to R_2 when $R_2 = R_5$ and $R_6 = R_7$

9-2-13 Audio Bridge Amplifier

Twice the output power can be obtained from the circuit shown in Figure 9-17. The LM 377 amplifiers are useful in this configuration to drive floating loads, such as loudspeakers or servo motors. The load impedance may be 8 or 16 Ω. Response of this circuit is 20 Hz to 160 kHz, with an output power up to 4 W.

9-2-14 DC Servo Amplifier

Op amps are extremely effective in controlling servo motors, as shown in Figure 9-18. The polarity and amplitude of the input voltage determine the speed and direction of the motor. This circuit has a gain of 10.

9-2-15 AC Servo Amplifier

An AC servo amplifier utilizes two op amps, as shown in Figure 9-19. The noninverting inputs are held at a DC reference voltage, while V_{in} controls the speed and direction of the motor.

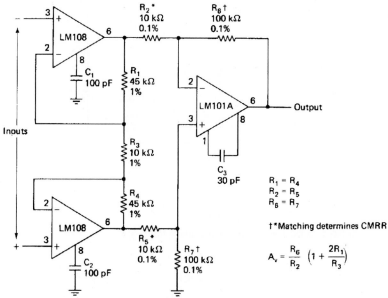

FIGURE 9-16 Differential input instrumentation amplifier with high common mode rejection. (Courtesy National Semiconductor Corp.)

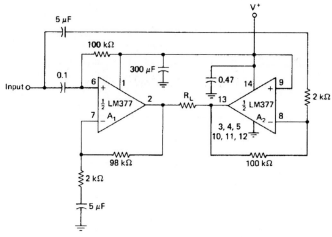

FIGURE 9-17 Audio bridge amplifier. (Courtesy National Semiconductor Corp.)

9-2-16 Absolute-Value Amplifier

The circuit in Figure 9-20 generates a positive output voltage for either polarity of input. For positive signals, it acts as a noninverting amplifier, and for negative signals, as an inverting amplifier. For the best accuracy, input signals should be greater than 1 V.

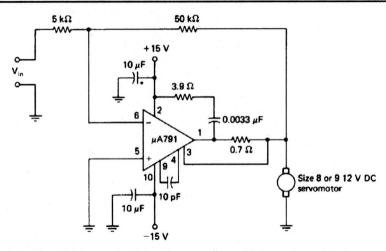

FIGURE 9-18 DC servo amplifier. (Courtesy National Semiconductor Corp.)

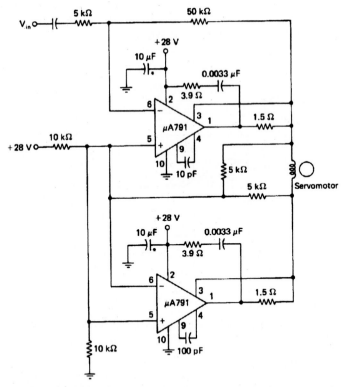

FIGURE 9-19 AC servo amplifier. (Courtesy National Semiconductor Corp.)

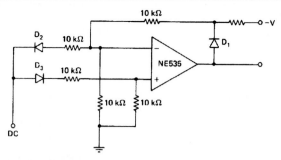

All resistor values are in ohms.

FIGURE 9-20 Absolute valve amplifier. (Permission to reprint granted by Signetics Corp., a subsidiary of U.S. Philips Corp., 811 E. Arques Ave., Sunnyvale CA 94086.)

SECTION 9-3 OSCILLATORS AND WAVEFORM GENERATORS

9-3-1 Phase-Shift Oscillator

The phase-shift oscillator in Figure 9-21 operates on positive feedback applied to the inverting input. The output is shifted about 60° across each resistor-capacitor combination ($3 \times 60°$ = 180°)—hence, oscillation.

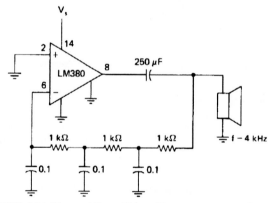

FIGURE 9-21 Phase shift oscillator. (Courtesy National Semiconductor Corp.)

9-3-2 Easily Tuned Sine-Wave Oscillator

The circuit shown in Figure 9-22 generates a sine wave by filtering a square wave. Two separate outputs are available. A voltage comparator produces the square wave, which is fed to the tuned circuit of the filter amplifier, producing only the sine-wave fundamental. The sine wave is fed to the comparator to produce the square wave. A total frequency of below 20 Hz to above 20 kHz can be produced in graduated ranges by changing C_1 and C_2 as shown in the table. Resistor R_3 sets the desired frequency within the range. Resistor R_8 is the amplitude adjustment. The zener diode stabilizes the square wave being fed to the filter.

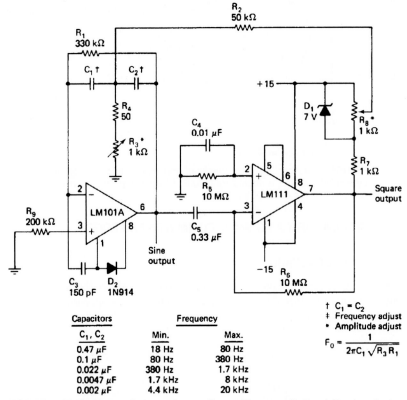

Capacitors	Frequency	
C_1, C_2	Min.	Max.
0.47 μF	18 Hz	80 Hz
0.1 μF	80 Hz	380 Hz
0.022 μF	380 Hz	1.7 kHz
0.0047 μF	1.7 kHz	8 kHz
0.002 μF	4.4 kHz	20 kHz

† $C_1 = C_2$
‡ Frequency adjust
* Amplitude adjust

$$F_0 = \frac{1}{2\pi C_1 \sqrt{R_3 R_1}}$$

FIGURE 9-22 Easily tuned sine wave oscillator. (Courtesy National Semiconductor Corp.)

9-3-3 Crystal Oscillator

The circuit in Figure 9-23 shows how a crystal oscillator is constructed using an LF111 voltage comparator. Similar to a standard square-wave generator, this circuit exhibits greater stability with positive feedback via the crystal.

9-3-4 Simple Staircase Generator

The circuit shown in Figure 9-24 is a basic integrator. The incoming pulses charge up the capacitor, causing the output to go in a negative direction. When the charge on the capacitor reaches the firing potential of the UJT emitter, the UJT conducts and discharges the capacitor. The output returns to zero and, with the UJT now open, the process starts over.

9-3-5 Free-Running Staircase Generator/Pulse Counter

An improved staircase generator using a quad op amp LM3900 IC is shown in Figure 9-25. This circuit is self-generating and uses one of the op amps as a pulse generator which feeds the noninverting input of a difference integrator. The output is positive-going, which feeds a voltage comparator. When the charge on the capacitor fires the comparator, a one-shot multi--vibrator resets the difference integrator.

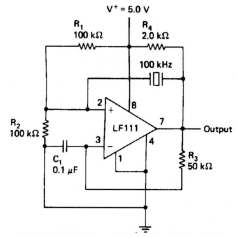

FIGURE 9-23 Crystal oscillator. (Courtesy National Semiconductor Corp.)

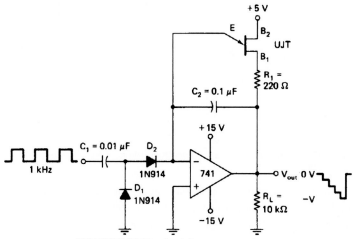

FIGURE 9-24 Simple staircase generator.

9-3-6 Digital-to-Analog Staircase Generator

Figure 9-26 shows a digital-to-analog converter circuit. A 7495 4-bit shift register is wired to produce a sequential counter whose outputs feed into an op-amp summing amplifier. The negative-going staircase output from the summing amplifier is fed to an inverting amplifier, producing a positive-going output with adjustable gain.

9-3-7 Monostable (One-Shot) Multivibrator

A positive-going-output one-shot multivibrator is shown in Figure 9-27a. Resistor R_2 keeps the output at zero in the quiescent state. A differentiated positive input pulse causes the output to switch to the positive voltage state where it is latched by R_5. When capacitor C_1 charges up to about $\frac{1}{4}$ of the +V supply, the circuit latches back to the quiescent state. The diode allows rapid retriggering.

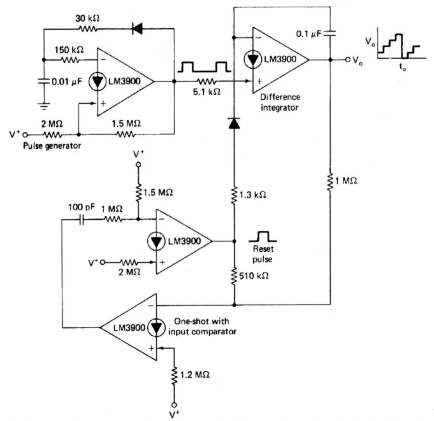

FIGURE 9-25 Free running staircase generator/pulse counter. (Courtesy National Semiconductor Corp.)

With slight modification the previous circuit can be used as a negative-going-output one-shot multivibrator, as shown in Figure 9-27b. Resistors R_2 and R_3 keep the inverting input essentially at ground, which forces V_{out} to the positive level. A differentiated negative input pulse causes the output to switch to zero. The output will remain low until C_1 discharges to about $\frac{1}{10}$ of the +V supply.

Moving the R_4C_2 network to the inverting input will allow the circuit to operate with a differentiated positive input pulse.

9-3-8 Schmitt Trigger

Op amps wired as voltage-level detectors perform exceptionally well as Schmitt triggers, shown in Figure 9-28. The inverting circuit in Figure 9-28a has a normally high output. When the voltage on the inverting input reaches the high trip point, the output goes to zero. When the input voltage is reduced to the low trip point, the output again goes high. The difference between these two input voltages is the circuit hysteresis. Resistors R_F and R_B, together with the +V supply, determine the high and low trip-point voltages.

The noninverting circuit shown in Figure 9-28b is similar except that the output is normally low. The input voltage is fed to the noninverting input and the hysteresis is somewhat

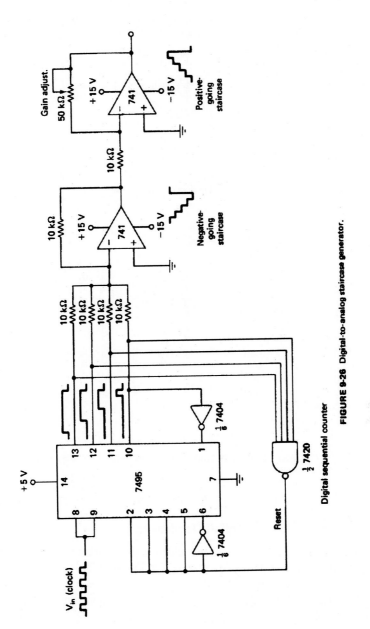

FIGURE 9-26 Digital-to-analog staircase generator.

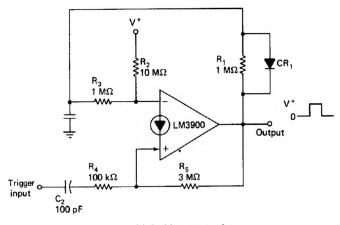

(a) Positive output pulse

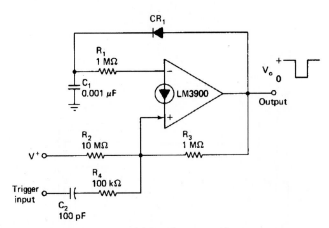

(b) Negative output pulse

FIGURE 9-27 Monostable (one-shot) multivibrator. (Courtesy National Semiconductor Corp.)

greater.

9-3-9 Programmable Unijunction Oscillator

If a diode and an RC charging circuit are added to the Schmitt trigger, a programmable unijunction oscillator can be produced, as shown in Figure 9-29. The output is normally high, and when the input voltage reaches the high trip point, the output falls to about zero and capacitor C discharges through the diode. The low trip point must be larger than +1 V to guarantee that the V_F of the diode plus the output voltage is less than the low trip-point voltage. Resistor R_2 can be made smaller to increase the discharge current.

9-3-10 Frequency Doubler

The simple frequency doubler shown in Figure 9-30 is very similar to the absolute-value

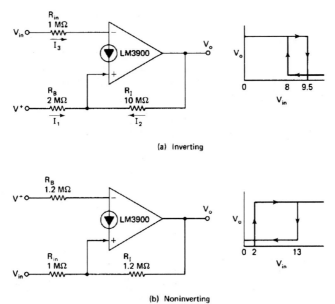

(a) Inverting

(b) Noninverting

FIGURE 9-28 Schmitt trigger. (Courtesy National Semiconductor Corp.)

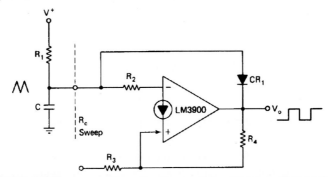

FIGURE 9-29 Programmable unijunction oscillator. (Courtesy National Semiconductor Corp.)

amplifier of Figure 9-20. A sine-wave signal input results in a full-wave rectified output at twice the frequency of the input signal. Other waveform-shaping circuits can follow this circuit to restore the pure sine wave or create other desired waveforms.

9-3-11 Pulse Generator

The pulse generator shown in Figure 9-31 is similar to a square-wave generator except that the output goes from zero to a positive level instead of from positive to negative. Frequency of the pulse generator is primarily determined by the capacitor, R_1, and the V_{ref}.

9-3-12 Two-Tone Alarm Circuit

Given in Figure 9-32 is a novel but very effective alarm circuit. Two tones are heard alter-

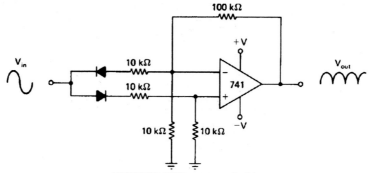

FIGURE 9-30 Frequency doubler.

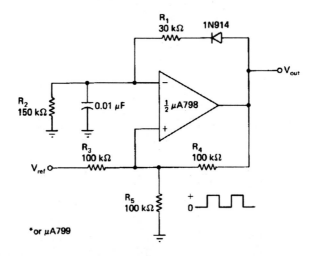

FIGURE 9-31 Pulse generator. (Courtesy National Semiconductor Corp.)

nately at the speaker. Varying C_2 changes the pitch of the two tones, while changing C_1 will change the switching time. Musically speaking, the two tones approximate tonic and minor third notes.

SECTION 9-4 SIMPLE TEST INSTRUMENTS

9-4-1 Sensitive Low-Cost DC Voltmeter

The voltmeter shown in Figure 9-33 has extremely high input impedance. Using the LF536 op amp as a noninverting amplifier, the input impedance for ranges up to 10 V is 5000 MΩ. The 30-V range has an input impedance of 30 MΩ, while the 100-V range has 100 MΩ. The diodes protect the input against overvoltage; however, the meter cannot withstand more than a 50 percent overload.

9-4-2 Wide-Band AC Voltmeter

The circuit shown in Figure 9-34 is a wide-band AC voltmeter capable of measuring AC signals as low as 15 mV up to 5 V at frequencies from 100 Hz to 500 kHz. Altering the values of

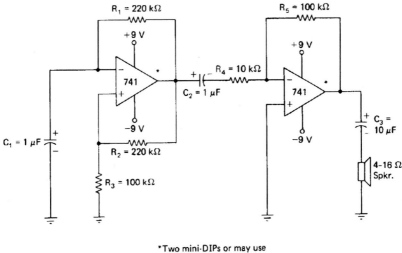

*Two mini-DIPs or may use
a dual op-amp 747 IC

FIGURE 9-32 Two-tone alarm circuit.

resistors R_1 through R_6 changes the full-scale sensitivity of the meter (R ≈ V_{in}/100 μA).

9-4-3 Triple-Range Ohmmeter

The ohmmeter shown in Figure 9-35 uses a linear scale, needs no calibration, and is insensitive to power-supply voltage. Resistances can be measured from 0 to 100 kΩ in three ranges. Like a standard voltmeter, resistance values are measured from a full-scale standpoint. A germanium diode protects the meter from overcurrent when the test points are left open.

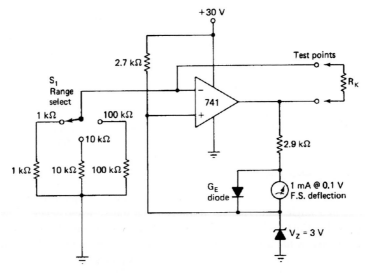

FIGURE 9-35 Triple range ohmmeter.

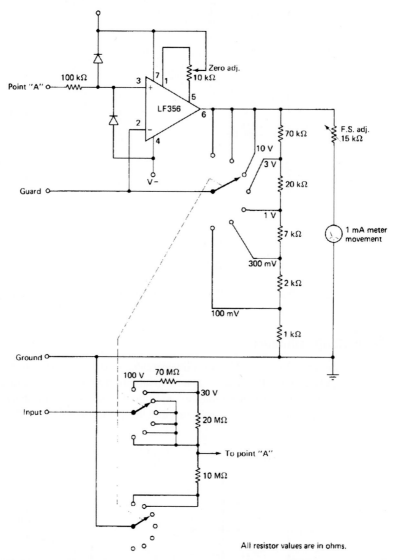

FIGURE 9-33 Sensitive low cost DC voltmeter. (Permission to reprint granted by Signetics Corp., a subsidiary of U.S. Philips Corp., 811 E. Arques Ave., Sunnyvale, CA 94086.)

9-4-4 Audio Circuit Tester

Shown in Figure 9-36 is a simple audio signal injector and signal tracer circuit that can be constructed in a single unit. The signal injector is a square-wave generator with a frequency selection ranging from 50 Hz to 20 kHz in four steps. An output adjustment can be set for the desired amplitude of the injected signal. The frequency ranges may be used to check the frequency response of a circuit. The signal tracer is a standard inverting amplifier with adjustable gain.

The injector is set for the desired frequency and amplitude, and the signal is then

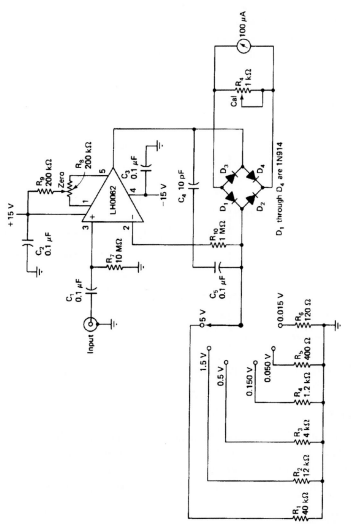

FIGURE 9-34 Wide band AC voltmeter. (Courtesy National Semiconductor Corp.)

249

entered into the circuit via the signal injector probe. The signal tracer probe is then used to trace the signal through the circuit under test at various points to locate the faulty section or stage.

SECTION 9-5 LOGIC CIRCUITS

9-5-1 AND Gate

The three-input AND gate shown in Figure 9-37 will give a high or 1 output ($\approx + 15$ V) when all of the inputs are high or 1 ($+ 15$ V). Resistors R_1 and R_2 set the $+ 375$-mV reference at the inverting input. In the "off state" this voltage forces the output to zero. When all inputs are high, sufficient current is drawn through R_6 to develop a voltage drop at the noninverting input that is more positive than the reference voltage. The output will now be in the "on state" or high potential.

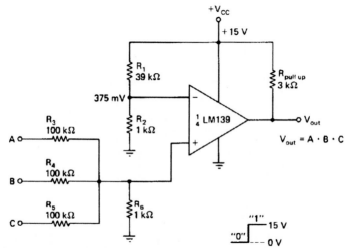

FIGURE 9-37 AND gate. (Courtesy National Semiconductor Corp.)

9-5-2 OR Gate

The OR-gate circuit in Figure 9-38 is identical to the AND gate in Figure 9-37 except that R_1 has been increased to set the reference voltage at the inverting input to 75 mV. The output will go high ($\approx +15$ V) when any one of the inputs goes high ($+15$ V). A 1 at any input will develop enough voltage drop across R_6 (≈ 150 MV) to cause the op amp to switch states.

9-5-3 NAND Gate

Unlike the op-amp AND gate, which uses an active noninverting input, the NAND gate uses the inverting input, as shown in Figure 9-39. Any low input (0 V) will cause the output to go high ($\approx +15$ V). When all diode inputs are high, the inverting input is pulled high and the output is low. When any one diode input is low, the inverting input is pulled low and the op-amp output goes high.

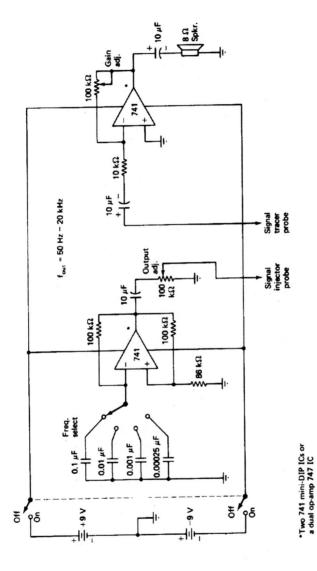

FIGURE 9-36 Audio circuit tester.

*Two 741 mini-DIP ICs or
a dual op-amp 747 IC

251

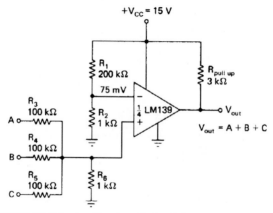

FIGURE 9-38 OR gate. (Courtesy National Semiconductor Corp.)

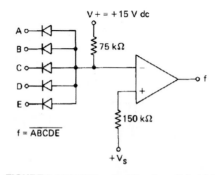

FIGURE 9-39 NAND gate. (Courtesy Fairchild Camera & Instruments Corporation.)

9-5-4 NOR Gate

Like the NAND gate in Figure 9-39, the NOR gate shown in Figure 9-40 uses an active inverting input. The output will go high ($\approx+15$ V) only if all inputs are low (0 V). If any input is high (+15 V), there will be sufficient positive voltage at the inverting input to cause the output to remain low. When all resistor inputs are low, the inverting input will be low, causing the op amp to switch to the high state.

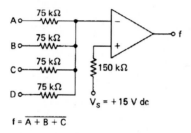

FIGURE 9-40 NOR gate. (Courtesy Fairchild Camera & Instruments Corporation.)

9-5-5 RS Flip-Flop

The RS flip-flop shown in Figure 9-41 is considered "off" when Q output is low (0 V) and its complementary $\overline{Q}$ output is high (+15 V). The low output of Q is fed back to the inverting input of OP-1, which keeps Q output high. Similarly, the high output of $\overline{Q}$ is fed back to the inverting input of OP-2, which keeps Q output low. When a positive-going pulse is placed at the set input, Q output goes high and $\overline{Q}$ output goes low. The circuit will remain in this "on" state due to the latching action previously mentioned. A positive-going pulse on the reset input will force the flip-flop to the original "off" state. This logic circuit can be used as a temporary memory device.

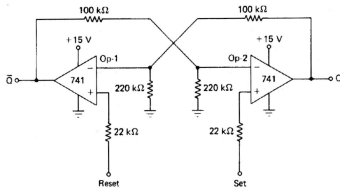

FIGURE 9-41 RS flip-flop.

SECTION 9-6 MISCELLANEOUS CIRCUITS

9-6-1 Feedforward Frequency Compensation

Op amps without internal frequency compensation can be modified with a simple feedforward network, as shown in Figure 9-42, which will increase the slew rate and bandwidth of a particular circuit. Feedforward frequency compensation is achieved by connecting C_1 from the input to one of the compensation terminals. High frequencies are bypassed around the initial stages of the op amp, thereby increasing the bandwidth. Capacitor C_2 is used for stability in the feedback loop. The diode may be added to increase slew rate with fast-rising inputs. This added high-frequency gain will also amplify high-frequency noise, and frequency-compensation techniques should only be applied to the extent required by the circuit.

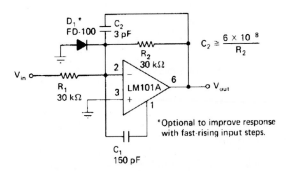

FIGURE 9-42 Feed-forward frequency compensation. (Courtesy National Semiconductor Corp.)

9-6-2 One-IC Intercom

The LM 38ON-8 (mini-DIP) IC can be used to construct a simple but effective intercom system, as shown in Figure 9-43. Both speakers are used as input (microphone) and output (speaker) transducers. The listen/talk switches are momentary (spring-return) types wired in the normal position, as shown. Operate only one switch at a time to prevent feedback oscillations. The audio output transformer steps up the speaker signal (when in the talk mode) to provide sufficient voltage to drive the amplifier. Resistor R_1 serves as a volume control. Capacitive filtering may be needed to prevent oscillation from occurring, depending on the distance of the remote speaker.

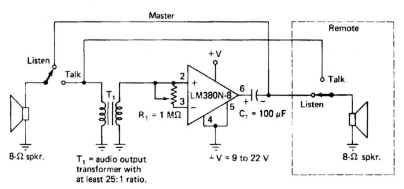

FIGURE 9-43 One IC intercom.

9-6-3 Simulated Inductor (Gyrator)

An op amp can be used to simulate an inductor (sometimes referred to as a gyrator), as shown in Figure 9-44. This type of circuit may be used to eliminate inductors from filters and tuned circuits. Inductance is characterized by an increase in output when frequency increases, with the effective inductance being equal to $L \approx R_1 R_2 C_1$.

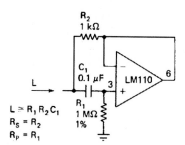

FIGURE 9-44 Simulated inductor (gyrator). (Courtesy National Semiconductor Corp.)

9-6-4 Op-Amp Tachometer

The basic op-amp tachometer shown in Figure 9-45a converts the input pulses to an average DC output via the *RC* averaging network. The output increases at a linear rate with an increase of input frequency. The resistor provides a discharge path for the capacitor to limit the integrating action. Therefore, the output voltage is directly proportional to the input frequency. A meter calibrated for RPM may be connected to the op-amp output.

A frequency-doubling tachometer, as shown in Figure 9-45b, reduces the ripple on the DC output voltage, which would result in a more precise meter indication. The operation of the circuit is to average the charge and discharge transient currents of the input capacitor, C_{in}. Resistor R_{in} converts the voltage pulses to current pulses and limits surge currents. Two current pulses are drawn from the RC averaging network for each cycle of the input frequency.

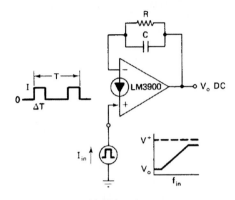

(a) Basic tachometer

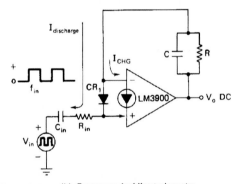

(b) Frequency-doubling tachometer

FIGURE 9-45 Op amp tachometer: (a) basic tachometer; (b) frequency doubling tachometer. (Courtesy National Semiconductor Corp.)

9-6-5 Low-Frequency Mixer

A frequency mixer that allows two input frequencies to produce a sum and a difference frequency is shown in Figure 9-46. Because a diode exists at the noninverting input of the LM3900, this op amp can be used for nonlinear signal processing. Filtering is accomplished by the 1-MΩ and 150-pF feed-back elements. The circuit has a gain of 10 with a corner frequency of 1 kHz. A signal with a larger amplitude can be placed at V_1 to serve as the local oscillator. The input diode is gated at this frequency (f_1). A smaller signal of a different frequency (f_2) is placed at V_2. The difference frequency ($f_2 - f_1$) is filtered from the resulting composite waveform and is present at the output. Relatively high frequencies can be applied at the inputs as long as the desired difference frequency is within the bandwidth capabilities of the amplifier and the RC low-pass filter.

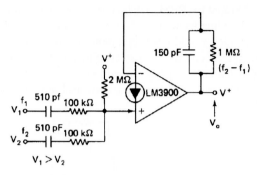

FIGURE 9-46 Low frequency mixer. (Courtesy National Semiconductor Corp.)

9-6-6 Window Voltage Detector

The window voltage detector shown in Figure 9-47 monitors an input voltage and indicates when this voltage goes either above or below the desired limits. The upper limit voltage (V_{UL}) is +5 V, and the lower limit voltage (V_{LL}) is +4 V. The input voltage (V_{in}) should be looking through a window whose limits are +4 V and +5 V. If V_{in} exceeds V_{UL}, the upper op amps output swings negative and the LED lights. If V_{in} drops below V_{LL}, the lower op amp's output swings negative and the LED lights. Window voltage detectors can be connected together to give multiple limit indications.

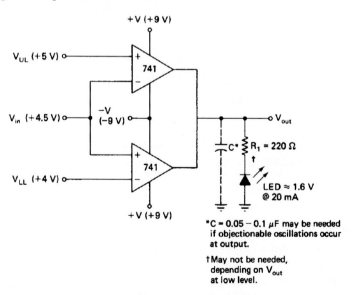

FIGURE 9-47 Window voltage detector.

9-6-7 Sample-and-Hold Circuit

A basic sample-and-hold circuit is shown in Figure 9-48a. The op amp is in the noninverting follower configuration. When switch S_1 is closed, capacitor C charges to $V_{in\ max}$. After S_1 is opened, C remains charged and the output will be at the same potential. Therefore, the circuit has sampled a voltage and is temporarily holding it.

However, leakages do occur, causing errors at the output, and this basic circuit is unable to sample rapidly changing transient voltages. An improved circuit using FET switches, which overcome the problems of the basic circuit, is shown in Figure 9-48b. Certain types of capacitors, such as paper and Mylar, exhibit a polarization phenomenon which causes the sampled voltage to drop off by about 50 mV and then stabilize when exercised over a 5-V range during the sample interval. Using the types of capacitors listed reduces this problem.

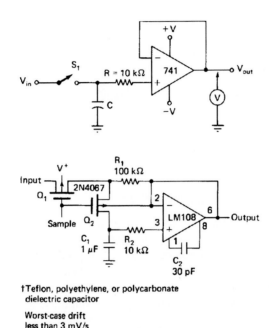

† Teflon, polyethylene, or polycarbonate dielectric capacitor

Worst-case drift less than 3 mV/s

FIGURE 9-48 Sample and hold circuit: (a) basic circuit; (b) improved circuit that eliminates leakages. (Courtesy National Semiconductor Corp.)

9-6-8 Bi-Quad Active Bandpass Filter

The bi-quad bandpass filter shown in Figure 9-49 is highly selective, with a center frequency of 1 kHz, a Q of 50, and a voltage gain of 100. However, this circuit is also called a state-variable filter and can simultaneously provide high-pass, low-pass, and bandpass outputs. The high-pass output can be taken from the output of the top op amp, the low-pass output from the output of the bottom op amp, and the bandpass output from the middle op amp, as shown. This circuit is easily tunable when $R_1 = R_3$, $R_5 = R_6$, and $C_1 = C_2$. Its center frequency is then determined as

$$f_c = \frac{1}{2\pi R_5 C_1}$$

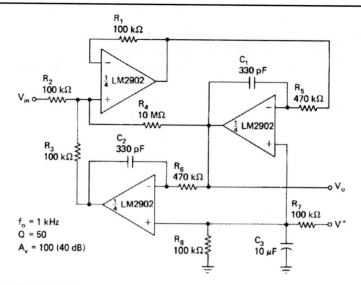

FIGURE 9-49 Bi-quad active bandpass filter. (Courtesy National Semiconductor Corp.)

9-6-9 Compressor/Expander Amplifiers

The circuit shown in Figure 9-50 has two functions. The compressor amplifier compresses high-amplitude input signals to prevent following circuits from clipping and creating other types of distortion. The resistor/diode networks, in parallel with the feedback resistor R_2, conduct on high peaks of the input signal, thereby reducing the gain of the amplifier.

The expander, being the counterpart of the compressor, receives the compressed signal (perhaps from a transmission line) and extends the amplitude to its full-amplitude range. In this case the resistor diode networks are placed in parallel with the input resistor. When the input signal reaches the compressed level, these networks conduct, thereby increasing the gain of the amplifier.

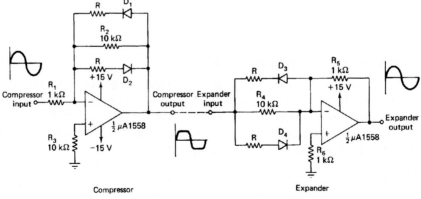

Maximum compression expansion ratio = R_1/R (10 kΩ > R $\geqslant$ 0)
Note: Diodes D_1 through D_4 are matched FD6666 or equivalent.

FIGURE 9-50 Compressor/expander amplifiers. (Courtesy Fairchild Camera & Instruments Corporation.)

9-6-10 Log Generator

By combining the characteristics of bipolar transistors and op amps, circuits can be constructed to generate logarithmic voltage outputs. The circuit shown in Figure 9-51 generates a logarithmic output voltage for a linear input current. This log (logarithmic) generator is a low-level circuit capable of handling input currents from 10 nA to 1.0 mA, with a dynamic range of 5 decades or 100 dB at an accuracy of 3.0 percent. With the values given, the scale factor is 1 V/decade and

$$E_{out} = -\left[\log 10\left(\frac{E_{in}}{R_{in}}\right) + 5\right]$$

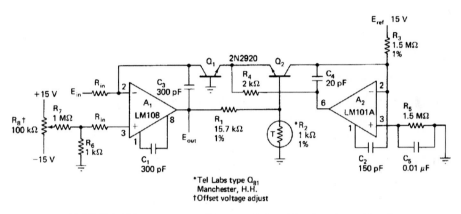

FIGURE 9-51 Log generator. (Courtesy National Semiconductor Corp.)

9-6-11 Antilog Generator

Slight modification of the log generator shown in Figure 9-51 will produce the antilog generator shown in Figure 9-52. A linear input current to this circuit produces an exponential (antilog) voltage output. With the values given

$$E_{out} = 10^{-(E_{in})}$$

9-6-12 Multiplier/Divider

Using logarithms for multiplication is a simple process of addition. Adding two numbers in log form produces a product in log form. Taking the antilog gives the product in conventional form. Similarly, division is a process of subtracting logs and then finding the antilog of the difference to obtain the conventional quotient.

The circuit shown in Figure 9-53 is a multiplier/divider. Basically, it consists of the log generator shown in Figure 9-51 and the antilog generator of Figure 9-52.

For multiplication, E_2 is set at a reference voltage and $E_{out} = 10 (E_1 \times E_3)$, while for a multiplication/division operation, $E_{out} = E_1E_3/10E_2$. If a single number is desired in the numerator, let E_1 or E_3 equal 1.

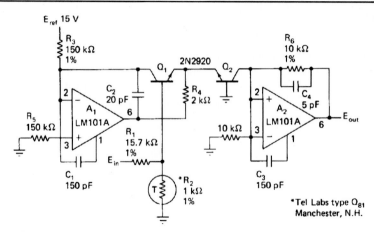

FIGURE 9-52 Antilog generator. (Courtesy National Semiconductor Corp.)

9-6-13 Cube Generator

A cube (X^3) generator is shown in Figure 9-54. It is similar to the multiplier/divider circuit of Figure 9-53 except for the addition of a few components, and inputs E_2 and E_3 are at a reference voltage. Actually, the circuit is capable of any power function by changing the values of R_9 and R_{10} as given by the expression

$$E_{out} = E_{in} \, 16.7 R_9 / R_9 + R_{10}$$

9-6-14 Root Extractor

Finding the root of a number using logs involves taking the log of the number, dividing it by, say, $\frac{1}{2}$ for the square root, and finding the antilog to convert it to conventional form. Such a root extractor is shown in Figure 9-55. Voltage divider $R_4 - R_5$ determines the ratio of the log voltage for the desired root.

9-6-15 High-Speed Warning Device

A high-speed warning device to be used for automotive applications is shown in Figure 9-56. The input signal uses the engine speed available at the primary of the spark coil, thus eliminating electromechanical transducers at the transmission or speedometer cable. A switch in the transmission closes in top gear and enables the display and audible alarm switch. The display shows the desired speed limit and is set by the 100-kΩ pot in accordance with the gear/axle ratios, number of cylinders, wheel/tire size, and so on. An LM2900 quad Norton op amp can be used to perform all the functions. Initially, A_1 amplifies and regulates the signal from the spark coil. A_2 converts frequency to voltage with the output proportional to engine RPM. A_3 compares this voltage with the reference voltage and turns on the output transistor at the set speed. When the vehicle speed exceeds the set limit, the tone generator will be energized. To extinguish these warnings, the driver will have to slow the vehicle to below the value set by the hysteresis.

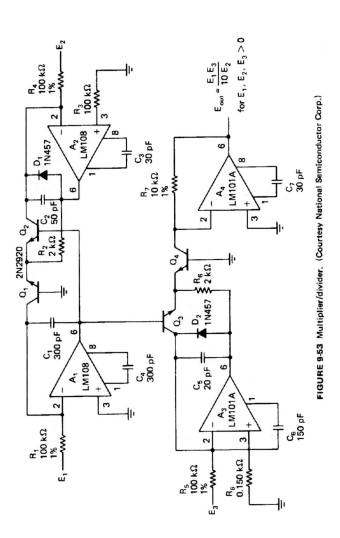

FIGURE 9-53 Multiplier/divider. (Courtesy National Semiconductor Corp.)

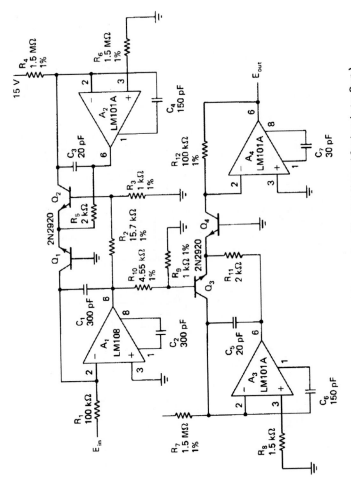

FIGURE 9-54 Cube generator. (Courtesy National Semiconductor Corp.)

262

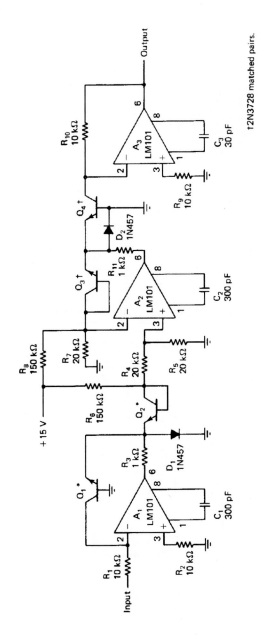

FIGURE 9-55 Root extractor. (Courtesy National Semiconductor Corp.)

263

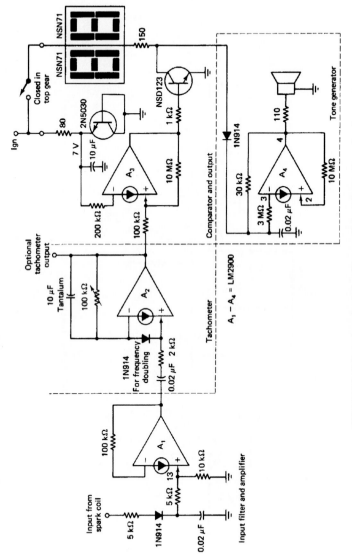

FIGURE 9-56 High speed warning device. (Courtesy National Semiconductor Corp.)

9-6-16 Pulse-Width Modulator

The pulse-width modulator shown in Figure 9-57 is basically a square-wave generator except that the pulse width can be modified via the input. The duty cycle of the output can be altered because the addition of the control voltage at the input alters the trip points of the generator.

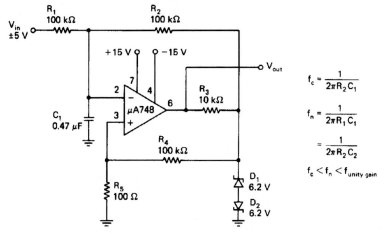

$$f_c = \frac{1}{2\pi R_2 C_1}$$

$$f_n = \frac{1}{2\pi R_1 C_1}$$

$$= \frac{1}{2\pi R_2 C_2}$$

$$f_c < f_n < f_{unity\ gain}$$

FIGURE 9-57 Pulse with modulator. (Courtesy Fairchild Camera & Instruments Corp.)

9-6-17 Capacitance Multiplier

In low-impedance systems where large capacitances are required, the circuit shown in Figure 9-58 might be used. Not intended for tuned circuits or filters because of low Q, the capacitance multiplier can be used in timing circuits on servo compensation networks. Capacitance C is determined by the formula shown.

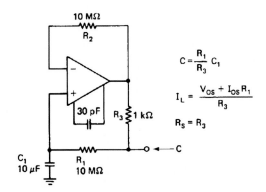

$$C = \frac{R_1}{R_3} C_1$$

$$I_L = \frac{V_{os} + I_{os} R_1}{R_3}$$

$$R_s = R_3$$

FIGURE 9-58 Capacitance multiplier. (Courtesy Fairchild Camera & Instruments Corporation.)

9-6-18 Precision Rectifiers

Normal diodes conduct only when the forward voltage across them exceeds 0.5 V, which leads to large errors when rectifying small signals. The precision rectifiers shown in Figure 9-59 provide accurate rectification. The half-wave rectifier of Figure 9-59a has a gain of 0 for positive signals and a gain of − 1 for negative signals. Output impedance differs for the two input polarities, and buffering may be needed. The output impedance for the full rectifier of Figure 9-59b is low for both input polarities, and the errors are small at all signal levels. Reversing the diodes in each circuit will invert the output polarity.

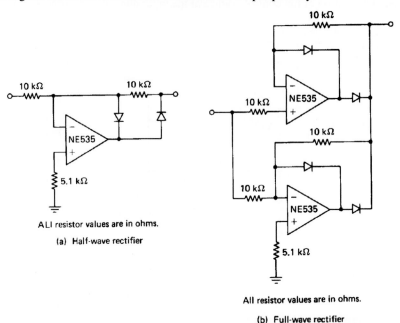

ALl resistor values are in ohms.

(a) Half-wave rectifier

All resistor values are in ohms.

(b) Full-wave rectifier

FIGURE 9-59 Precision rectifiers: (a) half wave rectifier; (b) full wave rectifier. (Permission to reprint granted by Signetic Corp., a subsidiary of U.S. Philips Corp., 811 E. Arques Ave., Sunnyvale, CA 94086.)

9-6-19 Phase Shifter

The phase shifter shown in Figure 9-60 can shift an input signal up to approximately 180°. The output V_{out} has the same frequency and amplitude as V_{in} except that it lags by so many degrees depending on the values of C_x, and R_x Making R_x variable allows for fine adjustment.

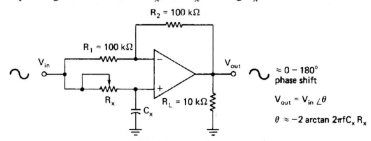

FIGURE 9-60 Phase shifter.

9-6-20 Phase-Locked Loop

The LM3900 quad op amp can be used in a phase-locked loop, as shown in Figure 9-61. Output signal phases from the input op amp are compared by the middle op amp. Any phase difference between these two signals is converted into a correction voltage and fed back to the input op amp. This causes the phase of the output signal to change so that it tracks the input reference signal. There is also a triangle wave available at the output of the phase comparator.

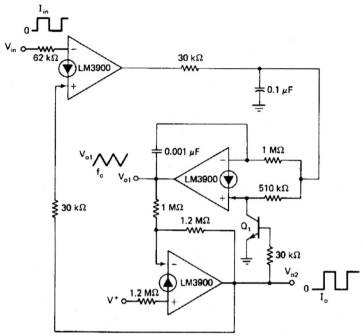

FIGURE 9-61 Phase-locked loop. (Courtesy National Semiconductor Corp.)

9-6-21 Voltage-Level Detector

Voltage-level detectors with LED indicators are shown in Figure 9-62. The supply voltage used can range up to ±15 V, but the input voltage sensed must be about 2 or 3 V below the maximum supply. The potentiometer can be used to set the reference voltage. When V_{in} goes beyond V_{ref}, the op-amp output changes states and the LED will light.

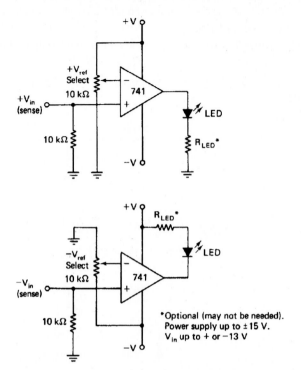

FIGURE 9-62 Voltage level detector: (a) positive indicator; (b) negative indicator.

APPENDIX A

VOLTAGE WAVEFORM PHOTOGRAPHS FOR SELECTED EXPERIMENTS

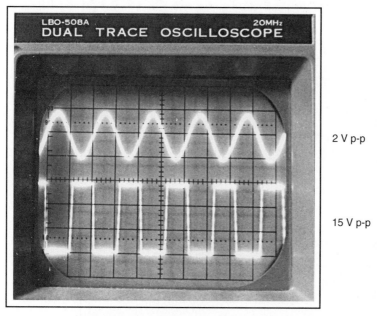

FIGURE A-1a Inverting Comparator

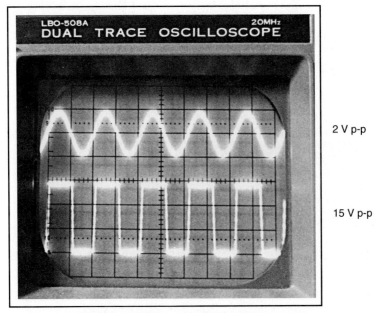

2 V p-p

15 V p-p

FIGURE A-1b Noninverting Comparator

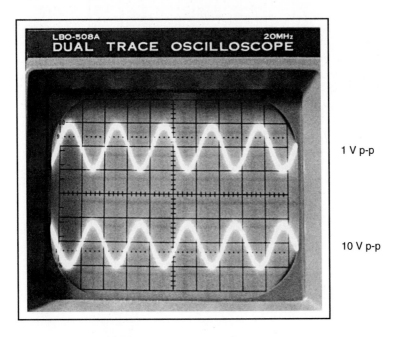

1 V p-p

10 V p-p

FIGURE A-2a Inverting amplifier

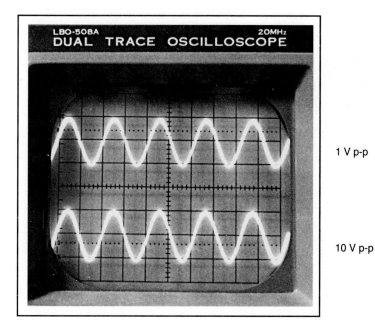

1 V p-p

10 V p-p

FIGURE A-2b Noninverting Amplifier

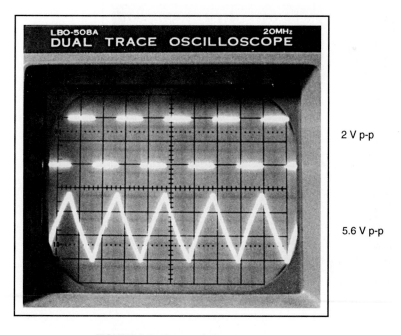

2 V p-p

5.6 V p-p

FIGURE A-3a Op amp Integrator

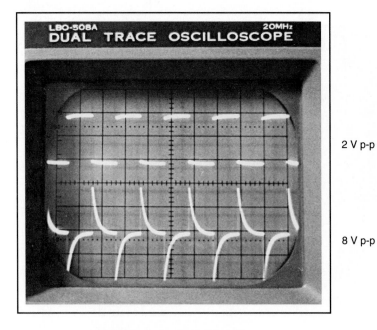

2 V p-p

8 V p-p

FIGURE A-3b Op Amp Differentiator

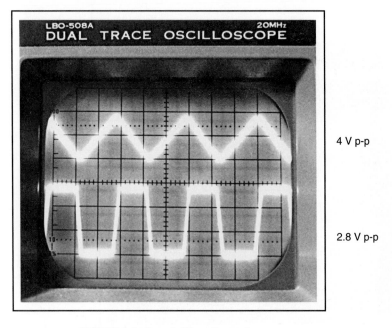

4 V p-p

2.8 V p-p

FIGURE A-4a Trangle Wave Generator

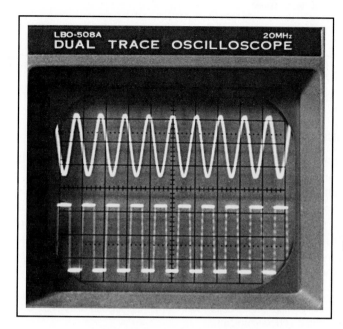

13.5 V p-p

28 V p-p

FIGURE A-4b Sine Wave Oscillator

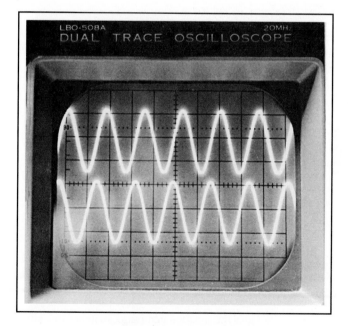

25 V p-p

26 V p-p

FIGURE A-5 Quadrature Oscillator

APPENDIX B

REVIEW OF TEST EQUIPMENT OPERATION AND USE

B-1-1 UNDERSTANDING MULTIMETERS

A multimeter is a general-purpose meter capable of measuring DC and AC voltage, current, resistance, and in some cases decibels. There are two types of meters: *analog,* using a standard meter movement with a needle, and *digital,* with an electronic numerical display (Figure B-1). Both types of meters have a positive (+) jack and a common jack (−) for the test leads; a function switch to select DC voltage, AC voltage, DC current, AC current, or ohms; and a range switch for accurate readings. The meters may also have other jacks to measure extended ranges of voltage (1 to 5 kV) and current (up to 10 A). There are some variations to the functions used for specific meters.

FIGURE B-1 Multimeters: (a) analog VOM; (b) digital VOM. (From F. Hughes, *Illustrated Guidebook to Electronic Devices and Circuits*, Prentice-Hall, Englewood Cliffs, N.J., © 1981, Fig. 1-38, p. 41. Reprinted with permission.)

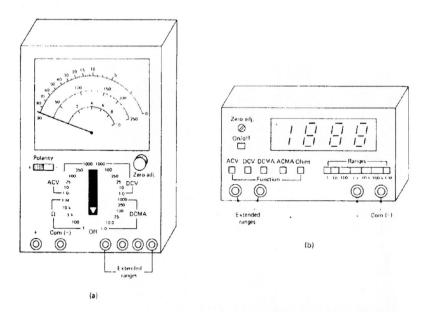

Current Source: Taken from *Fundamental Electronic Devices: Concepts and Experimentation*, 2nd ed., Fredrick W. Hughes, Prentice Hall Inc., 1990, Figure B-1, page 5.

The analog meter usually includes the function and range switches in a single switch. It may also have a polarity switch to facilitate reversing the test leads. The needle will have a screw for mechanical adjust to set it to zero and also a zero adjust control to compensate for weakening batteries when measuring resistance. An analog meter call be set to read positive and negative voltage by simply reversing the test leads or moving the polarity switch. A digital meter usually has an automatic indicator for polarity on its display.

A meter of reasonable quality will have an input resistance of 20 kΩ per volt or greater to prevent loading down a circuit, which causes an error in the reading. For example, if a DC voltmeter was set on the 10-V scale, its input resistance would be 200 kΩ. If it were placed across a 200-kΩ resistor in a circuit, the total effective resistance at that point would be 100 kΩ, which would certainly cause an erroneous reading.

Meters must be properly connected to a circuit to ensure a correct reading (see Figure B-2). A voltmeter is always placed across (in parallel with) the circuit or component to be measured. When measuring current, the circuit must be opened and the meter inserted in series with the circuit or component to be measured. When measuring the resistance of a component in a circuit, the voltage to the circuit must be removed and one end of the component opened for the circuit (to prevent any parallel paths from affecting the reading) and the meter placed in parallel with the component.

Special probes are used with meters for specific circuits. These include shielded cable, high-voltage, and capacitance types, and radio-frequency (RF) detectors.

FIGURE B-2 Proper meter connections: (a) measuring voltage (parallel); (b) measuring current (series); (c) measuring ohms (open circuit). (From F. Hughes, *Illustrated Guidebook to Electronic Devices and Circuits*, Prentice-Hall, Englewood Cliffs, N.J., © 1981, Fig. 1-39, p. 42. Reprinted with permission.)

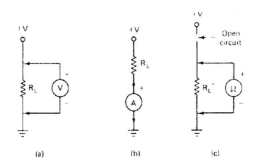

Current Source: Taken from *Fundamental Electronic Devices: Concepts and Experimentation*, 2nd ed., Fredrick W. Hughes, Prentice Hall Inc., 1990, Figure B-2, page 6.

B-1-2 READING MULTIMETERS

On a standard analog meter there is a scale for ohms, DC, and AC (see Figures B-3 to B-5). When the function switch is set on 250 V AC, a full-scale needle deflection indicates that the meter is measuring 250 V AC. If the needle is at 150, the meter is measuring 150 V AC. The various ranges of a specific function would use the same scale. Therefore, the individual gradient values have to be determined. For example, if the 250 V AC scale is used, there are 10 gradients between the numbers, and the value between numbers is 50 V. The value of each gradient can be found by dividing 50 by 10 (50/10 = 5), which results in 5 V per gradient. The same scale would be used for 25 V AC, except that the number 250 = 25, 200 = 20, 150 = 15, and so on. Now there is a 5-V difference between numbers, so each gradient is worth 0.5 V. If the range switch is set to 10 V AC, the same scale is used and each gradient is worth 0.2 V. When the range switch is set to 100 V AC, the number 10 = 100, 8 = 80, 6 = 60, and so on, and each gradient is worth 2 V. All voltage and current scales are used the same way, remembering that the AC voltage is the effective or root-mean-square (rms) value.

The ohm scale is a nonlinear scale that may be indicated in reverse to the other scales

(Figure B-6). The resistance function is used as a multiplier indicator. The function switch is placed to the desired range and the test leads are shorted together. The zero adj. (ohms adj.) control is then used to set the needle to zero on the scale. The leads are then opened and placed across the desired resistor to be read. If the function switch is set at 1 kΩ and the needle goes to 10, the value of the resistor being read is 10 kΩ. The meter may need to be zeroed each time a different range is selected.

With a digital meter, all values of DC, AC, and ohms measured will fall within the range selected. If the value being measured is greater than the range selected, an indication will be given, such as the display going blank or blinking, or perhaps only the most significant digit will light.

A user should spend some time getting oriented to meters and any test equipment being used. Equipment manuals will give detailed instructions as to their proper use.

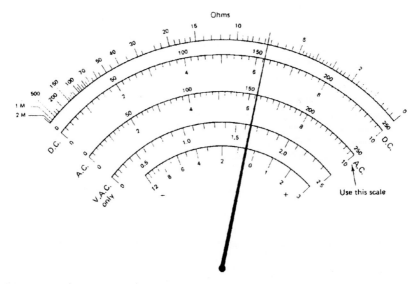

FIGURE B-3 Reading AC voltage (range switch set at 250 V AC, meter reads 155 V). (From F. Hughes, *Illustrated Guidebook to Electronic Devices and Circuits*, Prentice-Hall, Englewood Cliffs, N.J., © 1981, Fig. 1-39, p. 42. Reprinted with permission.)

Current Source: Taken from *Fundamental Electronic Devices: Concepts and Experimentation*, 2nd ed., Fredrick W. Hughes, Prentice Hall Inc., 1990, Figure B-2, page 7.

B-1-3 UNDERSTANDING THE OSCILLOSCOPE

The oscilloscope presents an accurate electronic picture of changing voltages within a circuit. An election beam is created, focused, accelerated, and properly deflected to display the voltage waveforms on the face of a cathode-ray tube (CRT). The basic circuits and controls of an oscilloscope (Figures B-7 and B-8) are:

FIGURE B-4 Reading DC voltage (range switch set at 10 V DC, meter reads 9.2 V). (From F. Hughes, *Illustrated Guidebook to Electronic Devices and Circuits*, Prentice-Hall, Englewood Cliffs, N.J., © 1981, Fig. 1-41, p. 43. Reprinted with permission.)

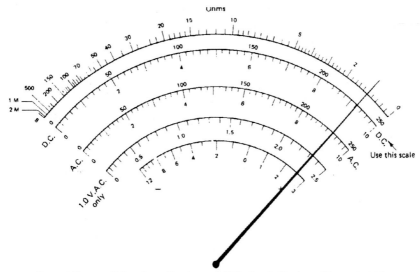

Current Source: Taken from *Fundamental Electronic Devices: Concepts and Experimentation*, 2nd ed., Fredrick W. Hughes, Prentice Hall Inc., 1990, Figure B-4, page 7.

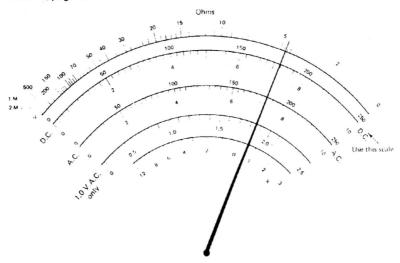

FIGURE B-5 Reading DC current range (range switch set at 25 mA DC, meter reads 18mA.) (From F. Hughes, *Illustrated Guidebook to Electronic Devices and Circuits*, Prentice-Hall, Englewood Cliffs, N.J., © 1981, Fig. 1-42, p. 44. Reprinted with permission.)

Current Source: *Taken from Fundamental Electronic Devices: Concepts and Experimentation*, 2nd ed., Fredrick W. Hughes, Prentice Hall Inc., 1990, Figure B-5, page 8.

FIGURE B-6 Reading ohms (range switch set at 1kΩ, meter reads 55 kΩ). (From F. Hughes, *Illustrated Guidebook to Electronic Devices and Circuits*, Prentice-Hall, Englewood Cliffs, N.J., © 1981, Fig. 1-43, p. 45. Reprinted with permission.)

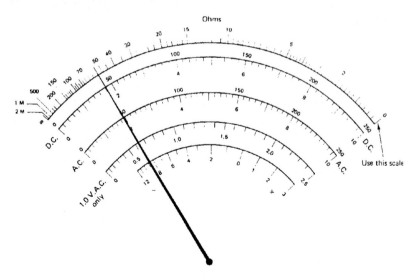

Current Source: Taken from *Fundamental Electronic Devices: Concepts and Experimentation*, 2nd ed., Fredrick W. Hughes, Prentice Hall Inc., 1990, Figure B-6, page 8.

Power supply: provides high DC voltage (up to a few thousand volts) for the CRT and lower DC voltages for other circuits

Intensity control: adjusts brightness of display

Focus control: adjusts sharpness of display

Time-base generator: provides the basic sawtooth voltage, which moves the trace on the face of the CRT from left to right horizontally

Time/ICM selector: adjusts the frequency of the time-base generator

Horizontal amplifier circuits: amplifies the output of the time-base generator and applies it to the horizontal deflection plates

Horizontal gain control: adjusts full trace horizontally on the face of the CRT

Horizontal positioning control: centers trace horizontally on the face of the CRT

Vertical input: accepts voltage to be measured, either DC or AC

Vertical attenuator: reduces input voltage amplitude so as not to overdrive trace on face of the CRT

V/CM selector: selects desired input voltage attenuation

Vertical amplifier circuits: amplifies input voltage and applies it to the vertical deflection plates

Vertical gain control: manually adjusts the amplitude of input voltage displayed on the face of the CRT

Vertical positioning control: centers trace vertically on the face of the CRT

Trigger circuit: synchronizes time-base generator with input frequency, another external frequency, or 60-Hz line frequency; enables trace to be stopped for accurate measurements

Stability control: manual control for locking in display

External horizontal input: synchronizes horizontal trace for special measurements and displays as Lissajous patterns

Z input: used for intensity modulation of electron beam, perhaps for frequency measurements

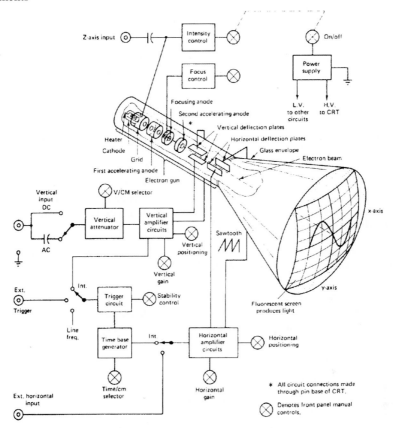

FIGURE B-7 Block diagram of basic oscilloscope. (From F. Hughes, *Illustrated Guidebook to Electronic Devices and Circuits*, Prentice-Hall, Englewood Cliffs, N.J., 1981, Fig. 1-44, page 46. Reprinted with permission.)

Current Source: Taken from *Fundamental Electronic Devices: Concepts and Experimentation*, 2nd ed., Fredrick W. Hughes, Prentice Hall Inc., 1990, Figure C-1, page 12.

B-1-4 READING THE OSCILLOSCOPE

The amplitude of a voltage waveform on an oscilloscope screen can be determined by counting the number of centimeters (cm) and/or fractions thereof, vertically, from one peak to the other peak of the waveform and then multiplying it by the setting of the volts/cm control. As an example, referring to the sine wave in Figure B-9 if the amplitude is 4 cm and the control is set on 1 V/cm, the peak-to-peak voltage is 4 V (4 cm × 1 V/cm = 4 V). If the control is set on 0.5 V/cm, the voltage is 2 V peak to peak (4 cm × 0.5 V/cm = 2 V).

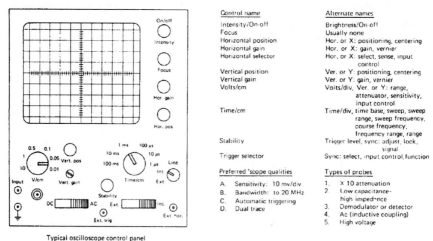

Typical oscilloscope control panel

FIGURE B-8 Oscilloscope controls. (From F. Hughes, *Illustrated Guidebook to Electronic Devices and Circuits*, Prentice-Hall, Englewood Cliffs, N.J., 1981, Fig. 1-45, page 47. Reprinted with permission.)

Current Source: Taken from *Fundamental Electronic Devices: Concepts and Experimentation*, 2nd ed., Fredrick W. Hughes, Prentice Hall Inc., 1990, Figure C-2, page 13.

The frequency of a waveform can be determined by counting the number of centimeters and/or fractions thereof, horizontally, in one cycle or period of the waveform and then multiplying it by the setting of the time/cm control. For example, if the waveform is 4 cm long and the control is set at 1 ms, the period is 4 ms (4 cm × 1 ms = 4 ms). The frequency can now be found from the formula

$$f = \frac{1}{p} = \frac{1}{4\,\text{ms}} = \frac{1}{4 \times 10^{-3}\,\text{s}} = 0.25 \times 10^3 = 250\,\text{Hz}$$

If the control is set on 100 μs, the period is 400 μs (4 cm × 100 μs = 400 μs) and the frequency is 2.5 kHz:

$$f = \frac{1}{p} = \frac{1}{400\,\text{ms}} = \frac{1}{4 \times 10^{-4}} = 0.25 \times 10^4 = 2500\,\text{Hz}$$

A dual-trace oscilloscope is advantageous to show the input signal and output signal simultaneously, to determine any defects, and to indicate phase relationships. The two traces may be placed over each other (superimposed) to indicate better the phase shift between two signals (Figure B-10).

B-1-5 USING THE BASIC SIGNAL GENERATOR

A signal generator converts DC to AC or varying DC in the form of sine waves, square waves, triangle waves, or other types of voltage waveforms. The signal generator is used to inject a signal into a circuit or piece of equipment for troubleshooting or for calibration.

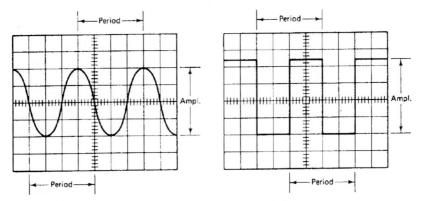

FIGURE B-9 Oscilloscope voltage waveforms: (a) sine wave; (b) square wave. (From F. Hughes, *Illustrated Guidebook to Electronic Devices and Circuits*, Prentice-Hall, Englewood Cliffs, N.J., 1981, Fig. 1-46, page 47. Reprinted with permission.)

Current Source: Taken from *Fundamental Electronic Devices: Concepts and Experimentation*, 2nd ed., Fredrick W. Hughes, Prentice Hall Inc., 1990, Figure C-3, page 13.

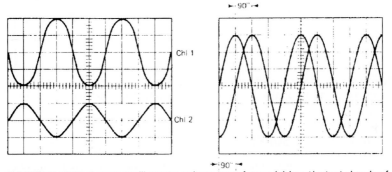

FIGURE B-10 Dual-trace oscilloscope voltage waveforms: (a) input/output signals of an amplifier; (b) both channels superimposed to show phase shift of two signals. (from F. Hughes, Illustrated Guidebook to Electronic Devices and Circuits, Prentice-Hall, Englewood Cliffs, N.J., 1981, Fig. 1-47, Page 49. Reprinted with permission.

Current source: Taken from Fundamental Electronic Devices: Concepts And Experimentation, 2nd ed., Fredrick W. Hughes, Prentice-Hall Inc., 1990, Figure C-4, Page

Some generators may be used for audio, RF, or higher frequencies, whereas others have overlapping frequency ranges. A standard function generator usually has three types of waveforms. All generators will have a frequency range switch, a fine adjustment control for selecting a specific frequency, an amplitude control for varying the peak-to-peak output voltage, and output terminals (Figure B-11).

To select a sine wave of, say, 5 kHz, the user sets the function switch to the sine wave and the range switch to 1 k, and then adjusts the frequency fine adjust control to 5. The amplitude control is then adjusted to establish the desired peak-to-peak voltage output.

Some generators may have a DC component at the output terminals that could upset the circuit to which they are connected. In this case, a capacitor connected in series with the positive output terminal and the circuit will block the DC component.

In some cases a very small signal is required from the generator, but the noise at the output terminals may be too objectionable or the signal too large when the amplitude control is turned way down. To remedy this, the user can place a large-value resistor (100 kΩ to 1 MΩ) in series with the positive output terminal and the circuit. Sufficient voltage can be developed at the output terminals to overcome the problems mentioned, while the resistor drops some of the voltage, which permits the correct signal amplitude to be placed on the circuit.

FIGURE B-11 Basic signal generator. (From F. Hughes, *Illustrated Guidebook to Electronic Devices and Circuits,* Prentice-Hall, Englewood Cliffs, N.J., 1981, Fig. 1-49, page 50. Reprinted with permission.)

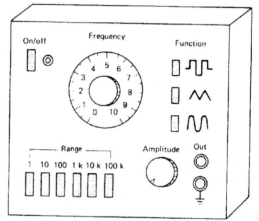

Current Source: Taken from *Fundamental Electronic Devices: Concepts and Experimentation,* 2nd ed., Fredrick W. Hughes, Prentice Hall Inc., 1990, Figure D-1, page 15.

B-1-6 USE OF A POWER SUPPLY

When batteries are used frequently, their energy becomes depleted and the circuits they are powering will in most cases have faulty operation. Power supplies are used to replace batteries. *A power supply is a device, that converts the 120-AC line voltage to DC voltage for operating other electrical/electronic circuits.* Power supplies are more efficient and dependable than batteries. Nearly every electronic device that operates on 120 V AC has an internal power supply built into it. Separate self contained power supplies are used for performing laboratory experiments and testing printed circuit (PC) boards or other discrete electronic components. There are various types of power supplies, but one very popular version is shown in Figure B-12.

The pilot light is an indication that the power supply is on or off. Even when this light is on, the output terminals should be measured to determine if voltage is present. The main output terminals are marked −V, GND, and +V or some other similar indication. The GND terminal is the common connection for most circuits. It is usually the color black with electronic circuits. Every circuit needs two connections to a power supply. The most used terminals are the GND and the +V. The +V terminal supplies a positive voltage with respect to the GND terminal, In many cases it is red in color. The +V control is a pot that adjusts the voltage level at the +V terminal. The −V terminal sup-plies a negative voltage with respect to the

GND terminal. The –V control is a pot that adjusts the voltage at the –V terminal.

Many circuits today, such as operational amplifiers (op amps), use a + and a – voltage power supply. These types of power supplies may also have a fixed +5 V terminal and ground terminal that are used with digital circuits.

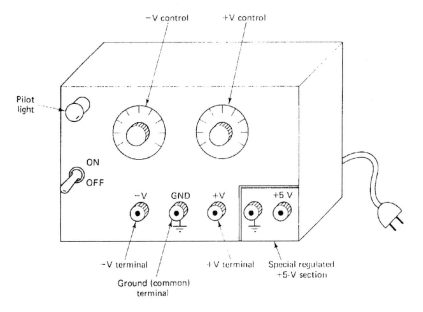

FIGURE B-12 Typical ± *V* power supply.

Current Source: Taken from *Fundamental AC/DC Circuits: Concepts and Experimentation*, Fredrick W. Hughes, Prentice Hall Inc., 1990, Figure 4-9, page 128.

Before you use a power supply, the voltage control should be turned all the way counterclockwise, so that zero or minimum voltage is present at the output terminals. The following sequence is the proper way to use a power supply.

1. Have the correct drawing or schematic diagram of the circuit being tested.
2. Connect the power supply to the circuit.
3. Place a voltmeter across the voltage terminals connected to the circuit.
4. Slowly adjust the voltage control until the voltmeter indicates the desired voltage.
5. Turn off the power supply when you are not testing or working with the circuit.

Caution!

Never short-out the terminals of the power supply with a wire or metal object. This can damage the power supply or create more problems.

B-1-7 PROCEDURE FOR EXPERIMENTING WITH TESTING A DISCRETE CIRCUIT

It may be necessary to disconnect a printed circuit board from a system to check it separately. The following procedure can be used aa a guide for setting up the equipment to check a PC board or for experimenting with a new circuit on a breadboard (see Figure B-13).

1. Have the proper circuit schematic in front of you.
2. Have the proper equipment, parts, and test leads in front of you.
3. Construct the circuit if it is an experiment.
4. Connect the power supply to the circuit, which may be positive and ground, negative and ground, or both positive-negative and ground.
5. Connect all equipment grounds to the common circuit ground (as indicated by the dashed lines).
6. Turn on the power supply and set the proper DC voltages. Measure with a voltmeter.
7. Use a voltmeter to check DC voltages on the circuit.
8. Connect the output device to the circuit.
9. Connect the input device to the circuit.
10. Set the desired input signal to the circuit.
11. Use the oscilloscope or voltmeter to check the input signal at point *A*.
12. Use the oscilloscope or voltmeter to check the output signals at point *B*.
13. Observe the output device for the correct indication.

FIGURE B-13 General setup for testing a discrete circuit. (From F. Hughes, *Illustrated Guidebook to Electronic Devices and Circuits*, Prentice-Hall, Englewood Cliffs, N.J., 1981, Fig 1-50, page 52. Reprinted with permission.)

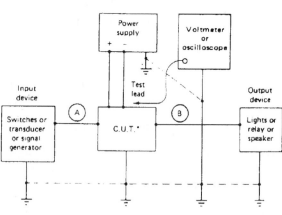

Current Source: *Taken from Fundamental Electronic Devices: Concepts and Experimentation,* 2nd ed., Fredrick W. Hughes, Prentice Hall Inc., 1990, Figure E-1, page 17.

APPENDIX C

SELECTED MANUFACTURERS' OP-AMP SPECIFICATION SHEETS

μA702
WIDEBAND DC AMPLIFIER
FAIRCHILD LINEAR INTEGRATED CIRCUIT

GENERAL DESCRIPTION — The μA702 is a monolithic DC Amplifier constructed using the Fairchild Planar* epitaxial process. It is intended for use as an operational amplifier in analog computers, as a precision instrumentation amplifier, or in other applications requiring a feedback amplifier useful from dc to 30 MHz.

- **LOW OFFSET VOLTAGE**
- **LOW OFFSET VOLTAGE DRIFT**
- **WIDE BANDWIDTH — 20 MHz TYP**
- **HIGH SLEW RATE — 5 V/μs TYP**

ABSOLUTE MAXIMUM RATINGS

Voltage Between V+ and V− Terminals	21 V
Peak Output Current	50 mA
Differential Input Voltage	±5.0 V
Input Voltage	+1.5 V to −6.0 V
Internal Power Dissipation (Note)	
Metal Can	500 mW
DIP	670 mW
Flatpak	570 mW
Operating Temperature Range	
Military (μA702)	−55°C to +125°C
Commercial (μA702C)	0°C to +70°C
Storage Temperature Range	−65°C to +150°C
Lead Temperature (Soldering, 60 seconds)	300°C

NOTE

Rating applies to ambient temperature up to 70 C. Above 70°C ambient derate linearly at 6.3 mW/°C for Metal Can, 8.3 mW/°C for DIP and 7.1 mW/°C for the Flatpak.

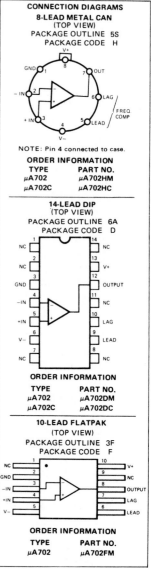

CONNECTION DIAGRAMS
8-LEAD METAL CAN
(TOP VIEW)
PACKAGE OUTLINE 5S
PACKAGE CODE H

NOTE: Pin 4 connected to case.

ORDER INFORMATION

TYPE	PART NO.
μA702	μA702HM
μA702C	μA702HC

14-LEAD DIP
(TOP VIEW)
PACKAGE OUTLINE 6A
PACKAGE CODE D

ORDER INFORMATION

TYPE	PART NO.
μA702	μA702DM
μA702C	μA702DC

10-LEAD FLATPAK
(TOP VIEW)
PACKAGE OUTLINE 3F
PACKAGE CODE F

ORDER INFORMATION

TYPE	PART NO.
μA702	μA702FM

EQUIVALENT CIRCUIT

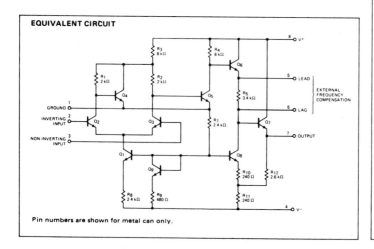

Pin numbers are shown for metal can only.

*Planar is a patented Fairchild process.

FAIRCHILD LINEAR INTEGRATED CIRCUITS • µA702

µA702

ELECTRICAL CHARACTERISTICS (T_A = 25°C unless otherwise specified)

PARAMETER	CONDITIONS	V+ = 12.0V, V− = −6.0V			V+ = 6.0V, V− = −3.0V			UNITS
		MIN	TYP	MAX	MIN	TYP	MAX	
Input Offset Voltage	$R_S \leqslant 2\ k\Omega$		0.5	2.0		0.7	3.0	mV
Input Offset Current			180	500		120	500	nA
Input Bias Current			2.0	5.0		1.2	3.5	µA
Input Resistance		16	40		22	67		kΩ
Input Voltage Range		−4.0		+0.5	−1.5		+0.5	V
Common Mode Rejection Ratio	$R_S \leqslant 2\ k\Omega$, f < 1 kHz	80	100		80	100		dB
Large Signal Voltage Gain	$R_L \geqslant 100\ k\Omega$, V_{OUT} = ±5.0 V	2500	3600	6000				
	$R_L \geqslant 100\ k\Omega$, V_{OUT} = ±2.5 V				600	900	1500	
Output Resistance			200	500		300	700	Ω
Supply Current	V_{OUT} = 0		5.0	6.7		2.1	3.3	mA
Power Consumption	V_{OUT} = 0		90	120		19	30	mW
Transient Response (unity-gain) Rise Time	CI = 0.01 µF, RI = 20 Ω, $R_L \geqslant 100\ k\Omega$, V_{IN} = 10 mV		25	120				ns
Overshoot	$C_L \leqslant 100\ pF$		10	50				%
Transient Response (x100 gain) Rise Time	C3 = 50 pF, $R_L \geqslant 100\ k\Omega$,		10	30				ns
Overshoot	V_{IN} = 1 mV		20	40				%
The following specifications apply for −55°C ≤ T_A ≤ +125°C:								
Input Offset Voltage	$R_S \leqslant 2\ k\Omega$			3.0			4.0	mV
Average Temperature Coefficient of Input Offset Voltage	RS = 50 Ω, T_A = 25°C to +125°C		2.5	10		3.5	15	µV/°C
	RS = 50 Ω, T_A = 25°C to −55°C		2.0	10		3.0	15	µV/°C
Input Offset Current	T_A = +125°C		80	500		50	500	nA
	T_A = −55°C		400	1500		280	1500	nA
Average Temperature Coefficient of Input Offset Current	T_A = 25°C to +125°C		1.0	5.0		0.7	4.0	nA/°C
	T_A = 25°C to −55°C		3.0	16		2.0	13	nA/°C
Input Bias Current	T_A = −55°C		4.3	10		2.6	7.5	µA
Input Resistance		6.0			8.0			kΩ
Common Mode Rejection Ratio	$R_S \leqslant 2\ k\Omega$, f < 1 kHz	70	95		70	95		dB
Supply Voltage Rejection Ratio	V+ = 12 V, V− = −6.0 V to V+ = 6.0 V, V− = −3.0 V, $R_S \leqslant 2\ k\Omega$		75	200		75	200	µV/V
Large Signal Voltage Gain	$R_L \geqslant 100\ k\Omega$, V_{OUT} = ±5.0 V	2000		7000				
	$R_L \geqslant 100\ k\Omega$, V_{OUT} = ±2.5 V				500		1750	
Output Voltage Swing	$R_L \geqslant 100\ k\Omega$	±5.0	±5.3		±2.5	±2.7		V
	$R_L \geqslant 10\ k\Omega$	±3.5	±4.0		±1.5	±2.0		V
Supply Current	T_A = +125°C, V_{OUT} = 0		4.4	6.7		1.7	3.3	mA
	T_A = −55°C, V_{OUT} = 0		5.0	7.5		2.1	3.9	mA
Power Consumption	T_A = +125°C, V_{OUT} = 0		80	120		15	30	mW
	T_A = −55°C, V_{OUT} = 0		90	135		19	35	mW

TYPICAL PERFORMANCE CURVE FOR µA702

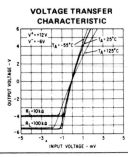

VOLTAGE TRANSFER CHARACTERISTIC

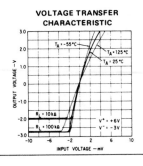

VOLTAGE TRANSFER CHARACTERISTIC

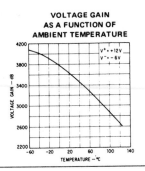

VOLTAGE GAIN AS A FUNCTION OF AMBIENT TEMPERATURE

μA709
HIGH PERFORMANCE OPERATIONAL AMPLIFIER
FAIRCHILD LINEAR INTEGRATED CIRCUITS

GENERAL DESCRIPTION — The μA709 is a monolithic High Gain Operational Amplifier constructed using the Fairchild Planar* epitaxial process. It features low offset, high input impedance, large input common mode range, high output swing under load and low power consumption. The device displays exceptional temperature stability and will operate over a wide range of supply voltages with little performance degradation. The amplifier is intended for use in dc servo systems, high impedance analog computers, low level instrumentation applications and for the generation of special linear and nonlinear transfer functions.

ABSOLUTE MAXIMUM RATINGS

Supply Voltage	±18 V
Internal Power Dissipation (Note)	
Metal Can	500 mW
DIP	670 mW
Flatpak	570 mW
Differential Input Voltage	±5.0 V
Input Voltage	±10 V
Storage Temperature Range	
Metal, Hermetic DIP, and Flatpak	−65°C to +150°C
Molded DIP	−55°C to +125°C
Operating Temperature Range	
Military (μA709A and μA709)	−55°C to +125°C
Commercial (μA709C)	0°C to +70°C
Lead Temperature	
Metal Can, Hermetic DIP, and Flatpak (Soldering 60 s)	300°C
Molded DIP	260°C
Output Short Circuit Duration	5 s

NOTE:
Rating applies to ambient temperature up to 70°C. Above 70°C ambient derate linearly at 6.3mW/°C for Metal Can, 8.3mW/°C for DIP, 7.1mW/°C for the Flatpak and 5.6mW/°C for the Mini DIP.

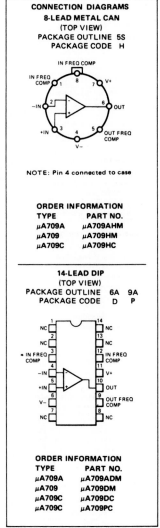

CONNECTION DIAGRAMS
8-LEAD METAL CAN
(TOP VIEW)
PACKAGE OUTLINE 5S
PACKAGE CODE H

NOTE: Pin 4 connected to case

ORDER INFORMATION

TYPE	PART NO.
μA709A	μA709AHM
μA709	μA709HM
μA709C	μA709HC

14-LEAD DIP
(TOP VIEW)
PACKAGE OUTLINE 6A 9A
PACKAGE CODE D P

ORDER INFORMATION

TYPE	PART NO.
μA709A	μA709ADM
μA709	μA709DM
μA709C	μA709DC
μA709C	μA709PC

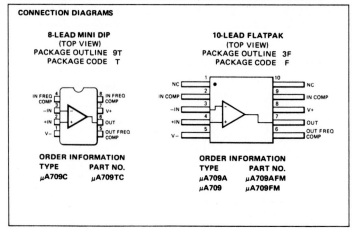

CONNECTION DIAGRAMS

8-LEAD MINI DIP
(TOP VIEW)
PACKAGE OUTLINE 9T
PACKAGE CODE T

10-LEAD FLATPAK
(TOP VIEW)
PACKAGE OUTLINE 3F
PACKAGE CODE F

ORDER INFORMATION

TYPE	PART NO.
μA709C	μA709TC

ORDER INFORMATION

TYPE	PART NO.
μA709A	μA709AFM
μA709	μA709FM

*Planar is a patented Fairchild process.

FAIRCHILD LINEAR INTEGRATED CIRCUITS • μA709

μA709A

ELECTRICAL CHARACTERISTICS (T_A = 25°C, ±9 V ≤ V_S ≤ ±15 V unless otherwise specified)

PARAMETER (see definitions)		CONDITIONS	MIN	TYP	MAX	UNITS
Input Offset Voltage		$R_S \leq 10$ kΩ		0.6	2.0	mV
Input Offset Current				10	50	nA
Input Bias Current				100	200	nA
Input Resistance			350	700		kΩ
Output Resistance				150		Ω
Supply Current		V_S = ±15 V		2.5	3.6	mA
Power Consumption		V_S = ±15 V		75	108	mW
Transient Response	Rise time	V_S = ±15 V, V_{IN} = 20 mV, R_L = 2 kΩ, C1 = 5 nF, R1 = 1.5 kΩ, C2 = 200 pF, R2 = 50Ω $C_L \leq 100$ pF			1.5	μs
	Overshoot				30	%

The following specifications apply for −55°C ≤ T_A ≤ +125°C:

PARAMETER		CONDITIONS	MIN	TYP	MAX	UNITS
Input Offset Voltage		$R_S \leq 10$ kΩ			3.0	mV
Average Temperature Coefficient of Input Offset Voltage		R_S = 50Ω, T_A = +25°C to +125°C		1.8	10	μV/°C
		R_S = 50Ω, T_A = +25°C to −55°C		1.8	10	μV/°C
		R_S = 10 kΩ, T_A = +25°C to +125°C		2.0	15	μV/°C
		R_S = 10 kΩ, T_A = +25°C to −55°C		4.8	25	μV/°C
Input Offset Current		T_A = +125°C		3.5	50	nA
		T_A = −55°C		40	250	nA
Average Temperature Coefficient of Input Offset Current		T_A = +25°C to +125°C		0.08	0.5	nA/°C
		T_A = +25°C to −55°C		0.45	2.8	nA/°C
Input Bias Current		T_A = −55°C		300	600	nA
Input Resistance		T_A = −55°C	85	170		kΩ
Input Voltage Range		V_S = ±15 V	±8.0			V
Common Mode Rejection Ratio		$R_S \leq 10$ kΩ	80	110		dB
Supply Voltage Rejection Ratio		$R_S \leq 10$ kΩ		40	100	μV/V
Large Signal Voltage Gain		V_S = ±15 V, $R_L \geq 2$ kΩ, V_{OUT} = ±10 V	25,000		70,000	V/V
Output Voltage Swing		V_S = ±15 V, $R_L \geq 10$ kΩ	±12	±14		V
		V_S = ±15 V, $R_L \geq 2$ kΩ	±10	±13		V
Supply Current		T_A = +125°C, V_S = ±15 V		2.1	3.0	mA
		T_A = −55°C, V_S = ±15 V		2.7	4.5	mA
Power Consumption		T_A = +125°C, V_S = ±15 V		63	90	mW
		T_A = −55°C, V_S = ±15 V		81	135	mW

PERFORMANCE CURVES FOR μA709A

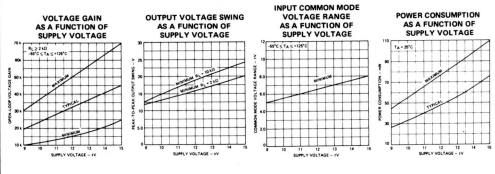

VOLTAGE GAIN AS A FUNCTION OF SUPPLY VOLTAGE

OUTPUT VOLTAGE SWING AS A FUNCTION OF SUPPLY VOLTAGE

INPUT COMMON MODE VOLTAGE RANGE AS A FUNCTION OF SUPPLY VOLTAGE

POWER CONSUMPTION AS A FUNCTION OF SUPPLY VOLTAGE

µA101 · µA201
GENERAL PURPOSE OPERATIONAL AMPLIFIERS
FAIRCHILD LINEAR INTEGRATED CIRCUITS

GENERAL DESCRIPTION — The 101 and 201 are General Purpose monolithic Operational Amplifiers constructed using the Fairchild Planar* epitaxial process. They are intended for a wide range of analog applications where tailoring of frequency characteristics is desirable. The 101 and 201 compensate easily with a single external component. High common mode voltage range and absence of "latch-up" make the 101 and 201 ideal for use as voltage followers. The high gain and wide range of operating voltages provide superior performance in integrator, summing amplifier, and general feedback applications. The 101 and 201 are short-circuit protected and have the same pin configuration as the popular µA741, µA748 and µA709.

- **SHORT-CIRCUIT PROTECTION**
- **OFFSET VOLTAGE NULL CAPABILITY**
- **LARGE COMMON-MODE AND DIFFERENTIAL VOLTAGE RANGES**
- **LOW POWER CONSUMPTION**
- **NO LATCH-UP**

ABSOLUTE MAXIMUM RATINGS

Supply Voltage	±22V
Internal Power Dissipation (Note 1)	
Metal Can	500mW
DIP	670mW
Differential Input Voltage	±30V
Input Voltage (Note 2)	±15V
Storage Temperature Range	
Metal Can, DIP	−65°C to +150°C
Operating Temperature Range (Note 3)	
Military (µA101)	−55°C to +125°C
Commercial (µA201)	0°C to +70°C
Lead Temperature (Soldering, 60 seconds)	300°C

EQUIVALENT CIRCUIT

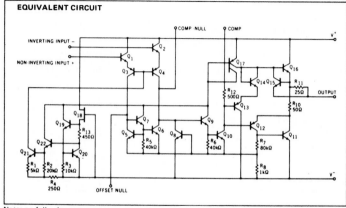

Notes on following pages

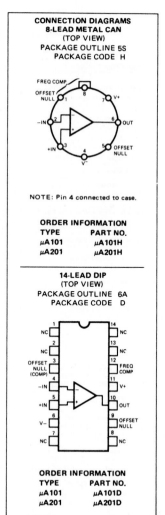

CONNECTION DIAGRAMS
8-LEAD METAL CAN
(TOP VIEW)
PACKAGE OUTLINE 5S
PACKAGE CODE H

NOTE: Pin 4 connected to case.

ORDER INFORMATION

TYPE	PART NO.
µA101	µA101H
µA201	µA201H

14-LEAD DIP
(TOP VIEW)
PACKAGE OUTLINE 6A
PACKAGE CODE   D

ORDER INFORMATION

TYPE	PART NO.
µA101	µA101D
µA201	µA201D

*Planar is a patented Fairchild process.

FAIRCHILD LINEAR INTEGRATED CIRCUITS • μA101 • μA201

ELECTRICAL CHARACTERISTICS FOR μA101 (± 5.0 V $\leqslant V_S \leqslant \pm 20$ V, $T_A = 25°$C, C1 = 30 pF unless otherwise specified)

PARAMETER	CONDITIONS		MIN	TYP	MAX	UNITS
Input Offset Voltage	$R_S \leqslant 10\,k\Omega$			1.0	5.0	mV
Input Offset Current				40	200	nA
Input Bias Current				120	500	nA
Input Resistance			300	800		$k\Omega$
Supply Current	$V_S = \pm 20$V			1.8	3.0	mA
Large Signal Voltage Gain	$V_S = \pm 15$V $V_{OUT} = \pm 10$V, $R_L \geqslant 2\,k\Omega$		50	160		V/mV
The following specifications apply for $-55°$C $\leqslant T_A \leqslant +125°$C:						
Input Offset Voltage	$R_S \leqslant 10\,k\Omega$				6.0	mV
Average Temperature Coefficient of Input Offset Voltage	$R_S \leqslant 50\,k\Omega$			3.0		μV/°C
	$R_S \leqslant 10\,k\Omega$			6.0		μV/°C
Input Offset Current	$T_A = +125°$C			10	200	nA
	$T_A = -55°$C			100	500	nA
Average Temperature Coefficient of Input Offset Current	$+25°$C $\leqslant T_A \leqslant +125°$C			0.01	0.1	nA/°C
	$-55°$C $\leqslant T_A \leqslant +25°$C			0.02	0.2	nA/°C
Input Bias Current	$T_A = -55°$C			0.28	1.5	μA
Supply Current	$T_A = +125°$C, $V_S = \pm 20$V			1.2	2.5	mA
Large Signal Voltage Gain	$V_S = \pm 15$V, $V_{OUT} = \pm 10$V $R_L \geqslant 2\,k\Omega$		25			V/mV
Output Voltage Swing	$V_S = \pm 15$V	$R_L = 10\,k\Omega$	± 12	± 14		V
		$R_L = 2\,k\Omega$	± 10	± 13		V
Input Voltage Range	$V_S = \pm 15$V		± 12			V
Common Mode Rejection Ratio	$R_S \leqslant 10\,k\Omega$		70	90		dB
Supply Voltage Rejection Ratio	$R_S \leqslant 10\,k\Omega$		70	90		dB

NOTES
1. Rating applies to ambient temperature up to 70°C. Above 70°C ambient derate linearly at 6.3mW/°C for the Metal Can and 8.3mW/°C for the DIP.
2. For supply voltages less than ± 15V, the absolute maximum input voltage is equal to the supply voltage.
3. Short circuit may be to ground or either supply. The 101 ratings apply to +125°C case temperature or +75°C ambient temperature. The 201 ratings apply to case temperatures up to +70°C.

μA741
FREQUENCY-COMPENSATED OPERATIONAL AMPLIFIER
FAIRCHILD LINEAR INTEGRATED CIRCUIT

GENERAL DESCRIPTION – The μA741 is a high performance monolithic Operational Amplifier constructed using the Fairchild Planar* epitaxial process. It is intended for a wide range of analog applications. High common mode voltage range and absence of latch-up tendencies make the μA741 ideal for use as a voltage follower. The high gain and wide range of operating voltage provides superior performance in integrator, summing amplifier, and general feedback applications. Electrical characteristics of the μA741A and E are identical to MIL-M-38510/10101.

- **NO FREQUENCY COMPENSATION REQUIRED**
- **SHORT CIRCUIT PROTECTION**
- **OFFSET VOLTAGE NULL CAPABILITY**
- **LARGE COMMON MODE AND DIFFERENTIAL VOLTAGE RANGES**
- **LOW POWER CONSUMPTION**
- **NO LATCH-UP**

ABSOLUTE MAXIMUM RATINGS

Supply Voltage	
μA741A, μA741, μA741E	±22 V
μA741C	±18 V
Internal Power Dissipation (Note 1)	
Metal Can	500 mW
Molded and Hermetic DIP	670 mW
Mini DIP	310 mW
Flatpak	570 mW
Differential Input Voltage	±30 V
Input Voltage (Note 2)	±15 V
Storage Temperature Range	
Metal Can, Hermetic DIP, and Flatpak	−65°C to +150°C
Mini DIP, Molded DIP	−55°C to +125°C
Operating Temperature Range	
Military (μA741A, μA741)	−55°C to +125°C
Commercial (μA741E, μA741C)	0°C to +70°C
Lead Temperature (Soldering)	
Metal Can, Hermetic DIPs, and Flatpak (60 s)	300°C
Molded DIPs (10 s)	260°C
Output Short Circuit Duration (Note 3)	Indefinite

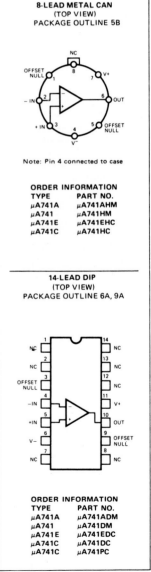

CONNECTION DIAGRAMS

8-LEAD METAL CAN
(TOP VIEW)
PACKAGE OUTLINE 5B

Note: Pin 4 connected to case

ORDER INFORMATION

TYPE	PART NO.
μA741A	μA741AHM
μA741	μA741HM
μA741E	μA741EHC
μA741C	μA741HC

14-LEAD DIP
(TOP VIEW)
PACKAGE OUTLINE 6A, 9A

ORDER INFORMATION

TYPE	PART NO.
μA741A	μA741ADM
μA741	μA741DM
μA741E	μA741EDC
μA741C	μA741DC
μA741C	μA741PC

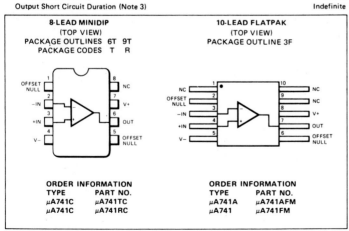

8-LEAD MINIDIP
(TOP VIEW)
PACKAGE OUTLINES 6T 9T
PACKAGE CODES   T   R

ORDER INFORMATION

TYPE	PART NO.
μA741C	μA741TC
μA741C	μA741RC

10-LEAD FLATPAK
(TOP VIEW)
PACKAGE OUTLINE 3F

ORDER INFORMATION

TYPE	PART NO.
μA741A	μA741AFM
μA741	μA741FM

Notes on following pages.

*Planar is a patented Fairchild process.

FAIRCHILD LINEAR INTEGRATED CIRCUITS • μA741

μA741A

ELECTRICAL CHARACTERISTICS ($V_S = \pm15V$, $T_A = 25°C$ unless otherwise specified)

PARAMETERS (see definitions)		CONDITIONS	MIN	TYP	MAX	UNITS
Input Offset Voltage		$R_S \leqslant 50\Omega$		0.8	3.0	mV
Average Input Offset Voltage Drift					15	$\mu V/°C$
Input Offset Current				3.0	30	nA
Average Input Offset Current Drift					0.5	$nA/°C$
Input Bias Current				30	80	nA
Power Supply Rejection Ratio		$V_S = +10, -20$; $V_S = +20, -10V$, $R_S = 50\Omega$		15	50	$\mu V/V$
Output Short Circuit Current			10	25	35	mA
Power Dissipation		$V_S = \pm20V$		80	150	mW
Input Impedance		$V_S = \pm20V$	1.0	6.0		$M\Omega$
Large Signal Voltage Gain		$V_S = \pm20V$, $R_L = 2k\Omega$, $V_{OUT} = \pm15V$	50			V/mV
Transient Response	Rise Time			0.25	0.8	μs
(Unity Gain)	Overshoot			6.0	20	%
Bandwidth (Note 4)			.437	1.5		MHz
Slew Rate (Unity Gain)		$V_{IN} = \pm10V$	0.3	0.7		$V/\mu s$
The following specifications apply for $-55°C \leqslant T_A \leqslant +125°C$						
Input Offset Voltage					4.0	mV
Input Offset Current					70	nA
Input Bias Current					210	nA
Common Mode Rejection Ratio		$V_S = \pm20V$, $V_{IN} = \pm15V$, $R_S = 50\Omega$	80	95		dB
Adjustment For Input Offset Voltage		$V_S = \pm20V$	10			mV
Output Short Circuit Current			10		40	mA
Power Dissipation		$V_S = \pm20V$ $-55°C$			165	mW
		$+125°C$			135	mW
Input Impedance		$V_S = \pm20V$	0.5			$M\Omega$
Output Voltage Swing		$V_S = \pm20V$, $R_L = 10k\Omega$	±16			V
		$R_L = 2k\Omega$	±15			V
Large Signal Voltage Gain		$V_S = \pm20V$, $R_L = 2k\Omega$, $V_{OUT} = \pm15V$	32			V/mV
		$V_S = \pm5V$, $R_L = 2k\Omega$, $V_{OUT} = \pm2 V$	10			V/mV

NOTES
1. Rating applies to ambient temperatures up to 70°C. Above 70°C ambient derate linearly at 6.3mW/°C for the metal can, 8.3mW/°C for the DIP and 7.1mW/°C for the Flatpak.
2. For supply voltages less than ±15V, the absolute maximum input voltage is equal to the supply voltage.
3. Short circuit may be to ground or either supply. Rating applies to +125°C case temperature or 75°C ambient temperature.
4. Calculated value from: $BW(MHz) = \dfrac{0.35}{Rise\ Time\ (\mu s)}$

HIGH PERFORMANCE OPERATIONAL AMPLIFIER   MC1456/1556

MC1456/1556-F,N,T

DESCRIPTION

The MC1456/1556 is an internally compensated precision monolithic operational amplifier featuring extremely low offset and bias currents and offset null capability. The MC1456/1556 is short circuit protected and its high common mode and differential input voltage range provides exceptional performance when used as an integrator, summing amplifier, and voltage follower.

PIN CONFIGURATIONS

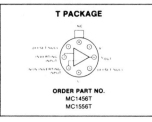

T PACKAGE

ORDER PART NO.
MC1456T
MC1556T

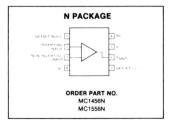

N PACKAGE

ORDER PART NO.
MC1456N
MC1556N

OFFSET ADJUST CIRCUIT

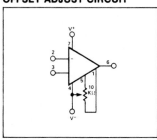

FEATURES

- Low input bias current—15nA maximum
- Low input offset current—2.0nA maximum
- Low input offset voltage—4.0mV maximum
- High slew rate—2.5V/μs typical
- Large power bandwidth—40kHz typical
- Low power consumption—45mW maximum
- Offset voltage null capability
- Output short circuit protection
- Input over-voltage protection
- Mil std 883A,B,C, available

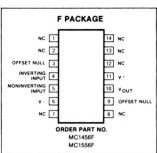

F PACKAGE

NC	1		14	NC
NC	2		13	NC
OFFSET NULL	3		12	NC
INVERTING INPUT	4		11	V +
NONINVERTING INPUT	5		10	V OUT
V -	6		9	OFFSET NULL
NC	7		8	NC

ORDER PART NO.
MC1456F
MC1556F

EQUIVALENT SCHEMATIC

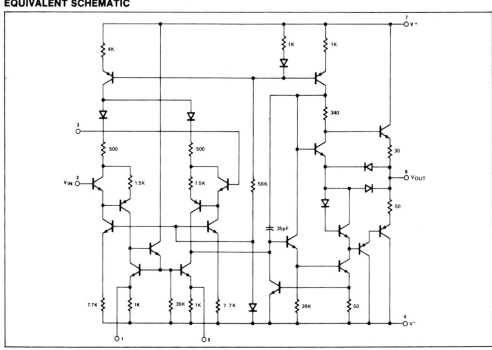

HIGH PERFORMANCE OPERATIONAL AMPLIFIER	MC1456/1556

MC1456/1556-F,N,T

ABSOLUTE MAXIMUM RATINGS

PARAMETER	RATING	UNIT
Power supply voltage MC1556	±22	V
MC1456	±18	V
Differential input voltage	± V_{CC}	V
Common mode input voltage	± V_{CC}	V
Load current	20	mA
Output short circuit duration	Continuous	
Power dissipation	680	mW
Derate above T_A = 25°C	4.6	mW/°C
Operating temperature range		
MC1556	–55 to +125	°C
MC1456	0 to +70	°C
Storage temperature range	–65 to +150	°C

DC ELECTRICAL CHARACTERISTICS T_A = 25°C, V_S = ± 15V unless otherwise specified

PARAMETER		TEST CONDITIONS	MC1556			MC1456			UNIT
			Min	Typ	Max	Min	Typ	Max	
V_{OS}	Offset voltage			2.0	4.0		5.0	10.0	mVdc
		Over temperature			6.0			14.0	mVdc
I_{OS}	Offset current			1.0	2.0		5.0	10.0	nA
		0°C ≤ T_A ≤ 70°C						14	nA
		25°C ≤ T_A ≤ 125°C			3.0				nA
		–55°C ≤ T_A ≤ 25°C			5.0				nA
I_{BIAS}	Input current			8.0	15		15.0	30.0	nA
		Over temperature			30			40	nA
V_{CM}	Common mode voltage range		±12	±13		±11	±12		V
CMRR	Common mode rejection ratio	R_S ≤ 10kΩ, T_A = 25°C, f = 100Hz	80	110		70	110		dB
Z_{IN}	Common mode input impedance	f = 20Hz		250			250		MΩ
V_{OUT}	Output voltage swing	R_L = 2kΩ	±12	±13		±11	±12		V
I_{CC}	Supply current			1.0	1.5		1.3	3.0	mA
P_D	DC quiescent power dissipation (V_O = 0)			30	45		40	90	mW
P_{SRR}	Supply voltage rejection ratio	R_S ≤ 10kΩ		50	100		75	200	μV/V
	Large signal voltage gain	R_L ≤ 2kΩ, V_{OUT} = ±10V, T_A = 25°C	100	200		70	100		V/mV
		Over temperature	40			40			V/mV

AC ELECTRICAL CHARACTERISTICS T_A = 25°C, V_S = ± 15V unless otherwise specified.

PARAMETER		TEST CONDITIONS	MC1556			MC1456			UNIT
			Min	Typ	Max	Min	Typ	Max	
	Differential input impedance								
c_p	Parallel input capacitance	Open loop f = 20Hz		6.0			6.0		pF
r_p	Parallel input resistance			5			3		MΩ
e_n	Equivalent input noise voltage	A_V = 100, R_S = 10kΩ, f = 1.0kHz, BW = 1.0Hz		45			45		nV/$\sqrt{Hz}$
BW_p	Power bandwidth	A_V = 1, R_L = 2kΩ, THD ≤ 5% V_{OUT} = ±10V		40			40		kHz
	Phase margin (open loop, unity gain)			70			70		degrees
	Gain margin			18			18		dB
S_R	Slew rate (unity gain)			2.5			2.5		V/μsec
Z_{OUT}	Output impedance	f = 20Hz		1.0	2.0		1.0	2.5	kΩ
BW	Unity gain crossover frequency (open loop)			1.0			1.0		MHz

HIGH PERFORMANCE JFET INPUT OP AMPS   LF155/155A/156/156A/157/157A SERIES

LF155/A/156/A/157/A, LF255/256/257,
LF355/A/356/A/357/A-T

DESCRIPTION

LF155, LF155A, LF255, LF355, LF355A (Low Supply Current)
LF156, LF156A, LF256, LF356, LF356A (Wide Band)
LF157, LF157A, LF257, LF357, LF357A (Wide Band)

The LF155, LF156, LF157 Series of operational amplifiers employ well matched, high voltage JFET input structures on the same monolithic chip as bipolar devices. These amplifiers feature low input bias and offset currents, low offset voltage and offset voltage drift, coupled with offset adjust which does not degrade drift or common mode rejection. The devices are also designed for high slew rate, wide bandwidth, extremely fast settling time and low noise.

COMMON FEATURES

(LF155A/156A/157A)

- Low input bias current 30pA
- Low input offset current 3pA
- High input impedance $10^{12}\Omega$
- Low input offset voltage 1mV
- Low V_{OS} temperature drift $3\mu V/°C$
- Low input noise current $0.01pA/\sqrt{Hz}$

SPECIFIC FEATURES

	LF155A	LF156A
Settling time (0.01%)	$4\mu s$	$1.5\mu s$
High slew rate	$5v/\mu s$	$12v/\mu s$
Wide bandwidth	2.5MHz	5MHz
Low input noise	$20nV/\sqrt{Hz}$	$12nV/\sqrt{Hz}$

- LF155, LF156—military qualifications pending

LF157A $(A_V = 5)$

- **Settling time** (0.01%) $1.5\mu s$
- **High slew rate** $50v/\mu s$
- **Wide bandwidth**   20MHz
- **Low input noise** $12nV/\sqrt{Hz}$

APPLICATIONS

- Precision high speed integrators
- Fast A/D, D/A converters
- High impedance buffers
- Wideband, low noise, low drift amplifier

PIN CONFIGURATION

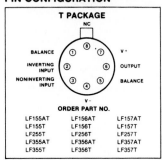

T PACKAGE

NC

BALANCE — (1)   (8) — V +
INVERTING INPUT — (2)   (6) — OUTPUT
NONINVERTING INPUT — (3)   (5) — BALANCE
(4)
V -

ORDER PART NO.

LF155AT	LF156AT	LF157AT
LF155T	LF156T	LF157T
LF255T	LF256T	LF257T
LF355AT	LF356AT	LF357AT
LF355T	LF356T	LF357T

EQUIVALENT SCHEMATIC

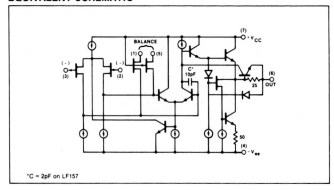

*C = 2pF on LF157

HIGH PERFORMANCE JFET INPUT OP AMPS   LF155/155A/156/156A/157/157A SERIES

LF155/A/156/A/157/A, LF255/256/257,
LF355/A/356/A/357/A-T

ABSOLUTE MAXIMUM RATINGS

PARAMETER	RATING	UNIT
Supply voltage		
LF155A/6A/7A, LF155/6/7	±22	V
LF255/6/7	±22	V
LF355A/6A/7A, LF355/6/7	±18	V
Power dissipation[1] TO-99 (T-package)		
LF155A/6A/7A, LF155/6/7	670	mW
LF255/6/7	570	mW
LF355A/6A/7A, LF355/6/7	500	mW
Operating temperature range		
LF155A/6A/7A, LF155/6/7	−55 to +125	°C
LF255/6/7	−25 to +85	°C
LF355A/6A/7A, LF355/6/7	0 to +70	°C
T_J (Max)		
LF155A/6A/7A, LF155/6/7	150	°C
LF255/6/7	115	°C
LF355A/6A/7A, LF355/6/7	100	°C
Input voltage range[2]		
LF155A/6A/7A, LF155/6/7	±20	V
LF255/6/7	±20	V
LF355A/6A/7A, LF355/6/7	±20	V
Output short circuit duration		
LF155A/6A/7A, LF155/6/7	Continuous	
LF255/6/7	Continuous	
LF355A/6A/7A, LF355/6/7	Continuous	
Storage temperature range		
LF155A/6A/7A, LF155/6/7	−65 to +150	°C
LF255/6/7	−65 to +150	°C
LF355A/6A/7A, LF355/6/7	−65 to +150	°C
Lead temperature (soldering, 10sec.)	300	°C
LF155A/6A/7A, LF155/6/7	300	°C
LF255/6/7	300	°C
LF355A/6A/7A, LF355/6/7	300	°C

NOTES

1. The TO-99 package must be derated based on a thermal resistance of 150°C/W
   junction to ambient or 25°C/W junction to case.
2. Unless otherwise specified, the absolute maximum negative input voltage is equal to
   the negative power supply voltage.

HIGH PERFORMANCE JFET INPUT OP AMPS   LF155/155A/156/156A/157/157A SERIES

LF155/A/156/A/157/A, LF255/256/257,
LF355/A/356/A/357/A-T

DC ELECTRICAL CHARACTERISTICS $T_A = 25°C$ unless otherwise specified. (See notes on following page.)

PARAMETER		TEST CONDITIONS	LF155A/6A/7A			LF355A/6A/7A			UNIT
			Min	Typ	Max	Min	Typ	Max	
V_{OS}	Input offset voltage	$R_s = 50\Omega$		1	2 2.5		1	2 2.3	mV mV
$\Delta V_{OS}/\Delta T$	Avg. TC of input offset voltage	$R_s = 50\Omega$		3	5		3	5	$\mu V/°C$
$\Delta TC/\Delta V_{OS}$	Change in average TC[2] with V_{OS} adjust	$R_s = 50\Omega$		0.5			0.5		$\mu V/°C$ per mV
I_{OS}	Input offset current[1,3]	$T_J = 25°C$ $T_J \leq T_{high}$		3	10 10		3	10 1	pA nA
I_B	Input bias current[1,3]	$T_J = 25°C$ $T_J \leq T_{high}$		30	50 25		30	50 5	pA nA
R_{IN}	Input resistance	$T_J = 25°C$		10^{12}			10^{12}		Ω
A_{VOL}	Large signal voltage gain	$V_s = \pm 15V$ $V_O = \pm 10V, R_L = 2k\Omega$ Over temp.	50 25	200		50 25	200		V/mV V/mV
V_O	Output voltage swing	$V_s = \pm 15V, R_L = 10k\Omega$ $V_s = \pm 15V, R_L = 2k\Omega$	± 12 ± 10	± 13 ± 12		± 12 ± 10	± 13 ± 12		V V
V_{CM}	Input common mode Voltage range	$V_s = \pm 15V$	± 11	$+15.1$ -12		± 11	$+15.1$ -12		V V V
CMRR PSRR	Common-mode rejection ratio Supply volt. rej. ratio[4]		85 85	100 100		85 85	100 100		dB dB

DC ELECTRICAL CHARACTERISTICS   (Cont'd) $T_A = 25°C$ unless otherwise specified. (See notes on following page.)

PARAMETER		TEST CONDITIONS	LF155/6/7			LF255/6/7			UNIT
			Min	Typ	Max	Min	Typ	Max	
V_{OS}	Input offset voltage	$R_s = 50\Omega$		3	5 7		3	5 6.5	mV mV
$\Delta V_{OS}/\Delta T$	Avg. TC of input offset voltage	$R_s = 50\Omega$		5			5		$\mu V/°C$
$\Delta TC/\Delta V_{OS}$	Change in average TC[2] with V_{OS} adjust	$R_s = 50\Omega$		0.5			0.5		$\mu V/°C$ per mV
I_{OS}	Input offset current[1,3]	$T_J = 25°C$ $T_J \leq T_{high}$		3	20 20		3	20 1	pA nA
I_B	Input bias current[1,3]	$T_J = 25°C$ $T_J \leq T_{high}$		30	100 50		30	100 5	pA nA
R_{IN}	Input resistance	$T_J = 25°C$		10^{12}			10^{12}		Ω
A_{VOL}	Large signal voltage gain	$V_s = \pm 15V$ $V_O = \pm 10V, R_L = 2k\Omega$ Over temp.	50 25	200		50 25	200		V/mV V/mV
V_O	Output voltage swing	$V_s = \pm 15V, R_L = 10k\Omega$ $V_s = \pm 15V, R_L = 2k\Omega$	± 12 ± 10	± 13 ± 12		± 12 ± 10	± 13 ± 12		V V
V_{CM}	Input common mode Voltage range	$V_s = \pm 15V$	± 11	$+15.1$ -12		± 11	$+15.1$ -12		V V V
CMRR PSRR	Common-mode rejection ratio Supply volt. rej. ratio[4]		85 85	100 100		85 85	100 100		dB dB

HIGH PERFORMANCE JFET INPUT OP AMPS   LF155/155A/156/156A/157/157A SERIES

LF155/A/156/A/157/A, LF255/256/257,
LF355/A/356/A/357/A-T

DC ELECTRICAL CHARACTERISTICS (Cont'd) T_A = 25°C unless otherwise specified.

PARAMETER		TEST CONDITIONS	LF355/6/7			UNIT
			Min	Typ	Max	
V_{os}	Input offset voltage	$R_s = 50\Omega$		3	10	mV
					13	mV
$\Delta V_{os}/\Delta T$	Avg. TC of input offset voltage	$R_s = 50\Omega$		5		$\mu V/°C$
$\Delta TC/\Delta V_{os}$	Change in average TC[2] with V_{os} adjust	$R_s = 50\Omega$		0.5		$\mu V/°C$ per mV
I_{os}	Input offset current[1,3]	$T_J = 25°C$		3	50	pA
		$T_J \leq T_{high}$			2	nA
I_B	Input bias current[1,3]	$T_J = 25°C$		30	200	pA
		$T_J \leq T_{high}$			8	nA
R_{IN}	Input resistance	$T_J = 25°C$		10^{12}		Ω
A_{VOL}	Large signal voltage gain	$V_s = \pm 15V$ $V_o = \pm 10V, R_L = 2k\Omega$	25	200		V/mV
		Over temp.	15			V/mV
V_o	Output voltage swing	$V_s = \pm 15V, R_L = 10k\Omega$	±12	±13		V
		$V_s = \pm 15V, R_L = 2k\Omega$	±10	±12		V
V_{CM}	Input common mode Voltage range	$V_s = \pm 15V$	±10	+15.1		V
						V
				-12		V
CMRR	Common-mode rejection ratio		80	100		dB
PSRR	Supply volt. rej. ratio[4]		80	100		dB

DC ELECTRICAL CHARACTERISTICS T_A = 25°C, $V_s = \pm15V$ unless otherwise specified.

PARAMETER	LF155A/355A LF155/255			LF355			LF156A/LF156/256			UNIT
	Min	Typ	Max	Min	Typ	Max	Min	Typ	Max	
Supply current		2	4		2	4		5	7	mA

DC ELECTRICAL CHARACTERISTICS (Cont'd) T_A = 25°C, $V_s = \pm 15V$ unless otherwise specified.

PARAMETER	LF356A/LF356			LF157A/LF157/257			LF357A/LF357			UNIT
	Min	Typ	Max	Min	Typ	Max	Min	Typ	Max	
Supply current		5	10		5	7		5	10	mA

NOTES

1. These specifications apply for $\pm15V \leq V_S \leq \pm 20V$, -55°C $\leq T_A$ $\pm125°C$ and T_{HIGH} = +125°C unless otherwise stated for the LF155A/6A/7A and the LF155/6/7. For the LF255/6/7, these specifications apply for $\pm15V \leq V_S \leq \pm20V$, -25°C $\leq T_A \leq +85°C$ and T_{HIGH} = 85°C unless otherwise stated. For the LF355A/6A/7A, these specifications apply for $\pm15V \leq V_S \leq \pm20V$, 0°C $\leq T_A \leq +70°C$ and T_{HIGH} = +70°C, and for the LF355/6/7 these specifications apply for $V_S = \pm15V$ and 0°C $\leq T_A \leq +70°C$. V_{OS}, I_B and I_{OS} are measured at $V_{CM}= 0$.

2. The Temperature Coefficient of the adjusted input offset voltage changes only a small amount (0.5$\mu V/°C$ typically) for each mV of adjustment from its original unadjusted value. Common mode rejection and open loop voltage gain are also unaffected by offset adjustment.

3. The input bias currents are junction leakage currents which approximately double for every 10°C increase in the junction temperature, T_J. Due to limited production test time, the input bias currents measured are correlated to junction temperature. In normal operation the junction temperature rises above the ambient temperature as a result of internal power dissipation, Pd. $T_j = T_A + \theta_{jA}$ Pd where θ_{jA} is the thermal resistance from junction to ambient. Use of a heat sink is recommended if input bias current is to be kept to a minimum.

4. Supply Voltage Rejection is measured for both supply magnitudes increasing or decreasing simultaneously, in accordance with common practice.

HIGH PERFORMANCE JFET INPUT OP AMPS   LF155/155A/156/156A/157/157A SERIES

LF155/A/156/A/157/A, LF255/256/257,
LF355/A/356/A/357/A-T

AC ELECTRICAL CHARACTERISTICS $T_A = 25°C$, $V_s = \pm 15V$ unless otherwise specified.[1]

PARAMETER		TEST CONDITIONS	LF155A/LF355A			LF156A/356A			LF157A/357A			UNIT
			Min	Typ	Max	Min	Typ	Max	Min	Typ	Max	
SR	Slew rate	LF155/156 LF155A/6A: $A_v = 1$	3	5		10	12		40	50		V/μs
GBW	Gain bandwidth product			2.5		4	4.5		15	20		MHz
t_s	Settling time[5] to 0.01%			4			1.5			1.5		μs
e_n	Equiv. input noise volt.	$R_s = 100\Omega$ f = 100Hz f = 1000Hz		25 20			15 12			15 12		nV/$\sqrt{Hz}$ nV/$\sqrt{Hz}$
i_n	Equiv. input noise current	f = 100Hz f = 1000Hz		0.01 0.01			0.01 0.01			0.01 0.01		pA/$\sqrt{Hz}$ pA/$\sqrt{Hz}$
C_{IN}	Input capacitance			3			3			3		pF

AC ELECTRICAL CHARACTERISTICS (Cont'd) $T_A = 25°C$, $V_s = \pm 15V$ unless otherwise specified.[1]

PARAMETER		TEST CONDITIONS	LF155/255/355			LF156/256			LF356			UNIT
			Min	Typ	Max	Min	Typ	Max	Min	Typ	Max	
SR	Slew rate	LF155/156 LF155A/6A: $A_v = 1$,		5		7.5	12			12		V/μs
GBW	Gain bandwidth product			2.5			5			5		MHz
t_s	Settling time[5] to 0.01%			4			1.5			1.5		μs
e_n	Equiv. input noise volt.	$R_s = 100\Omega$ f = 100Hz f = 1000Hz		25 20			15 12			15 12		nV/$\sqrt{Hz}$ nV/$\sqrt{Hz}$
i_n	Equiv. input noise current	f = 100Hz f = 1000Hz		0.01 0.01			0.01 0.01			0.01 0.01		pA/$\sqrt{Hz}$ pA/$\sqrt{Hz}$
C_{IN}	Input capacitance			3			3			3		pF

LF155/A/156/A/157/A, LF255/256/257,
LF355/A/356/A/357/A-T

AC ELECTRICAL CHARACTERISTICS (Cont'd) $T_A = 25°C$, $V_S = \pm 15V$ unless otherwise specified.[1]

PARAMETER		TEST CONDITIONS	LF157/257			LF357			UNIT
			Min	Typ	Max	Min	Typ	Max	
SR	Slew rate	LF157A/LF157: $A_V = 5$	30	50			50		V/μs
GBW	Gain bandwidth product			20			20		MHz
t_s	Settling time[5] to 0.01%			1.5			1.5		μs
e_n	Equiv. input noise volt.	$R_s = 100Ω$ f = 100Hz f = 1000Hz		15 12			15 12		nV/√Hz nV/√Hz
i_n	Equiv. input noise current	f = 100Hz f = 1000Hz		0.01 0.01			0.01 0.01		pA/√Hz pA/√Hz
C_{IN}	Input capacitance			3			3		pF

NOTE

5. Settling time is defined here, for a unity gain inverter connection using 2kΩ resistors for the LF155/6. It is the time required for the error voltage (the voltage at the inverting input pin on the amplifier) to settle to within 0.01% of its final value from the time a 10V step input is applied to the inverter. For the LF157, $A_V = -5$, the feedback resistor from output to input is 2kΩ and the output step is 10V (See Settling Time Test Circuit).

TYPICAL DC PERFORMANCE CHARACTERISTICS (curves are for LF155, LF156 and LF157 unless otherwise specified.)

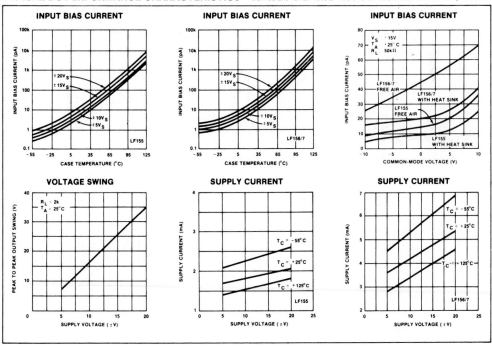

LM377 dual 2 watt audio amplifier

Consumer Circuits

general description

The LM377 is a monolithic dual power amplifier which offers high quality performance for stereo phonographs, tape players, recorders, and AM-FM stereo receivers, etc.

The LM377 will deliver 2W/channel into 8 or 16Ω loads. The amplifier is designed to operate with a minimum of external components and contains an internal bias regulator to bias each amplifier. Device overload protection consists of both internal current limit and thermal shutdown.

features

- A_{VO} typical 90 dB
- 2W per channel
- 70 dB ripple rejection
- 75 dB channel separation
- Internal stabilization
- Self centered biasing

- 3 MΩ input impedance
- 10–26V operation
- Internal current limiting
- Internal thermal protection

applications

- Multi-channel audio systems
- Tape recorders and players
- Movie projectors
- Automotive systems
- Stereo phonographs
- Bridge output stages
- AM-FM radio receivers
- Intercoms
- Servo amplifiers
- Instrument systems

schematic diagram

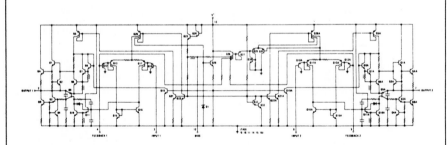

connection diagram

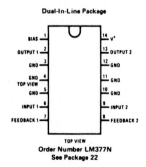

TOP VIEW
Order Number LM377N
See Package 22

typical applications

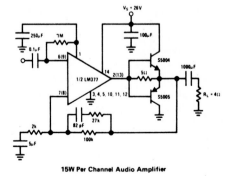

15W Per Channel Audio Amplifier

absolute maximum ratings

Supply Voltage	26V
Input Voltage	0V – V_{SUPPLY}
Operating Temperature	$0°C$ to $+70°C$
Storage Temperature	$-65°C$ to $+150°C$
Junction Temperature	$150°C$
Lead Temperature (Soldering, 10 seconds)	$300°C$

electrical characteristics

V_S = 20V, T_{TAB} = 25°C, R_L = 8Ω, A_V = 50 (34 dB), unless otherwise specified.

PARAMETER	CONDITIONS	MIN	TYP	MAX	UNITS
Total Supply Current	P_{OUT} = 0W		15	50	mA
	P_{OUT} = 1.5W/Channel		430	500	mA
DC Output Level			10		V
Supply Voltage		10		26	V
Output Power	T.H.D. = < 5%	2	2.5		W
T.H.D.	P_{OUT} = 0.05W/Channel, f = 1 kHz		0.25		%
	P_{OUT} = 1W/Channel, f = 1 kHz		0.07	1	%
	P_{OUT} = 2W/Channel, f = 1 kHz		0.10		%
Offset Voltage			15		mV
Input Bias Current			100		nA
Input Impedance		3			MΩ
Open Loop Gain	R_S = 0Ω	66	90		dB
Output Swing			V_S–6		V_{P-P}
Channel Separation	C_F = 250μF, f = 1 kHz	50	70		dB
Ripple Rejection	f = 120 Hz, C_F = 250μF	60	70		dB
Current Limit			1.5		A
Slew Rate			1.4		V/μs
Equivalent Input Noise Voltage	R_S = 600Ω, 100 Hz – 10 kHz		3		μVrms

Note 1: For operation at ambient temperatures greater than 25°C the LM377 must be derated based on a maximum 150°C junction temperature using a thermal resistance which depends upon device mounting techniques.

Note 2: Dissipation characteristics are shown for four mounting configurations.

   a. Infinite sink – 13.4°C/W

   b. P.C. board +V_7 sink – 21°C/W. P.C. board is 2 1/2 square inches. Staver V_7 sink is 0.02 inch thick copper and has a radiating surface area of 10 square inches.

   c. P.C. board only – 29°C/W. Device soldered to 2 1/2 square inch P.C. board.

   d. Free air – 58°C/W.

Consumer Circuits

LM378 dual 4 watt audio amplifier

general description

The LM378 is a monolithic dual power amplifier which offers high quality performance for stereo phonographs, tape players, recorders, and AM-FM stereo receivers, etc.

The LM378 will deliver 4W channel into 8 or 16Ω loads. The amplifier is designed to operate with a minimum of external components and contains an internal bias regulator to bias each amplifier. Device overload protection consists of both internal current limit and thermal shutdown.

features

- A$_{VO}$ typical 90 dB
- 4W per channel
- 70 dB ripple rejection
- 75 dB channel separation
- Internal stabilization

- Self centered biasing
- 3 MΩ input impedance
- Internal current limiting
- Internal thermal protection

applications

- Multi-channel audio systems
- Tape recorders and players
- Movie projectors
- Automotive systems
- Stereo phonographs
- Bridge output stages
- AM-FM radio receivers
- Intercoms
- Servo amplifiers
- Instrument systems

schematic diagram

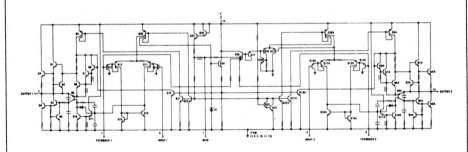

connection diagram

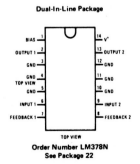

Dual-In-Line Package

TOP VIEW

Order Number LM378N
See Package 22

typical applications

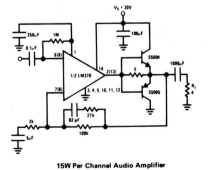

15W Per Channel Audio Amplifier

absolute maximum ratings

Supply Voltage	35V
Input Voltage	$0V - V_{SUPPLY}$
Operating Temperature	$0°C$ to $+70°C$
Storage Temperature	$-65°C$ to $+150°C$
Junction Temperature	$150°C$
Lead Temperature (Soldering, 10 seconds)	$300°C$

electrical characteristics

V_S = 24V, T_{TAB} = 25°C, R_L = 8Ω, A_V = 50 (34 dB), unless otherwise specified.

PARAMETER	CONDITIONS	MIN	TYP	MAX	UNITS
Total Supply Current	P_{OUT} = 0W		15	50	mA
	P_{OUT} = 1.5W/Channel		430	500	mA
DC Output Level			12		V
Supply Voltage		10			V
Output Power	T.H.D. = < 5%, R_L = 8Ω	4	5		W
	T.H.D. = < 5%, R_L = 16Ω	4	5		W*
T.H.D.	P_{OUT} = 0.05W/Channel, f = 1 kHz		0.25		%
	P_{OUT} = 1W/Channel, f = 1 kHz		0.07	1	%
	P_{OUT} 2W/Channel, f = 1 kHz		0.10		%
Offset Voltage			15		mV
Input Bias Current			100		nA
Input Impedance		3			MΩ
Open Loop Gain	R_S = 0Ω	66	90		dB
Channel Separation	C_F = 250μF, f = 1 kHz	50	70		dB
Ripple Rejection	f = 120 Hz, C_F = 250μF	60	70		dB
Current Limit			1.5		A
Slew Rate			1.4		V/μs
Equivalent Input Noise Voltage	R_S = 600Ω, 100 Hz − 10 kHz		3		μVrms

Note 1: For operation at ambient temperatures greater than 25°C the LM378 must be derated based on a maximum 150°C junction temperature using a thermal resistance which depends upon device mounting techniques.

Note 2: Dissipation characteristics are shown for four mounting configurations.

    a. Infinite sink − 13.4°C/W

    b. P.C. board +V_7 sink − 21°C/W. P.C. board is 2 1/2 square inches. Staver V_7 sink is 0.02 inch thick copper and has a radiating surface area of 10 square inches.

    c. P.C. board only − 29°C/W. Device soldered to 2 1/2 square inch P.C. board.

    d. Free air − 58°C/W.

*Tested at V_S = 30V.

Consumer Circuits

LM387 low noise dual preamplifier

general description

The LM387 is a dual preamplifier for the amplication of low level signals in applications requiring optimum noise performance. Each of the two amplifiers is completely independent, with an internal power supply decoupler-regulator, providing 110 dB supply rejection and 60 dB channel separation. Other outstanding features include high gain (104 dB), large output voltage swing ($V_{CC}-2V$)p-p, and wide power bandwidth (75 kHz, 20 Vp-p). The LM387 operates from a single supply across the wide range of 9 to 40V.

The amplifiers are internally compensated for. All gains greater than 10. The LM387 is available in an 8 lead dual-in-line package.

features

- Low noise $0.8\mu V$ total input noise
- High gain   104 dB open loop
- Single supply operation
- Wide supply range   9 to 40V
- Power supply rejection   110 dB
- Large output voltage swing ($V_{CC}-2V$)p-p
- Wide bandwidth 15 MHz unity gain
- Power bandwidth 75 kHz, 20 Vp-p
- Internally compensated
- Short circuit protected

schematic and connection diagrams

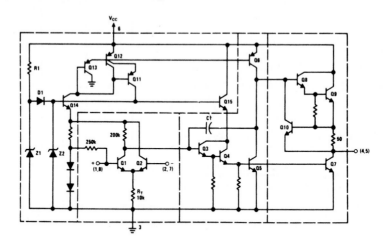

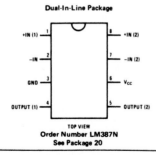

Dual-In-Line Package

+IN (1)	1	8	+IN (2)
−IN	2	7	−IN (2)
GND	3	6	V_{CC}
OUTPUT (1)	4	5	OUTPUT (2)

TOP VIEW
Order Number LM387N
See Package 20

absolute maximum ratings

Supply Voltage	+40V
Power Dissipation	660 mW
Operating Temperature Range	$0°C$ to $+70°C$
Storage Temperature Range	$-65°C$ to $+150°C$
Lead Temperature (Soldering, 10 seconds)	$300°C$

electrical characteristics $T_A = 25°C$, $V_{CC} = 14V$, unless otherwise stated.

PARAMETER	CONDITIONS	MIN	TYP	MAX	UNITS
Voltage Gain	Open Loop		160,000		V/V
Supply Current	V_{CC} 9 to 40V, $R_L = \infty$		10		mA
Input Resistance					
Positive Input			100.		$k\Omega$
Negative Input			200		$k\Omega$
Input Current					
Negative Input			0.5		μA
Output Resistance	Open Loop		150		Ω
Output Current	Source		8		mA
	Sink		2		mA
Output Voltage Swing	Peak-to-Peak		$V_{CC}-2$		V
Small Signal Bandwidth			15		MHz
Power Bandwidth	20 Vp-p (V_{CC} = 24V)		75		kHz
Maximum Input Voltage	Linear Operation			300	mVrms
Supply Rejection Ratio	f = 1 kHz		110		dB
Channel Separation	f = 1 kHz		60		dB
Total Harmonic Distortion	75 dB Gain, f = 1 kHz		0.1		%
Total Equivalent Input Noise	$R_S = 600\Omega$, 100 – 10,000 Hz		0.8	1.4	$\mu Vrms$
Noise Figure	50 kΩ, 10 – 10,000 Hz		1.0		dB
	10 kΩ, 10 – 10,000 Hz		1.6		dB
	5 kΩ, 10 – 10,000 Hz		2.8		dB

Operational Amplifiers

LM747/LM747C dual operational amplifier

general description

The LM747 and the LM747C are general purpose dual operational amplifiers. The two amplifiers share a common bias network and power supply leads. Otherwise, their operation is completely independent.

features

- No frequency compensation required
- Short-circuit protection
- Wide common-mode and differential voltage ranges

- Low-power consumption
- No latch-up
- Balanced offset null

Additional features of the LM747 and LM747C are: no latch-up when input common mode range is exceeded, freedom from oscillations, and package flexibility.

The LM747C is identical to the LM747 except that the LM747C has its specifications guaranteed over the temperature range from $0°C$ to $70°C$ instead of $-55°C$ to $+125°C$.

schematic diagram (each amplifier)

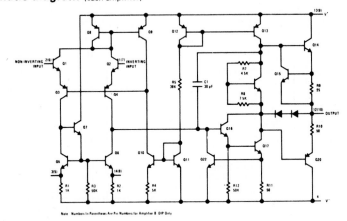

Note: Numbers In Parentheses Are Pin Numbers for Amplifier B DIP Only

connection diagrams

Metal Can Package

Order Number LM747H or LM747CH
See Package 14

Flat Package

Order Number LM747F or LM747CF
See Package 4

Dual-In-Line Packages

Order Number LM747D or LM747CD
See Package 1

Order Number LM747CN
See Package 22

**V⁺A and V⁺B are internally connected.

absolute maximum ratings

Supply Voltage LM747	±22V
LM747C	±18V
Power Dissipation (Note 1)	800 mW
Differential Input Voltage	±30V
Input Voltage (Note 2)	±15V
Output Short-Circuit Duration	Indefinite
Operating Temperature Range LM747	$-55°C$ to $125°C$
LM747C	$0°C$ to $70°C$
Storage Temperature Range	$-65°C$ to $150°C$
Lead Temperature (Soldering, 10 sec)	$300°C$

electrical characteristics (Note 3)

PARAMETER	CONDITIONS	LM747 MIN	LM747 TYP	LM747 MAX	LM747C MIN	LM747C TYP	LM747C MAX	UNITS
Input Offset Voltage	$T_A = 25°C$, $R_S \le 10 k\Omega$		1.0	5.0		1.0	6.0	mV
Input Offset Current	$T_A = 25°C$		80	200		80	200	nA
Input Bias Current	$T_A = 25°C$		200	500		200	500	nA
Input Resistance	$T_A = 25°C$	0.3	1.0		0.3	1.0		MΩ
Supply Current Both Amplifiers	$T_A = 25°C$, $V_S = \pm15V$		3.0	5.6		3.0	5.6	mA
Large Signal Voltage Gain	$T_A = 25°C$, $V_S = \pm15V$ $V_{OUT} = \pm10V$, $R_L \ge 2 k\Omega$	50	160		50	160		V/mV
Input Offset Voltage	$R_S \le 10 k\Omega$			6.0			7.5	mV
Input Offset Current				500			300	nA
Input Bias Current				1.5			0.8	μA
Large Signal Voltage Gain	$V_S = \pm15V$, $V_{OUT} = \pm10V$ $R_L \ge 2 k\Omega$	25			25			V/mV
Output Voltage Swing	$V_S = \pm15V$, $R_L = 10 k\Omega$	±12	±14		±12	±14		V
	$R_L = 2 k\Omega$	±10	±13		±10	±13		V
Input Voltage Range	$V_S = \pm15V$	±12			±12			V
Common Mode Rejection Ratio	$R_S \le 10 k\Omega$	70	90		70	90		dB
Supply Voltage Rejection Ratio	$R_S \le 10 k\Omega$	77	96		77	96		dB

Note 1: The maximum junction temperature of the LM747 is $150°C$, while that of the LM747C is $100°C$. For operating at elevated temperatures, devices in the TO-5 package must be derated based on a thermal resistance of $150°C$/W, junction to ambient, or $45°C$/W, junction to case. For the flat package, the derating is based on a thermal resistance of $185°C$/W when mounted on a 1/16-inch-thick epoxy glass board with ten, 0.03-inch-wide, 2-ounce copper conductors. The thermal resistance of the dual-in-line package is $100°C$/W, junction to ambient.

Note 2: For supply voltages less than ±15V, the absolute maximum input voltage is equal to the supply voltage.

Note 3: These specifications apply for $V_S = \pm15V$ and $-55°C \le T_A \le 125°C$, unless otherwise specified. With the LM747C, however, all specifications are limited to $0°C \le T_A \le 70°C$ $V_S = \pm15V$.

Operational Amplifiers

LM3900 quad amplifier
general description

The LM3900 consists of four independent, dual input, internally compensated amplifiers which were designed specifically to operate off of a single power supply voltage and to provide a large output voltage swing. These amplifiers make use of a current mirror to achieve the non-inverting input function. Application areas include: AC amplifiers, RC active filters; low frequency triangle, squarewave and pulse waveform generation circuits, tachometers and low speed, high voltage digital logic gates.

features

- Wide single supply voltage range   4 V_{DC} to 36 V_{DC}
  or dual supplies ±2 V_{DC} to ±18 V_{DC}
- Supply current drain independent of supply voltage
- Low input biasing current   30 nA
- High open-loop gain   70 dB
- Wide bandwidth   2.5 MHz (Unity Gain)
- Large output voltage swing $(V^+ -1)$ V_{p-p}
- Internally frequency compensated for unity gain
- Output short-circuit protection

schematic and connection diagrams

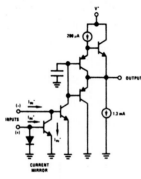

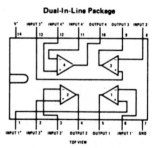

Dual-In-Line Package

Order Number LM3900N
See Package 22

typical applications $(V^+ = 15 V_{DC})$

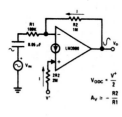

Inverting Amplifier

$$V_{ODC} = \frac{V^+}{2}$$
$$A_V \geq -\frac{R2}{R1}$$

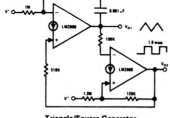

Triangle/Square Generator

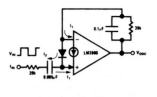

Frequency-Doubling Tachometer

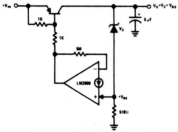

Low $V_{IN}-V_{OUT}$ Voltage Regulator

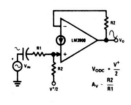

Non-Inverting Amplifier

$$V_{ODC} = \frac{V^+}{2}$$
$$A_V = \frac{R2}{R1}$$

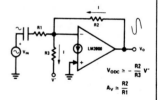

Negative Supply Biasing

$$V_{ODC} = -\frac{R2}{R3} V^-$$
$$A_V \geq \frac{R2}{R1}$$

absolute maximum ratings

Supply Voltage	+32 VDC
	±18 VDC
Power Dissipation (T_A = 25°C) (Note 1)	570 mW
Input Currents, $I_{IN}+$ or $I_{IN}-$	20 mA DC
Output Short Circuit Duration — One	Continuous
Amplifier T_A = 25°C	
(See Application Hints)	
Operating Temperature Range	0°C to +70°C
Storage Temperature Range	–65°C to +150°C
Lead Temperature (Soldering, 10 seconds)	300°C

electrical characteristics (V^+ = +15 VDC and T_A = 25°C unless otherwise noted)

PARAMETER	CONDITIONS	MIN	TYP	MAX	UNITS
Open Loop					
Voltage Gain	f = 100 Hz	1200	2800		V/V
Input Resistance	Inverting Input		1		MΩ
Output Resistance			8		kΩ
Unity Gain Bandwidth	Inverting Input		2.5		MHz
Input Bias Current	Inverting Input		30	200	nA
Slew Rate	Positive Output Swing		0.5		V/µs
	Negative Output Swing		20		V/µs
Supply Current	R_L = ∞ On All Amplifiers		6.2	10	mA DC
Output Voltage Swing	R_L = 5.1k				
V_{OUT} High	$I_{IN}-$ = 0, $I_{IN}+$ = 0	13.5	14.2		VDC
V_{OUT} Low	$I_{IN}-$ = 10 µA, $I_{IN}+$ = 0		0.09	0.2	VDC
Output Current Capability					
Source		3	18		mA DC
Sink	(Note 2)	0.5	1.3		mA DC
Power Supply Rejection	f = 100 Hz		70		dB
Mirror Gain	$I_{IN}+$ = 200 µA (Note 3)	0.9	1	1.1	µA/µA
Mirror Current	(Note 4)		10	500	µA DC
Negative Input Current	(Note 5)		1.0		mA DC

Note 1: For operating at high temperatures, the device must be derated based on a 125°C maximum junction temperature and a thermal resistance of 175°C/W which applies for the device soldered in a printed circuit board, operating in a still air ambient.

Note 2: The output current sink capability can be increased for large signal conditions by overdriving the inverting input. This is shown in the section on Typical Characteristics.

Note 3: This spec indicates the current gain of the current mirror which is used as the non-inverting input.

Note 4: Input V_{BE} match between the non-inverting and the inverting inputs occurs for a mirror current (non-inverting input current) of approximately 10 µA. This is therefore a typical design center for many of the application circuits.

Note 5: Clamp transistors are included on the IC to prevent the input voltages from swinging below ground more than approximately –0.3 VDC. The negative input currents which may result from large signal overdrive with capacitance input coupling need to be externally limited to values of approximately 1 mA. Negative input currents in excess of 4 mA will cause the output voltage to drop to a low voltage. This maximum current applies to any one of the input terminals. If more than one of the input terminals are simultaneously driven negative smaller maximum currents are allowed. Common-mode current biasing can be used to prevent negative input voltages; see for example the "Differentiator Circuit" in the applications section.

ANSWERS TO SELF-CHECKING QUIZZES

Chapter 1

1. c, 1	11. False
2. f, k	12. True
3. a	13. False
4. i	14. True
5. h	15. True
6. e	16. True
7. d	17. True
8. i	18. False
9. g	19. True
10. b	20. True

Chapter 2

1. f	11. b
2. d	12. a
3. e	13. c
4. a	14. f
5. c	15. b
6. b	16. a
7. a	17. b
8. c	18. c
8. a	19. b
10. d	20. d

Chapter 3

1. e	11. b
2. f	12. f
3. b	13. True
4. c	14. False
5. a	15. False
6. d	16. True
7. e	17 True
8. c	18. True
9. d	19. False
10. a	20. True

Chapter 4

1. c	6. True
2. a	7. True
3. e	8. False
4. b	9. True
5. d	10. False

Chapter 5

1. OP-3	6. T.C.-2
2. OP-4	7. b
3. T.C.-1	8. c
4. R_{11}	9. a
5. OP-1	10. d

Chapter 6

1. b	6. e
2. g	7. a
3. d	8. d
4. c	9. b
5. f	10. d

Chapter 7

1. b	6. a
2. c	7. d
3. a	8. c
4. c	9. b
5. c	10. b

OP AMP FINAL EXAMINATION

Select the most correct answer for each question.

1. A standard op amp has:
   a. Low input impedance, high gain, and low output impedance
   b. Low input impedance, high gain, and high output impedance
   c. High input impedance, high gain, and high output impedance
   d. High input impedance, high gain, and low output impedance

2. An op amp may:
   a. Operate on a + dual power supply
   b. Have two inputs
   c. Have one output
   d. All of the above
   e. None of the above

3. The maximum rate of change of an op amp's output voltage to an input voltage change is called:
   a. Common-mode rejection
   b. Bandwidth
   c. Slew rate
   d. Latch-up

4. If a signal of the same amplitude and phase angle is applied to both inputs of an op amp simultaneously, and the output is nearly zero, the op amp is said to have a:
   a. Low gain
   b. High slew rate
   c. High common-mode rejection ratio
   d. None of the above

5. An error voltage occurring at the output of an op amp when the input voltages are the same is referred to as:
   a. Output offset voltage
   b. Input offset current
   c. Common-mode amplification
   d. None of the above

6. The heart of an op amp is:
   a. The emitter-follower output stage
   b. The differential input amplifier circuit
   c. Tthe low-gain voltage amplifier
   d. None of the above

7. The arrangement of components in the output stage of an op amp is referred to as the:
   a. Differential amplifier
   b. Emitter-follower output
   c. Totem-pole output
   d. Current amplifier

8. Offset nulling can be accomplished by:
   a. Adjusting special potentiometers at the inputs
   b. Using a potentiometer connected between special pins on the op amp
   c. Both of the above
   d. None of the above

9. The highest frequency at which the op amp output gain falls to 70.7percent of the maximum output is called:
   a. The unity gain point
   b. The frequency response
   c. Frequency compensation
   d. All of the above

10. The type of feedback generally applied to an op amp to control gain and stability is:
   a. Negative feedback
   b. Positive feedback
   c. Regenerative feedback
   d. None of the above

11. The output voltage of the circuit shown in Figure A is approximately:
   a. + 8.1 V
   b. + 5.25 V
   c. − 5.25 V
   d. + 0.25 V

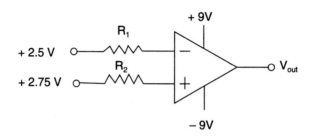

FIGURE A

12. Referring to Figure B, V_{ref} is approximately:
   a. + 7.0 V
   b. − 12 V
   c. + 4.9 V
   d. − 9.0 V

13. Referring to Figure B, when the input voltage is 0 V, the output voltage of the op amp will be:
   a. + 4.9 V
   b. + 10.8 V
   c. − 10.8 V
   d. None of the above.

14. Referring to Figure B, when the input voltage reaches +5.0 V, the output voltage will be:
   a. + 4.9 V
   b. + 10.8 V
   c. − 10.8 V
   d. − 7.0 V

15. Referring to Figure C, the gain of the circuit is:
   a. 4.7
   b. 9.5
   c. 47

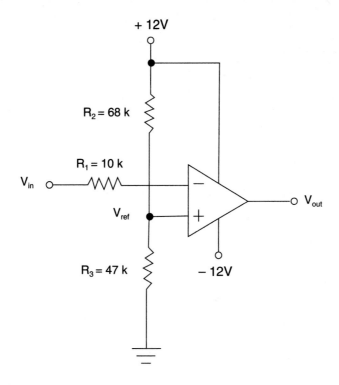

FIGURE B

    d.   None of the above
16. Referring to Figure C, if $V_{in} = 1.5$ V p-p, then V_{out} is:
    a.   4.7 V p-p
    b.   7.05 V p-p
    c.   14.25 V p-p
    d.   in + saturation
17. Referring to Figure D, the gain of the circuit is:
    a.   5
    b.   10
    c.   11
    d.   None of the above
18. Referring to Figure D, if $V_{in} = 0.5$ Vp-p, then V_{out} is:
    a.   5.0 V p-p
    b.   0.55 V p-p
    c.   11 V p-p
    d.   5.5 V

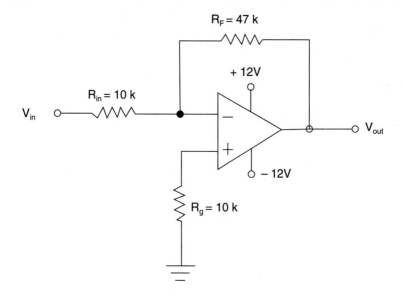

FIGURE C

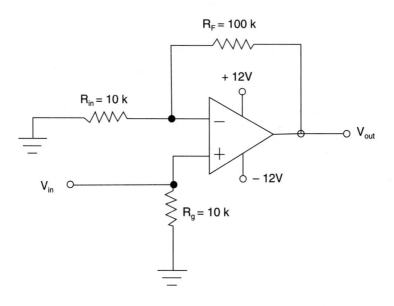

FIGURE D

19. Virtual ground is also referred to as the:
    a.   Common ground
    b.   Earth ground
    c.   Summing point
    d.   None of the above

20. Which of the following is *not* true for a voltage follower?
    a.   Has a gain of 1
    b.   Has low output impedance
    c.   Used as a buffer amplifier
    d.   Has low input impedance

21. Referring to Figure E, all resistors are 10 kΩ. When $V_1 = +5$ V, $V_2 = 9$ V and $V_3 = +2$ V, V_{out} is:
    a.   +2 V
    b.   +16 V
    c.   –2 V
    d.   –11 V

22. Referring to Figure E, $R_1 = 10$ kΩ, $R_2 = 5$ kΩ, $R_3 = 2$ kΩ and $R_F = 10$ kΩ. When $V_1 = +1$ V, $V_2 = +2$ V, and $V_3 = 3$ V, V_{out} is:
    a.   0 V
    b.   –15 V
    c.   –6 V
    d.   +10 V

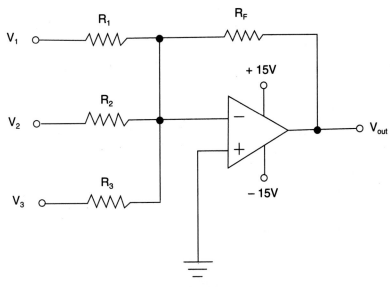

FIGURE E

23. A noninverting voltage-follower amplifier with an input of –3.5 V will have an output of:
    a.   +7 V
    b.   –7 V
    c.   –3.5 V
    d.   +3.5 V

24. Referring to Figure F, all resistors are 10 kΩ. When $V_1 = +5$ V, and $V_2 = 3$ V, V_{out} will be:
    a.   +2 V
    b.   −2 V
    c.   +8 V
    d.   −8 V

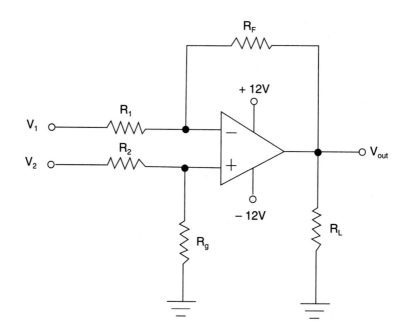

FIGURE F

25. If an inverting voltage-follower amplifier has an input resistor of 22 kΩ , then the feedback resistor should have a value of:
    a.   2.2 kΩ
    b.   22 kΩ
    c.   1.1 kΩ
    d.   11 kΩ
26. The audio frequency range is from:
    a.   60Hz–1 kHz
    b.   300Hz–3 kHz
    c.   20Hz–20 kHz
    d.   50Hz–100 kHz
27. The term used to refer to low audio frequencies is:
    a.   Octave
    b.   Bass
    c.   Treble
    d.   None of the above

28. Some op amps are designed to be used with single-polarity power supplies.
    a.   True
    b.   False
29. A circuit capable of selecting sound from one of two speakers or both is known as:
    a.   A tone control
    b.   A crossover network
    c.   An octave equalizer
    d.   A panning circuit
30. The best circuit used to eliminate 60-Hz hum is:
    a.   A rumble filter
    b.   A speech filter
    c.   A scratch filter
    d.   An octave equalizer
31. An audio system requires a preamplifier with a gain of 200 to match a 50 kΩ impedance microphone. The best amplifier configuration to use is:
    a.   A non-inverting follower
    b.   A summing amp
    c.   A non-inverting amp
    d.   An inverting amp
32. A summing amplifier used in audio frequency work is referred to as:
    a.   A panning circuit
    b.   A mixer
    c.   A crossover network
    d.   None of the above
33. A 10-section octave equalizer can adjust the frequency response of:
    a.   Low frequencies
    b.   Middle frequencies
    c.   High frequencies
    d.   All of the above
34. Input protection devices to op amps are:
    a.   Normal diodes
    b.   Zener diodes
    c.   Resistors
    d.   All of the above
35. If the output of an op amp becomes saturated at one or the other polarity of the power supply voltage and remains there, the condition is referred to as:
    a.   Overvoltage
    b.   Latch-up
    c.   Shorting
    d.   None of the above
36. Power supply decoupling involves the use of:
    a.   Inductors
    b.   Capacitors
    c.   Transistors
    d.   Diodes
37. Referring to Figure G, if V_{out} is at −V saturation, the probable cause is:
    a. R_{in} open
    b. R_L open

    c.   + 15 V supply open

    d. C_{out} shorted

38. Referring to Figure G, the input signal is 2 V p-p. The output signal is undistorted at 10 V p-p.

    a.   The circuit is okay

    b. R_L is open

    c. R_{in} increased in value

    d. C_1 is shorted

39. Referring to Figure G, V_{out} is at + V_{sat}. The probable cause is:

    a. R_F open

    b. C_1 shorted

    c. R_{in} open

    d.   None of the above

40. Referring to Figure G, the output waveform is clipped (flat) on a portion of the negative alternation. The probable cause is:

    a. R_F open

    b.   The $-V$ supply voltage is low

    c. R_G open

    d. C_2 shorted

41. Referring to Figure G, there is no output voltage. All resistors are the proper value. The probable cause is:

    a. C_1 shorted

    b. C_{out} shorted

    c. R_L open

    d.   The op amp is defective

42. If both inputs of an op amp are at the same potential, the output should be at:

    a.   + V supply voltage

    b.   - V supply voltage

    c.   Zero volts

    d.   Depends on A_v factor

43. Low voltage at a power supply terminal of an op amp could be caused by:

    a.   A leaky protection diode

    b.   An open decoupling capacitor

    c.   An open feedback resistor

    d.   A shorted stabilizing feedback capacitor

44. When the output of an op amp is pulled toward ground, the conducting circuit is referred to as the:

    a.   Bias circuit

    b.   Mirror circuit

    c.   Source circuit

    d.   Sink circuit

45. The op amp that produces an output voltage proportional to the difference of the currents at its inputs is the:

    a.   JFET-input op amp

    b.   CDA

    c.   OTA

    d.   None of the above

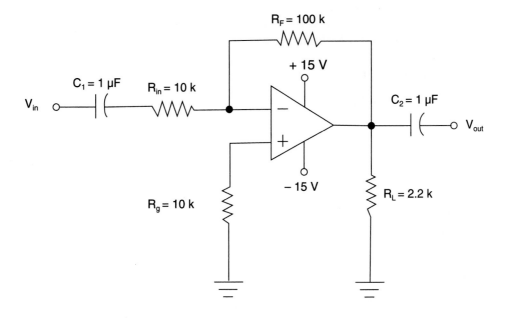

FIGURE G

46. A current mirror circuit:
    a.   Produces an output current twice as large as the input current
    b.   Produces an out-of-phase output current of the same value as the input current applied to it
    c.   Produces an in-phase output current very close to the value of input current applied to it
    d.   Is seldom used in op amps
47. An op amp that produces an output voltage proportional to the difference of the voltages at its inputs is the:
    a.   JFET-input op amp
    b.   CDA
    c.   OTA
    d.   All of the above
48. If the output of an op amp is pulled up toward $+V_{cc}$, the conducting circuit is referred to as the:
    a.   Bias circuit
    b.   Mirror circuit
    c.   Source circuit
    d.   Sink circuit
49. An op amp that produces a proportional output current with respect to a voltage difference at its inputs is the:
    a.   JFET op amp
    b.   CDA
    c.   OTA

    d.   None of the above

50. If it is desired to have the maximum output swing from a Norton op amp, you bias the quiescent output, V_Q, so that it would be:

    a. $2/+ V_{cc}$

    b. $+ V_{cc}/2$

    c. $2+ V_{cc}$

    d.   None of the above

Index